NARSES
HAMMER OF THE GOTHS

NARSES
HAMMER OF THE GOTHS

The Life and Times of Narses the Eunuch

LAWRENCE FAUBER

ALAN SUTTON · GLOUCESTER

ST. MARTIN'S PRESS · NEW YORK

First published in the United States of America 1990
All rights reserved. For information write:
Scholarly & Reference Books Division,
St. Martin's Press, 175 Fifth Avenue,
New York, NY 10010.

ISBN 0-312-04126-8

Library of Congress Cataloging-in-Publication Data

Fauber, L.H. (Lawrence Herbert)
Narses : the hammer of the Goths / L.H. Fauber.
p. cm.
ISBN 0-312-04126-8 : $29.95
1. Italy—History—476-774. 2. Narses, ca. 478-ca. 573.
3. Italy—History, Military. 4. Goths—Italy—History. I. Title.
DG512.6.F38 1990
945′.01—dc20 89-70035
CIP

First published in the United Kingdom in 1990 by
Alan Sutton Publishing Limited
30 Brunswick Road
Gloucester GL1 1JJ

British Library Cataloguing in Publication Data

Fauber, L.H.
Narses: the hammer of the Goths.
1. Byzantine Empire. Narses, 480–574
I. Title
949.5′01′0922

ISBN 0-86299-659-7

Typeset in 11/12pt Ehrhardt.
Typesetting and origination by Alan Sutton Publishing Limited.
Printed in Great Britain by Dotesios Printers.

Contents

List of Figures
(Drawn by Richard Bryant)

List of Plates

Part 1
The Origins and Early Career of Narses the Eunuch

Chapter 1

The Background of Narses

> '. . .and the emperor's steward, Narses, received them (for he too happened to be a Persarmenian by birth), and he presented them with a large sum of money.'
>
> Procopius of Caesarea[1]

This citation is the first historical reference to the individual generally known as Narses the Eunuch. The time is around AD 530, shortly after the Battle of Daras which was fought in July of that year. The occasion, the desertion of two Persarmenian brothers, who were generals in the service of the Great King of Persia. This could have been either the old ruler, Kavad (488–531) or his son and successor, Khosrau, or Chosroes I Anoushivan (531–79). In any case, these two renegades came, with their mother, to the Court of the East Roman Emperor, Justinian I, in Constantinople. The names of the two brothers, received and rewarded by their fellow-countryman, were Aratius and Narses (Narsez).

This latter name appears to have been a fairly common one in that region which lay between Assyria, Mesopotamia and the Caucasus. In fact, one source of reference lists no fewer than seventeen men with this name in late antiquity: a name borne by generals, governors, bishops, patriarchs, saints, theologians and even kings.[2]

The immediate and future problem, however, is to differentiate between the two individuals with this name referred to above. To resist the temptation of using Thomas Hodgkin's designation for the brother of Aratius as 'Narses the less', perhaps the symbolic device of Narses^2 will suffice to prevent any possible confusion.

Narses^2 was also an able general in his own right and served Justinian ably and loyally in Egypt and Italy before dying bravely in battle back in Armenia some thirteen years later (543). He and his brother, Aratius, must have impressed the Imperial authorities by an advantage gained a few years earlier in conflict with the rising military genius of the Empire, Belisarius.

This victory took place during the course of the hostilities between the East Romans and the Persians on the frontiers of the former Kingdom of Armenia.

By virtue of a treaty, or 'friendly partition' made in AD 387 between the Emperors Theodosius I (378–95) and Sapor III (385–88), Armenia had been divided into two separate states under 'nakharars' or vassal princes. The region west of a line passing from Erzerum in the north to the city of Mush in the south (i.e. about one fifth of Greater Armenia) was allotted to the East Roman Empire; the remainder went to Persia.

The Roman portion was added to the Diocesis Pontica; the Persian was that Persarmenia cited as the birthplace of the two Narses's.

Hostilities in Armenia

Belisarius, sharing his first command with an equally young fellow officer, Sittas, made a destructive raid into the eastern, or Persian, portion of Armenia. The date of his earliest recorded achievement is generally reckoned as either 525 or 526. Procopius (*c.*500–564/65), who became his legal advisor and private secretary in 527, did not give the year of the incursions made with Sittas. Instead, he contented himself with a Homeric allusion from both the Iliad and the Odyssey: 'both youths and wearing their first beards.'[3]

Born in 'Germania', between Thrace and Illyricum (the present village of Sapareva Banya, due south of Sofia) around the year 505, Belisarius would have been about twenty-one years old. He and Sittas had been body-guards of the future Emperor Justinian when he was commander-in-chief of the troops garrisoned in the Capital (magister equitum et peditum praesentalis).

Sittas was appointed duke of Armenia and after the year 528 became a brother-in-law of the Empress Theodora when he married her older sister Comita. Later, in 538, he was to lose his life fighting in Armenia.

In any event, a second inroad into Persarmenia made by Belisarius and Sittas was met and checked by Aratius and Narses[2]. The eagle eyes of the East Roman diplomatic service, 'the Barbarian Office' must have made note of these Armenian officers in the pay of Persia. Its far reaching diplomacy could not only bribe and buy individuals and entire tribes, but even whole nations.

Not long afterwards, members of the family of Narses[2] were at the Court of the late enemy being personally rewarded by the Emperor Justinian's own steward or treasurer. In fact, according to Procopius, Narses was so generous to his fellow-countrymen that a third, youngest brother, Isaac,

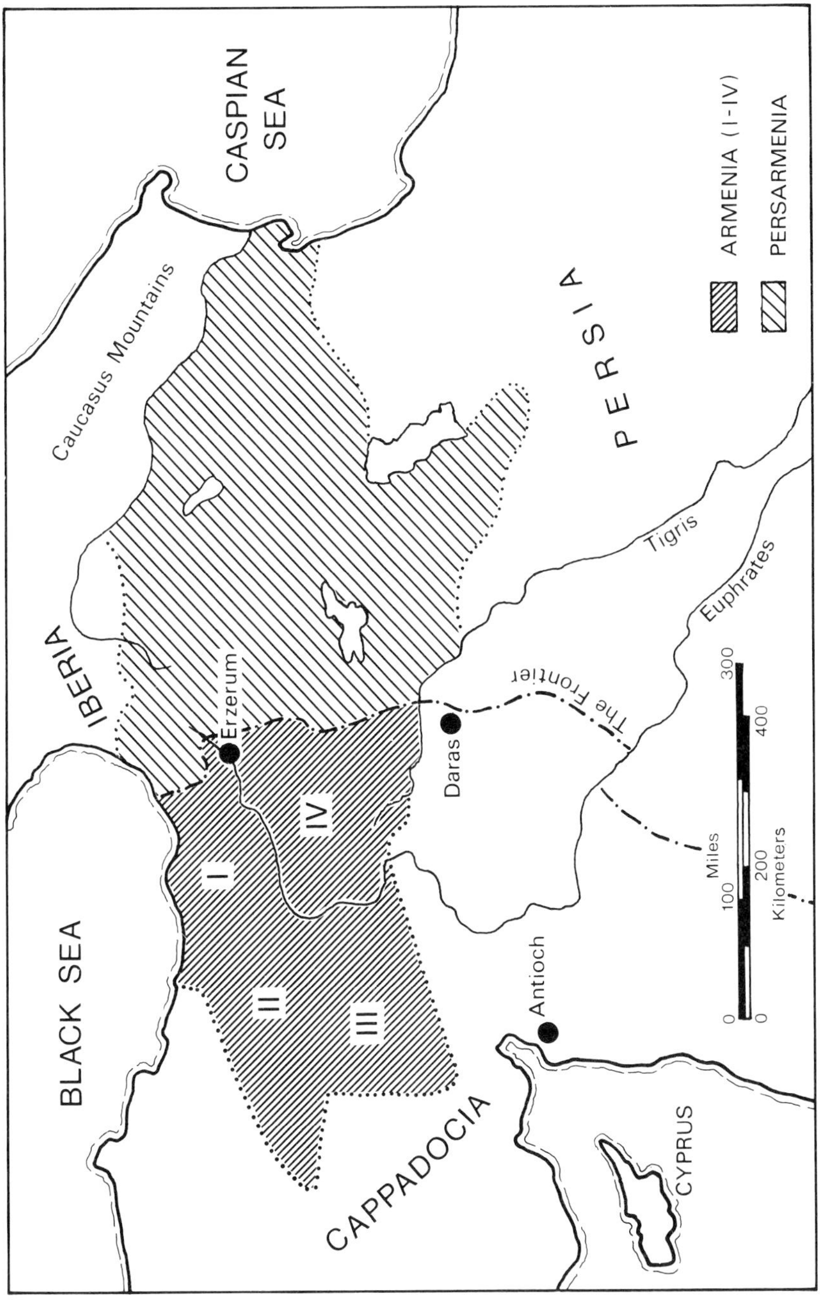

Fig. 1. Armenia and Persarmenia during the reign of Justinian. Armenia was divided into four parts. Parts I and IV probably represent the original area of Armenia that fell within the boundaries of the Roman Empire after partition.

hearing of his liberality, secretly entered into negotiations to betray the fortress of Bolum.[4] This was effected by opening a small gate at night, and thus one more Armenian was attracted to Constantinople and the Imperial service.

Armenians In The Empire

This race contributed many distinguished personages, besides craftsmen, scholars and administrators, who played important roles as State functionaries in the East Roman, and then later Byzantine Empire; generals, officials and even emperors. A generally accepted list of the latter would include:

Maurice	(582–602)
Heraclius	(610–41)
Bardanes-Philippicus	(711–13)
Artabasdus (Artavazd)	(742–43)
Leo V the Armenian	(813–20)
Romanus I Lecapenus	(920–44)
John I Tzimisces	(969–76)

Maurice, however, was actually a Cappadocian of Arabissus, said to be descended from the aristocracy of ancient Rome, but his policy of recruiting Armenians for his armies may have led to the later tradition that he himself was Armenian.

This would be perfectly in keeping with the well-known martial qualities of the race. Already in the fifth century, after the final separation of the Eastern and Western Roman Empires, (following the death of Theodosius I in 395) Armenians were picked by their excellence for the honour of serving in the Eastern Scholarii, or Palace Guard.[5]

On the other side of the border, these 'excellent' soldiers had always been reviewed by the Great King in person at Ctesiphon. Later, after being a fugitive from his own throne, King Chosroes would cede the greater part of Armenia to the 'Armenian' Emperor Maurice. This was testimony to its growing importance as a recruiting ground for the Eastern Empire, Maurice being the first emperor to fully realize its significance in this respect.

Armenian generals would be renowned for their military skill and courage during later Byzantine history, but already in Justinian's reign Artabanes, his kinsman Arsaces and the three brothers, Aratius, Narses[2] and Isaac were to prove their value and worth. Besides the famous Narses,

Procopius mentions sixteen Armenian generals of Justinian. As for Narses himself, he was to show not only the Armenian 'genius for war', but for administration as well. Furthermore, he also shared its reputation for having the 'best business brains' in the Empire.[6]

Initially the movements of the Armenians within the Empire were those of individual adventurers, rather than the migration of entire tribes, except when forcibly transported. For example, 10,000 Armenians were forcefully settled on Cyprus in 578.[7] Since the race was too prolific for its restricted valleys, its more enterprising sons were sent out to seek power and fortune in Constantinople.[8]

Narses and Artabanes have been seen as the most eminent examples of men of this race, leading the increasing movement towards the centre of the Imperial service at the Capital. This movement was encouraged by Justinian's reorganization of the provinces of Armenia in 536, and eventually led to a general westward movement of the Armenian population in the centuries following Justinian's death.[9]

The Armenians, along with the Arabs, Copts and Syrians, were among the races of the Empire who never gave up their own native language. They also kept their nationality alive in their own Church, founded by St Gregory the Illuminator (*c.*AD 300) with the ecclesiastical tenacity of the Jews. As a Kingdom they were actually the first to officially adopt Christianity. The Armenian Church rejected the Council of Chalcedon (AD 451), therefore Armenian immigrants had to renounce their 'heresy' and accept the Council's doctrine.[10]

The Armenians also have their own national system of chronology with the reform of the calendar after the death of the patriarch Narses in AD 551. It began on 11 July 552 and continues to the present day.

Other Races of the Empire

The Eastern Roman Empire, ultimately to be known as the 'Byzantine', was during Narses' day extremely cosmopolitan.

The question has been raised: 'Who, in the sixth century, were the Romans?'[11] The citizens of the ancient city of Rome itself could almost be dismissed as they were either under siege or actually under alien barbarian rule. As for the personages connected with the Court at the 'New Rome' of Constantinople their origins were very questionable indeed.

The Emperor himself was originally an Illyrian; the Empress Theodora, 'an Oriental', possibly from Cyprus or perhaps Syria; Belisarius was a Thracian, as was John, the nephew of Vitalian; the father and grandfather of Antonina, Belisarius' wife, had been charioteers in Thessalonica and the Capital; the Patrician Solomon was a eunuch from Mesopotamia.

From Asia Minor came the jurist Tribonian, who was born at Side in Pamphylia, and the two Isidores of Miletus (uncle and nephew). Peter Barsymes was a 'Syrian'; Corippus, a Court poet, came all the way from Carthage. Others who can be defined geographically were Anthemius of Tralles, John the Cappadocian and, of course, Procopius of Caesarea, in Palaestina.

Yet all of these personages would have thought of themselves in their own time and place as being 'Romans' or, at the very least, as serving as such.

The Emperor Justinian I

The origins and career of the central figure of this entire period, Justinian, are fairly well-known. This is no doubt due to the 'forest' of literature that has grown up around his name; leading in turn, however, to the most contradictory portrayals of his character and qualities.

In the case of his consort, the Empress Theodora, there has sprouted a veritable thicket of fictional accounts. Her character and qualities are, however, generally appreciated.

Belisarius has also fared fairly well, being the central character of medieval romances, political verses, an opera, plays and historical novels. 'Date obolum Balisario' was the title of the first important painting by Jacques-Louis David (1748–1825). In Italy there are gates and towers named for him, and in Marche even wine.

Only Narses (or Narsete) is little more than a name in the country where he accomplished epic feats on battlefields long forgotten and, as an 'Exarch' affected its history for centuries to come. In literature his name, character and even physical appearance have been submerged in a fictional scrub-undergrowth.

The exalted Emperor Justinian I, whom both Belisarius and Narses served so faithfully, was of obscure barbarian origins. He was born on 11 May 482 in the mountain village of Tauresium near Scupi (Skopje) which was the capital of the province of Dardania, and is now the capital of Macedona, the southernmost Republic of Yugoslavia.[12]

His mother Bigleniza (Vigilantia) was the sister of Justin, an illiterate Illyrian peasant. Justin had been a husbandman or shepherd, and was even said to have herded swine, before journeying on foot to Constantinople to become a soldier. There, he rose from rank to rank in a long service, beginning with the Emperor Leo, to become ultimately the Commander of the Emperor Anastasius' Excubitors (Imperial Bodyguards).

Justin's nephew, said to have been christened Uprauda, was also to make his way from his native hamlet to the Capital at his uncle's request, as his aunt was childless. She was a rustic barbarian captive, named Lupicina, whom Justin had purchased for a concubine and then married. Later, she would be crowned Augusta as Euphemia. It was intended that Uprauda should receive a 'Roman' and Christian education. He was to be known by the Romanized name of Flavius Petrus Sabbatius Justinianus. Sabbatius was his father's Latin name (from Istok) while Justinianus was taken from his uncle's.

Upon the death, in his eighty-seventh year, of the Emperor Anastasius (491–518) who left no surviving children, Justin, the illiterate Illyrian, was raised to the purple by the Army and Senate. It has been charged that the sixty-eight-year-old soldier misused funds entrusted to him to facilitate the election of Theocritus, the candidate promoted by Amantius, head of the Palace eunuchs.

The educated nephew, thirty-six years of age by now, may also have had a hand in the behind-the-scenes manoeuvring after the death of Anastasius on the night of 8–9 July 518.

At any rate, Anastasius' own three nephews, the sons of his sister Secundinus, Hypatius, Pompeius and Probus, were effectively by-passed in the succession to the throne. Among the darker accusations against Justinian is that he helped to frame the charges against Amantius and his man Theocritus that were the excuse for executing these rivals. Darkest yet is the story of his conduct towards the dangerous orthodox rebel, Vitalian, who had been recalled to Constantinople by Justin.

Vitalian, a native of Zaldaba in Lower Moesia, was a chief of possible Gothic descent who had been a count of the foederati of Thrace as had his father Patriciolus before him. He was the leader of an unsuccessful revolt against Anastasius, during 513–15, having marched at the head of an army of 50,000 men upon Constantinople. Under the new regime of Justin, he was given the title of 'magister militum praesentalis' and made a Consul. Besides being exceptionally small in stature he was also afflicted with a stammer, but even enemies acknowledged his courage and cunning in war. He was the uncle of Narses' friend, and future lieutenant, John.

Justinian had given a pledge of safety by sharing the Christian sacrament, and then had him, together with his followers, murdered during a banquet in the Palace during the seventh month of his consulship in 520.[13] Vitalian was said to have been stabbed seventeen times.

Justin I (518–27), as an uneducated barbarian, 'without the alphabet', had to painfully trace his signature on to edicts through a wooden stencil with the letters of his Imperial title.[14] His near contemporary, Theodoric, the Ostrogothic King in Italy (493–526) is said to have used a golden stencil with the word 'legi' ('I have read').[15]

The case has been made that Justinian being educated, particularly in law and theology, did govern in actual fact, in the name of Justin, from 518 to 527.

Procopius, in his Secret History, virtually treats Justin's reign as part of Justinian's. Three days before the feast of Easter in the year 527 (*c.*1–4 April) the nephew was adopted as a son and made a Caesar by the dangerously ill uncle.

With the death of Justin four months later (1 August), from an ulcer in the foot that had developed from an old arrow wound, Justinian officially ascended the throne.

However, instead of the usual reign of thirty-eight years generally assigned to him, Justinian I (527–65) could be credited with 'ruling' for forty-seven. Charles Diehl summed it up in this manner:

> 'Thus during nearly half a century, from 518 to 565 Justinian's will guided the destinies of the Roman Empire in the East.'[16]

Nonetheless, Justinian is not remembered for the longevity of his reign, but for the quality of its achievements.

First, he established the universal and permanent benefits of the principles of law and order, together with those of equity and justice, by his Code of Laws, the so-called Justinian Code. This was initially a consolidation and revision of all previous Roman law; in 527 Justinian had already appointed a commission of ten: eight high officials and two practising lawyers, including an eminent jurist Tribonian.

Six months after his official accession (13 February 528) he ordered the previous collections of laws to be put into a 'Codex', or book-form, as opposed to a roll; the Codex-Justinianius. The following year, 529 (7 April) the Codex Constitutionum was promulgated, taking force on 15 April. At the end of 530 (15 December) Tribonian, as chairman, chose the members of a new commission of sixteen; eminent lawyers and professors who worked in the Imperial Palace for three years (there was to be the interruption of the 'Nika' insurrection in 532).

The end of the year 533 saw the publication of the Digesta, or Digest (in Latin) and Pandectae, or Pandects (in Greek translation). These equalled fifty books in seven parts with 432 titles. On 30 December 533 they took effect as Imperial statute or law.

Also published during this period (21 November 533) was the Institutiones, or Institutes, which was a textbook for students. This was written by Tribonian, Theophilus, professor of law at Constantinople, and Dorotheus, professor of the law school at Berytus. They were assisted by Anatolius and Cratinus, who had also been members of the commission of sixteen. This manual was in fact based on the arrangement and divisions of the elementary standard textbook of Roman law by Gaius (*c.*115–*c.*180).

At the end of the year 534 (31 December), a second, revised edition of the 'Code' took effect; this was the *Codex Repetitae Praelectionis*. The unofficial, or semi-official, collections of Justinian's own laws, the Novellae, or Novels, (new constitutions) making three 'compilations' were published by 565, the year of his death. These Novels, or laws, were originally drawn up in Greek (except those relating to Africa and Italy) as they were addressed to John the Cappadocian who was ignorant of Latin.

Together, the Codex, Digest, Institutes and Novels are known as the Corpus Juris Civilis. This body of Justinian's Roman law became the foundation of medieval canon, and modern western civil law.

His consort the Empress Theodora also concerned herself with checking social crime, i.e. 'sins against the body'.[17] She initiated a law against very young girls being used in the white slavery traffic (Novel. 14, 535).

She even went so far as to round up over 500 adult prostitutes who plied their trade in the brothels or market-place (at the subsistence rate of three obels). They were all sent over to the Asiatic shore of the Bosphorus to be confined in a converted palace, the Convent of Metanoia. From this unwelcomed transformation, some, at least, escaped, by jumping to their deaths at night into the sea from the heights of the upper windows or the roof.[18]

Procopius put forth such tit-bits of tittilating gossip in his Anecdota, or 'Secret History', infamous for its condemnation of Justinian and Theodora, together with their Court. Narses was one of the very few public men of the reign at whom he threw no mud.

Besides the 'Secret History', and the history of the Persian, Vandalic and Gothic wars, there was a later work in adulation on Justinian's 'Buildings' (*De Aedificiis*). This is summed up in Gibbon's pronouncement:

> 'Procopius successively composed the history, the panegyric, and the satire of his own times.'[19]

For his many and varied building activities (churches, fortresses, towns, walls, etc.), Justinian was called 'reparator orbis' by his contemporaries. The greatest architectural achievement, however, of his time, is the Basilica of Divine Wisdom (Santa Sophia) with its great central dome.

The original church was built in 325 by Constantine and later enlarged by his son Constantius. It was destroyed by fire in 404, to be rebuilt in 415 under Theodosius II, only to be burnt again during the 'Nika' riots in January, 532.

Santa Sophia was erected in the comparatively short interval between 23 February 532 and 27 December 537. The architect was Anthemius of Tralles and the engineer, or mason, Isidore of Miletus; there were over 10,000 workmen.

Some twenty years later, on 14 December 557, an earthquake caused the fall of the highest portion of the roof of the central dome. As Anthemius was dead by then, it was repaired by Isidore the younger (a nephew) together with other architects.

Then, on 7 May 558, while the main dome was being repaired, part of the eastern hemicycle fell. The central dome's original circular form was changed to an ellipse, and an elevation of twenty more feet given to it; thus it had a shorter radius and became more convex and compact. By 24 December 563, the new dome was completed and St Sophia re-dedicated; it has lasted to the present day.

One trait professedly shared by Justinian with Narses was devotion to the Virgin; one invoked her aid in the administration of his Empire, the other was to seek tokens of her approval before his battles. Thus, both emperor and eunuch were motivated by the same piety.

Justinian personally attended to theological studies, and even controversy; he was constantly striving for 'orthodoxy'. He was as concerned with dogma as much as civil law, practically setting himself up as a Doctor of the Church. He was certainly looked upon by his own age as the living representative of two universal ideas – The Empire and Christianity.[20]

Yet it was Justinian's over-riding dream to literally restore the Roman Empire to its former extent that was ultimately to give Narses his great chance in a new military career. He was to complete this 'Imperial Restoration', begun by Belisarius in Africa, but left unfinished in Italy, by overthrowing the Ostrogothic Kingdom there. Then, this 'Hammer of the Goths' was to secure the reconquest by an annihilating victory over an overwhelming host of Alamanni-Frankish invaders.

Unlike Belisarius, Narses was not a mere military man but also possessed the administrative abilities of a statesman. After realizing Justinian's goal of a reconquered Italy, Narses was to remain there as his emperor's 'Exarch' or viceroy, and alter ego. He served Justinian as loyally as Belisarius; both men being compared in their faithfulness with the loyalty of Marcus Vipsanius Agrippa and Tiberius to the Emperor Augustus.

Furthermore, Narses maintained his master's confidence until the very end; only after the death of Justinian himself was disgrace, recall and exile to be the fate of the enigmatic eunuch.

The Origins Of Narses

Justinian often appears very 'senior' in relationship to many of the contemporaries of his Court and reign; Belisarius, Eudaimon, Germanus, Tribonian, John the Cappadocian, and then Peter Barsymes. He was already in his forties when he married his future consort, Theodora (*c*.525), she being a young ex-actress between twenty and twenty-five years of age. Justin had conveniently abrogated the ancient law forbidding alliances between senators and actresses or 'courtesans'.

Yet Narses was born between two and four years earlier than Justinian, and survived his Imperial master by estimates of from one to nine years. Indeed, the great question in the life span of Narses is not whether he was born in AD 478, 479 or even 480, but the year of his death, which historians have dated all the way from 566 to 574. Therefore, he may have lived anything from eighty-six to ninety-six years.

The date generally accepted for his birth is the 'probable' year of 478, assigned by Thomas Hodgkin. However, French and Italian authorities such as Ernest Stein[21] and Angelo Pernice,[22] in considering the problem of his extremely advanced old age, subject even the year 480 to 'caution'.

When first brought to our attention by Procopius in *c*.530, Narses would have already been at the advanced age of fifty, or even a year or two beyond, and yet, at that time, the greatest exploits of Narses the Eunuch General lie another twenty-two to twenty-four years in the future. It should also be added that he governed the ancient province of Italy for another twelve years or so after his military victories, before vanishing into the mists of myth and saga. Thus, historians have been confronted with a man whose greatest, history-making achievements were all realised after the age of seventy!

Equally enigmatic is the possible origin of his condition in life, being a eunuch. Only the bare fact that he was 'a Persarmenian by birth' is known of Narses, his genealogical and social background being unknown.

As there is no definite information that Narses was of servile origins, Hodgkin suggested that Narses' own parents could have had him 'prepared' and educated for service in an oriental court as a eunuch.[23] Hodgkin further supported this idea in his book *Italy and her Invaders*.[24] On the other hand, William Plate, while admitting that nothing was known of his earlier life, had Narses 'of quite obscure parentage'.[25] Indeed, his parents either sold him, or he was made a captive of war, when young, and suffered the fate of many such boys – he was castrated. George Finley implied the same result by stating that he 'was a Pers-Armenian captive'.[26]

In literary accounts of the origins of Narses there is often far more embellished detail regarding his physical condition, and even personal appearance.

Robert Graves, in his novel *Count Belisarius*, filled in the gaps of the surviving records with the fiction that Narses came of a well-known Armenian military family. Furthermore, that already at the tender age of eleven he had killed a man with his little sword before being captured in battle. Interestingly enough, Graves narrated the story of his heroic, noble general through the first person report of a eunuch. The character was one Eugenius, born Goronwy in his native Britain; carried away, at the age of six, by Saxon pirates; sold into slavery to a dealer in 'relics' from Palestine, where he was castrated. Eventually, he ended up in Constantinople as a servant in the household of Belisarius' wife, Antonina, to whom Eugenius has Narses relate his life story with his origins and background.[27]

John W. Vandercook in his fictionalized study *Empress Of The Dusk. A Life of Theodora of Byzantium* limited his version of Narses being a eunuch to 'an accident in childhood'. In this Vandercook may have confused Narses with Solomon the Eunuch who, according to Procopius, had an accident while in his swaddling clothes. Vandercook also anticipated events near the very end of Narses' long life by having him entirely spending his youth among women, being taught to cook as well as to spin and sew,[28] these later attributes already having been alleged by Gibbon:

> 'His youth had been employed in the management of the loom and distaff . . .'[29]

René Kraus, an Austrian journalist, listed as an 'authority on Byzantine history and culture' created a Persian background for Narses in his novel *Theodora The Circus Empress*. The Persians had given him the nickname of 'the mule'; apparently because of his having been born sterile. In order to escape the execution of the sentence, from the sacred book the Avesta, of being burnt alive, Narses as a boy of twelve or thirteen escaped across the Syrian border.[30]

So the full range of causes by which a man could have become a eunuch: being born sterile; having an accident in childhood; being 'prepared' by one's own parents for service at Court; sold into slavery, made captive or a prisoner-of-war, and then castrated; the whole job lot has been assigned to Narses by historical and literary interpreters. All that is lacking is the self-castration of the religious eunuch.

His Character and Appearance

A brief description of Narses' person was given by the contemporary chronicler Agathias Scholasticus, 'The Advocate' of Myrina (*c*.530–580) from whom so many historical and literary sketches have been drawn:

> 'He was above all, a man of sound mind, keen and clever in adapting himself to the times; and though he was not versed in literature nor

> practised in oratory, he made up for these deficiencies by the fertility of his wit, and did not lack words with which to express his opinions, which was an extraordinary thing for a eunuch brought up among the follies of the royal palace.'

Agathias described the physical characteristics of Narses very briefly indeed:

> 'In stature he was small and of a lean habit, but stronger and more high-spirited than would have been believed'[31]

From this rather short account of his person there have followed descriptions of Narses that seem to bear out those psychological experiments which show how an original version gains added links of detail and embellishment in the chain of its re-telling.

To Edward Gibbon in the eighteenth century, with his wealth of allusion, the eunuch Narses had 'a feeble diminutive body' that 'concealed the soul of a statesman and a warrior'. Eunuchs, as such, were generally among the objects of his greatest scorn, but in his treatment of Narses he showed much discrimination and impartiality.

In a declaration that deserves to be cited, Gibbon asserted:

> 'But the eunuch Narses is ranked among the few who have rescued that unhappy name from the contempt and hatred of mankind.'[32]

Then again, Narses was in general the only eunuch who was well spoken of; not only by Procopius, but with the other historians of his time he bore the character of an 'honourable man'. Even as a eunuch he was still one of the big men of his era.

James E. Dunlap in an elaboration of his doctoral thesis, *The Office Of The Grand Chamberlain In The Later Roman And Byzantine Empires*, devoted an entire section to Narses in a chapter on 'The Careers Of Prominent Grand Chamberlains'. Paraphrasing from Agathias, he described Narses as being short of stature and frail; not very well educated, or eloquent, yet a clear and forceful speaker; of exceptional prudence, industry and adaptability, of elegant manners and energetic enough to be equal to the greatest tasks.[33]

Other historians have drawn the conclusions that he was mentally strenuous and decisive in character, or of immense courage, and possessing a superb intelligence. Charles Diehl credited Narses with concealing under his frail appearance 'indomitable energy, prodigious activity and a strong will'.[34]

Unfortunately, from Agathias' original coinage of his character and physique, there has been a tendency to drive Narses' good characteristics out of circulation. From being merely 'keen and clever', Narses descends to being very shrewd, then calculating and ambitious, and then extremely ambitious. C.W.C. Oman describes him as 'clever, pushing and persistent'.[35]

Physically, he is reduced from being merely 'small' in stature to a little, or undersized, man and then to being very small; almost a dwarf.

William Plate went so far as to give him the body of a boy, and the voice of a woman.[36] Recently, Gillian Bradshaw, in her novel *The Bearkeeper's Daughter*, introduces Narses as small and frail-looking with a child's 'high sweet voice'.[37] Adding poetic licence to the meager record of Agathias, Robert Graves alleged that Narses was not only repulsively ugly with a squint and a twisted lip, but also dwarfish and big-buttocked to boot. Graves may have considered all of these physical deformities necessary in presenting Narses as a foil to his manly hero Belisarius.

Adding to his deformities, he goes from being bent and undersized to a round-backed little man. René Kraus even has him cunningly arranging the folds of his tunic to conceal his hunchback.

Perhaps the terse response of the Duke of Luxemburg, Francois Henride Montmorency-Bouteville (1628–95) to the complaint of William III would be in order:

> 'How does he know I have a hump? He has never seen my back.'

The best, and final, response to all of this glorified gossip about his person was the suggestion made by G.P. Baker:

> 'It has always been the custom to look with a certain amount of surprise and patronage upon Narses. That personage was doubtless accustomed to the same sort of insult when he was alive, so that he is not likely to bother himself about it now that he is dead.'[38]

To this can be added the suggestion that a likeness of Narses has come down to us, unrecognized. Behind Justinian's left shoulder, on the famous mosaic in S. Vitale, Ravenna, stands an older, unbearded courtier. Clearly he must have been a close and trusted advisor. Might this not be Narses?[39]

One generally accepted redeeming quality Narses was credited with possessing was that of piety. The original authority for this is Evagrius Scholasticus, (536–*c*.600) in his Ecclesiastica Historica. Evagrius was by profession an advocate, or lawyer. He testified that those about Narses' person affirmed that he propitiated the Deity with prayers and other acts of piety. Also, that he paid due honour to the Virgin as the mother of God; in return, she distinctly announced to him the proper time for military action.

Consequently, Narses never engaged in battle until he had received a signal from her. Thus, even in his own day, because of his religious fervour and profession of a special devotion to the Virgin, Narses was supposed to be under her direct protection. Evagrius ended his testimony by admitting that the later actions of Narses in Italy recounted by Agathias the Rhetorician had not reached his hands.[40]

Paulus Diaconus (Paul the Deacon) in his *History Of The Langobards*, near the end of the eighth century, after reviewing the early offices and honours of Narses, went on to describe his piety. As a very pious man, an orthodox Catholic in his religion, he was generous to the poor and very zealous when it came to restoring churches. He was so devoted to prayers and vigils that his victories were obtained more by pouring forth supplications to God than by the 'arms of war'.[41]

Early Offices and Titles

Whatever his birth, and original condition in life, Narses probably arrived at a very early age in Constantinople where he attained a footing in the officium of the Grand Chamberlain. In 491, the first year of Anastasius' reign he would have been between eleven and thirteen years old.

By his subtle and quick mind, threading a course through the labyrinth of bureaucratic offices, he rose, stage by stage, until in middle age, having grown grey in the service of emperors, he occupied a high position at Court. Around the year 530 he was cited by Procopius as being already the Emperor Justinian's 'steward'.

He was actually a sort of 'High Treasurer'; the bureaucratic designations listing a 'comes sacrarum largitionum' (Count of the Sacred Largesses) and a 'comes rerum privatarum' (Count of the Privy Purse). In any case, he was involved with the emperor's finances, and all payments from the Imperial treasury. It is known that he was a 'saccellarius' for at least seven or eight years (*c.*530–38).

In the year 531, Narses was sent into Armenia to take in Justinian's name the rich spoil found in a Persian town that had fallen into the hands of the East Romans. In this same year he is described as also being a cubicular, or chamberlain. These cubicularii were a highly 'peculiar' group; as eunuchs, they were, almost as a necessity, imported barbarian slaves (but acquired their freedom on entering imperial service).

By 532, Narses had joined the school of the Chartularii, which involved the custody of the archives of the Imperial household, or the 'Sacred

Bedchamber'. Contrary to the comments of Agathias, this position implied some literary attainment, and Narses and two colleagues held the positions of Spectabiles, which carried Proconsular status.

Narses was among the cubicularii, or eunuch chamberlains, of the emperor and empress in the sixth century who were also spatharii. These eunuch protospatharii, or first sword-bearers, had a special dress, or uniform; a white tunic adorned with gold, and a red doublet with gold facings. As insigne, they wore a necklet which was probably different in shape from the collar of the other protospatharii; pearls were probably a further differentiation. In addition, they carried a gold-handled sword. As commander of the eunuch body-guard, Narses was the Emperor Justinian's confidant.

Then, around the year 540 (i.e. when in his sixties) Narses rose to the greatest of all the offices for eunuchs, as the most trusted servants in the Imperial household. This was the exalted position of the Praepositus Sacri Cubiculi; or, in other words, the Grand Chamberlain of the Court.

The Grand Chamberlain (Praepositus Sacri Cubiculi)

The designation of 'praepositus' may have had a military or a more humble palace origin. There is nothing to indicate which, if either, of these two sources was the real origin of the title praepositus sacri cubiculi. However, it is known that this official designation of the head chamberlain had been changed from a 'cubiculo' at the time of Diocletian's reorganization (AD 284–305).[42]

Theoretically this chief of the chamberlains was originally an official of lowly station whose duties may have been limited to only controlling the servants and staff in the emperor's bedchamber.[43] There are inscriptions from the period of the Principate (the early Empire) recording the presence of praepositi who directed other small corps of servants about the palace. A list of their titles and duties would include:

praepositi cocorum	chief cooks
praepositi structorum	chief carvers
praepositi cellariorum/cellaris	chief cellarers
praepositus argenti or auri	chief custodians of the plate
praepositi pistorum	chief bakers

There was even a praepositus opificibus domus Augustae – a chief artisan of the palace. As these titles were, in their way, comparable to that of the praepositus cubiculi it could be assumed that he was at first merely the chief of the chamberlains.[44]

Nonetheless, there was a mighty host of palatine servants under his immediate direction. The office had grown in importance from the time of the Emperor Theodosius I (378–95); from the palace staff, and the bedchamber itself, there was to be control over the affairs of the divisions of the Imperial residences, estates and domains.

With the decline of statesmanship, this branch of administration in the Imperial or 'Sacred' Household was to assume more and more importance. In time, the Grand Chamberlain came to exercise a great personal extra-constitutional influence over the emperor himself; with a weak ruler, he could easily become the most powerful person in the entire Empire.

In addition, he could become one of the richest, a powerful praepositus virtually selling by auction the great offices of State. Furthermore, he received bribes for private audiences with the emperor. By Narses' time however, Justinian had authorized customary fees, and had suppressed the sale of offices.[45]

There are only two known cases where Roman citizens served as cubicularii. In one the pretender Magnus Maximus (383–88) made a short-lived break with tradition by appointing an elderly man of free birth as his first praepositus sacri cubiculi. In fact, it was said that he would not have eunuchs about his Court. This high position was however, within a year or two, once more occupied by a eunuch.

By a constitution of Theodosius II (408–450) the Patriciate had, in 422, been closed to eunuchs; thereafter the Grand, or High, Chamberlain was not a magistrate, but a 'minister'. There were two of these at the Eastern Court, the second serving the empress. Justinian, however, decided that all officials of the rank of Illustres should be eligible for the Patriciate and Narses, therefore, ultimately came to be admitted (he became honorary consul as well).[46] As the Grand Chamberlain he was an Illustris, one of four high offices that conferred on the holder membership in the Consistorium, or the Emperor's Imperial Council of State. This was a sort of Most Honourable Privy Council. It also served as a High Court of Justice, depending on the will, or discretion, of the emperor. Narses was to be equal in honour to the other three officers with the same rank, the Praetorian Prefects and the Master of Soldiery.

Furthermore, his position gave him the exclusive right to enter the emperor's presence unannounced. He was the head of the cubicularii, of whom there were eight ranks; their insignia were ivory tablets. Besides supervising the duties of his immediate subordinates, six in number, he had under his disposition three decuriones, who in turn were over thirty body-guards or silentiaries.[47]

These silentiaries derived their name from their chief duty which was to act as marshalls, or ushers, at a silentium nuntiare. This was the technical phrase for calling a meeting of an Imperial audience or council. Therefore, with their insigne of office, a gold staff, called 'the golden band', they constituted a 'series' leading to the inner chamber or veil.[48] Four of them were appropriated to the additional duty of serving the empress. Anastasius had been a silentiary at the Court of the Emperor Zeno, the Isaurian (474–91) and was nominated by the Empress Ariadne as his successor; less than six weeks later he married her.

The silentiaries also attended the Grand Chamberlain at the races in the Hippodrome where, during Justinian's reign, he sat in the Kathisma, the royal reviewing box, from where he actually directed the proceedings.

In addition, the Grand Chamberlain had administrative and financial duties relative to the Crown Lands with a large number of other subordinate officials under his direction. These were the canonicarii, or special agents, to assist the regular tax-gatherers in the payment of taxes.[49]

Together with this general authority, his office also had a certain control over the divina domus per Cappadocian, the Imperial Estates in Cappadocia, which were extra-territorial blocks of Royal land composed of thirteen estates in all.

If Narses occupied this high office from *c.*540 until his final departure for Italy, he would have had a full decade of wielding power at its very centre. Yet this in itself would scarcely have rescued him from the fate of countless other castrated men, that of being a contemptible eunuch. At best, most cubicularii retired into obscurity with their ill-gotten gains.

Dunlap set forth his real claim to fame:

> 'The story of Narses the famous minister of Justinian is less that of a Grand Chamberlain than that of a successful general, and if told in detail would almost constitute a history of the Gothic Wars of Justinian's reign.'[50]

Unfortunately for Narses and his exploits as a heroic 'condottiero', the observation made by J.M. Wallace-Hadrill may help to explain his historical neglect: 'No epic poet celebrated the reconquest of Italy.'[51]

It may have been a near thing after all, as Torquato Tasso (1544–95) in hesitating among six subjects for heroic epic poetry, had considered the conquests of Italy by Belisarius and by Narses.

Chapter II

The New Rome and the Rise of the Greens and the Blues

'. . .for Constantinople was the last and greatest
colony of Rome . . .'
H.M. Gwatkin[1]

In order to understand and follow the events that occurred in Constantinople between Sunday 11 January 532, and the following Sunday of the 18th, it is desirable to trace the background of the city; its citizens, factions and, particularly, its Hippodrome.

The Emperor Constantine had re-founded it in AD 330 as 'New Rome'. Such was its official title, but it has always been known as the City of Constantine and even as the 'Queenly City'. The original settlement of Byzantium was almost a thousand years earlier, founded traditionally in 657 BC.

From its very inception it was a truly cosmopolitan city. Constantine (306–37) not only brought members of the Senate from the old Rome to the new, but also encouraged immigration from all parts of the far-flung Roman Empire. Its population would not be predominantly Greek until the last centuries of its existence. As 'Byzantium', it would survive for yet another thousand years, falling to the Turks on 29 May 1453.

Its heyday was to be around the year 1000 when it would stand as a bastion of urban and 'classical' values during the early years of Medieval Europe.

For Justinian's reign, population estimates have ranged from *c.*600,000 up to about a million inhabitants; one method of judging being by the amount of corn imported annually.[2] Plague during the sixth century may have caused a temporary reduction in the population. It almost claimed the Emperor himself during the epidemic in the year 543.

Ancient Rome was to suffer far more than a 'temporary' decline; it may have reached a population of *c.*1,200,000 in the third century AD but by the middle of the fifth century it had fallen below 250,000. A century later, Narses as the conquering general from the new capital would find it to be a vast and empty mass of tumbling ruins; it would descend to a village in a graveyard of monuments during the Middle Ages. When Rome became the Capital of the reunited Kingdom of Italy in 1870 its population was only 226,022.

Of the other great cities of the Classical World, by the sixth century Alexandria was half the size of Constantinople, probably with about 330,000 inhabitants, while Antioch was about half as large, i.e. around 150,000. Since there is no statistical imformation available, there can only be plausible guesses at the population in the Eastern Empire. In the West, Carthage and Milan were other cities of large size. In the early sixth century the latter may have had a population of half a million, having been restored by the first Ostrogothic Kings in Italy. Milan had become the first city of the West for size, population, employment and wealth, but its prosperity came to a sudden end in 539, a victim of the warfare between the Empire and the Goths. Over a decade later, in 554, it would be revived to some extent by Narses after he became the administrator of the Italy he had re-conquered for the Empire.

The Factions

As for the quality of the citizens of the transplanted Rome on the Bosphorus, many of their values were to be found in the old Capital on the Tiber. In the words of Gibbon: 'Constantinople adopted the follies though not the virtues of ancient Rome' – licence without the freedom of democracy had been revived there and at Antioch as well.[3]

This was nowhere more apparent than in the passionate support given to the 'factiones' that championed the rival colours of the race-course. These factions which had agitated the Roman circus were to rage with re-doubled fury in the streets and Hippodrome of Constantinople. The passions and mass partisanship reached a peak of intensity that bordered on civil war during Justinian's reign.

The origins of the four factions in Rome known by their colours, the Blues, Greens, Reds and Whites, are obscure. At least two, the Reds and Whites, existed during Cicero's time in the last age of the Republic (106–43 BC). It is thought that the Blues and Greens arose under the Empire; the Blues, at least, by Augustan times.[4]

During the Republic chariot-racing had been an amateur sport for the upper classes; by the time of the Empire it had become a professional affair. Horace (65–8 BC) in his first Satire, The Race For Wealth And Position, gave the simile of the chariot-race and the contest for riches:

'Tis as when chariots are let loose from the barriers
and swept onwards behind the hoofed steeds:
hard on the horses that outstrip his own presses the charioteer,
caring naught for that other whom he passed and left in the rear.'[5]
(For the greedy there is always a richer rival ahead).

Not long after the time of Horace, the passion for betting, speculation and the universal craze for the colours had converted this circus sport into a frenzied institution.

Under the Principate, or early Empire, there were already four factions at Rome which were companies, or guilds, that furnished the chariots to the magistrates who gave the games. Each 'factio' provided one chariot for each race and was recompensed by the prize money. The losing factions presumably received some payment; the Government may have paid each group by a regular tariff. This organization was extended to other cities during the later Empire and acquired special importance at Constantinople, the Eastern Capital.

The Roman Notitia recorded four stables of the factions, where not only were horses kept prior to the races, but a standing stock was maintained. Their numbers were kept up by the emperors, consuls and praetors. The emperors had a number of stud farms in the provinces; Palmatius and Hermogenes being specially prized.

In the later Empire the factions no longer seem to have supplied the horses; the givers of the games, the emperors, senators, even humble decurions bought or bred their own. The games were in fact an obligation and required large sums of money. The factions still had their own stables, keeping the horses received as their due, or as free gifts from the emperors et al. Perhaps they still furnished teams to indigent or parsimonious senators.

The chariots continued to run under the colours of the factions who supplied the charioteers and the other personnel needed. The charioteers wore caps with the colours of the factions, and the Roman spectators displayed their favourite colour and betted on it. The tradition of racing colours has survived up to the present day.

As late as the Ostrogothic Kingdom, Cassiodorius, in Rome, writing a letter for Theodoric The Great to Faustus, the Preatorian Praefect at Ravenna, mentioned that when the Green charioteer flashed by, there was despair, if the Blue got the lead, even larger misery, etc.

As for the actual colours themselves that represented the factions, their original meanings are not very clear. Their names however, may be fairly translated as follows:[6]

Albata or Albati	white
Russata/Russati	[a russet] red
Prasina/Prasini (from the Greek word signifying a leek)	[a light] green
Veneta/Veneti (which could be explained by cerulean blue; properly, as the sky reflected in the sea)	blue

John Malalas (*c.*491–*c.*548) in his Chronographia, linked the factions with the origins of Rome; their colours being referred back to the roots of the four ancient elements. They have even been traced all the way back to Babylonia, as being related to the elements, planets, levels of space, etc. (Heaven, Air, Earth and Underworld).

At Antioch, were Malalas reported that every idle blackguard in the city had a hereditary attachment to the one or the other, the factions stood for the four city-quarters. Illustrative of this, Wallachian towns in the early nineteenth century still had their quarters marked by colours.

Cassiodorius, in the letter of King Theodoric noted above, said that the colours denoted the seasons. He interpreted the various appearances of nature during the four seasons as: blue – cloudy winter; green – verdant spring; red – flaming summer; white – frosty autumn.

Sources of Justinian's own period in the sixth century claimed that their names corresponded to the four elements: blue – water; green – the earth; red – fire; white – air.

A possibly contemporary allusion to the struggle of the Greens and Blues suggested that they represented the conflict of the earth and sea. The feuds and riots of the Blues and Greens at Constantinople were recorded by all the historians.

To give some notion of the disturbances there, in its arena, the Blues and Greens could be likened to two rival crowds at a football match; shouting abusive epithets at each other, then tearing down the barriers and breaking in upon the grounds. Personal rivalries would add to the tension and ultimately this strain would culminate into frightful outbursts of bloodshed. Constantinople was never really 'Romanized' – its crowds were Eastern, with barbarians thrown in.

It has been suggested, however, that these factions were something more than mere partisans of the colours of the races, the modern theory being that in the later Empire they were also political or religious groups.

Already by the fifth century at Constantinople the four factions were mentioned, but only two, the Blues and Greens, counted for anything. In the course of time the Reds joined with the Blues and the Whites with the Greens. Then, the Blues and Greens, if not the Reds and Whites, came to be associated with political and religious tendencies. As such organizations, and not merely for the races, the Blues were said to have drawn their leaders from the great landowners, and the Greens from trade and industry, in addition to court servants from the Empire's eastern lands.

In general, the Blues were for orthodoxy, being Catholic and imperialistic; while the Greens were Monophysites, or for other eastern heresies, and nationalistic. However, George Ostrogorsky warned that it was not true that the Blues were aristocratic, and the Greens were supported by the lower social classes; the general masses were to be found in both parties.[7]

At Antioch, as well as Constantinople itself, the support of a faction was necessary for candidates for civil or ecclesiastical honours, wires probably being pulled by a caucus of political agitators.

A further connection of the factions was with the demes. 'Demos' referred to the people as a whole (often the mass of poor citizens) and the ward or parish of the city or district where they lived. At Constantinople there were four demes in the city itself and its Asiatic suburbs.

Thus, there were the Blues and Greens of the city under Demarchs. The suburban Blues were under Domestic of the Schools, while the suburban Greens were under Domestic of the Excubiti. The rest of the populace ranged behind the Blues, or the Greens, either supporting, or attacking, the one faction or the other.

The demes, as sections of the urban population, were organized as a local militia forming the basis of a city guard. Their leaders were appointed by the Government and also had the duty of keeping in repair the local sections of the city walls. They raised and administered the taxes for these activities.

Inscriptions on the walls themselves testify to the work of construction entrusted to the factions as demes-men. In the year 413, the Praetorian Prefect, Anthemius, as 'regent' for the twelve-year-old Theodosius II, after razing the old fortifications (last repaired in 401) built the new line of walls; since called the Theodosian.

The Blues and Greens, between them, had furnished 16,000 labourers for this project; it is known that one Charisius was the head of the Blue faction at the time. Three decades later, in 447, the landward towers of the Theodosian fortifications were repaired and extended after being thrown down by an earthquake. They were rebuilt in three months under the Prefect Cyrus; once again, the colours, or demes men, must have supplied a full quota of labourers.

By the sixth century the factions had also come to include the keepers of wild beasts, dancers and probably all members of the entertainment professions. Theodora's father, Acacius, as keeper of the bears in the

Hippodrome, had belonged to the Greens. While the military and political importance of the factions is fully recognized, there is no explanation of how they became connected with the Circus parties.

One further attribute of the word 'demoi' was that it also applied to the places in the Hippodrome allotted to the factions. The Blues and the Greens each had their 'corners' at the two ends of the racecourse. This was to be a significant factor on the last fateful Sunday of 'Nika'.

Justinian and the Blues

The Emperor Anastasius was said to have only favoured the Red Faction so that he could chastize the Blues and Greens with impartial severity. Another, perhaps more plausible, version is that being partial to the Monophysites, he had shown favour to the Greens. Justinian, almost as a matter of course, patronised the Blues.

Actually, even when the power behind the throne during the reign of Justin I, Justinian had been sustained by the orthodox ecclesiastics, and he had further sought to secure his position by the devotion of one of the factions. In each party, there was a turbulent section, often a standing menace to public order, known as the 'Partisans'. He was alleged to have enlisted the Blue Partisans by procuring them official posts and favours.

Once safely seated on the throne, however, he resolved to no longer tolerate the license of the factions. A first edict, often repeated and sometimes even executed, had the firm resolution to support the innocent and chastize the guilty of every colour or denomination. Still, the balance of justice was in favour of the Blues. Judges were inclined to look less into the conduct and rights, and more into the colour of the party of an individual who stood before them. Justinian may have tried to maintain impartiality, but he has been accused of submitting to the 'implacable passions' of Theodora.[8]

As part and parcel of their general lawlessness, the dissolute youth of the factions adopted a distinct mode of dress and even hairstyle. Their attire consisted of cloaks, tunics fitted close about the wrists, with billowing sleeves, drawers and shoes. They affected the untrimmed 'Persian' type of beard, or moustache, together with the Massagetae or 'Hunnic' fashion of hair style (the hair cut off in front, back to the temples, leaving the rest to hang long).[9] The Blues, in particular, had become insolent with Justinian's royal favour and, as expressed by Gibbon, adopted 'the blue livery of disorder.'[10] They struck terror with their unorthodox appearance combined with a lofty step and sonorous voice.

The manufacture of weapons was a monopoly of the Government and they were only to be issued to the regular soldiers, but the young men of both the

Blues and Greens managed to get their hands on them. With these, they committed robberies, arson, even murder. Whatever his policy may have been regarding the factions, Justinian's very throne was almost lost in January 532 during a week of riot, ruin and revolution. Its culmination, in which Narses played no small part, was to be an appalling massacre in the Hippodrome.

The Hippodrome

Constantinople's race-course had been largely built by the 'African' Emperor, Septimius Severus (193–211) while it was still the old Byzantium in 203. He had however, left the edifice unfinished owing to his departure for the West (he was to die in Britain at York on 4 February 211). It was completed by Constantine. Originally rectangular in shape, the Hippodrome was enlarged at its south-west end by a semi-circular addition on a huge substructure of arches, or massive vaults (the sphendone), suspended over the uneven ground-level. The number of its tiers of seats was increased from sixteen to forty, giving it a seating capacity of 60,000. The overall length of the track of the Hippodrome was *c*.320 yards (see Appendix 1).

After its completion, it was to be more than a race-course; it was to become the 'axis' of the East Roman-Byzantine world. It became what the Forums were to Rome, or the Agora had been to Athens. It was the centre of the city where people came to gossip; the place where political views were voiced and rallies held. Triumphal celebrations, religious ceremonies, circuses and shows were also held there. In a certain sense, the circus took the place of a parliament.

As an assembly it was a substitute for the vanished Comitia, being the last asylum of the liberties of the 'Populus Romanus'. New emperors first showed themselves to their subjects there. There were riots against the Emperor, or even for him. Emperors in bad years (or just bad emperors) faced the people if they dared.

The Hippodrome's own axis, or centre, was the 'spina' which divided the race-course into two equal parts. In Rome this was a brick wall, about four feet high and twelve feet wide, with sufficient space at each end for the chariots to turn with freedom and safety. The two ends of the Hippodrome's spina were rounded for the same purpose and were called the 'corners'.

At the south-western end was the Green corner, while the north-eastern end was the Blue corner. The space between the latter and the Imperial reviewing stand was called the 'stama'; the Imperial guards were stationed there.

Placed on the spina, standing in a line down its middle, were three ancient monuments:

1. A sixty foot Egyptian Obelisk of Thothmes III (1479–47 BC) brought from Heliopolis via Alexandria by Theodosius I.
2. The Serpentine Pillar, or Column of Delphi, with a three-headed serpent commemorating the victory of the Greeks over Xerxes at Plataea in 479 BC. (Constantine had removed it from Delphi.)
3. The Four-Sided Brazen, or Bronze, Column

The 'carceres', or barriers, were the starting gates for the chariot races located at the southwest curve, or open-end of the course. At the far northeast end was the Manganon which held the stables for the horses and chariots, etc. In front of this was the 'Kathisma', the Imperial Stand, or Royal Box, which was the middle point of the race-course.

The Kathisma

This regal reviewing stand had been built in imitation of the 'pulvinar' or Podium in the Roman Circus. It was actually a two-storied building; the lower storey consisted of a number of porticos, or vaulted porches, closed in by strong fences. Here waited the charioteers and horses about to race.

On the upper storey of the Kathisma was a throne, extended like a bridgehead from the exclusive imperial residences. These palaces to the east of the Hippodrome were related to the race-course much as the Palace of the Caesars was to the Circus Maximus at Rome. The throne on the Imperial Stand made it the 'Palace of the Kathisma'. From it, the Basileus, or Emperor, addressed the people, making the chief announcements of the reign after his coronation.

An interesting decoration of this Royal Box was the four 'Bronze Horses' that were presumably the work of Lysippus (*c.*336–270 BC). They were to have as chequered a history as any emperor on an unstable throne.

Originally made for Chios, they were of the so-called Corinthian bronze that had been discovered by pure chance, being a mixture of ordinary bronze with gold and silver. They had been taken from Greece by Nero (AD 54–68) to decorate his triumphal arch at Rome.

In the first half of the fifth century, Theodosius II had the horses brought to Constantinople where they were set either in pairs on both sides of the Kathisma, or all four on top of its roof.

In 1204 they were dispatched to Venice by the Venetian ambassador and plenipotentiary, Marco Zeno, in Domenico Morosini's galley as part of the

Fourth Crusader's loot taken by the 'Franks' and Venetians. Only one hoof was broken off in transit.

From the Arsenal, Doge Pieto Ziani (1205–29), the successor of Enrico Dandolo, who had led the storming and sack of Constantinople, alloted the four horses their familiar abode above the west portal of St Mark's. (At least, they are said to have been in its central window by the middle of the thirteenth century.)

For over five hundred years, the 'Golden Stallions' stood as symbols of Venice's freedom. Then, in December 1797, Napoleon's specially appointed commissioners sent them to Paris, where they were placed on the Arc de Carrousel. After a comparatively short exile of eighteen years, they were returned (by 13 December 1815) to Venice where they still remain.

During both World Wars, however, the Horses of St Mark's were removed and sent to Rome for safety. At the present time, replicas have been placed on the balcony of the façade of St Mark's while the originals are nearby in the San Marco museum being protected from pollution.

The Races

As for the flesh and blood horses of Narses' day, they were part of a definite calendar and programme, not to mention ritual.

The main shows in the Hippodrome were held during the first week of January when the Consuls were inaugurated; on 11 May, Constantinople's dedication-day (and, coincidently, Justinian's birthday); and on other dates of national importance to the Empire as a whole. Chariot-races were also run in honour of an emperor's funeral.

These races were supervised by the Praetors, who were chosen yearly. When held there were twenty-four in a single day, with intervals in between for fights between men and beasts.

Each race was seven times the length of the course, said to be about one and a half miles. At the finish, the victors, with delegates of the winning faction carrying crosses of flowers, waited on the Emperor for their awards.

At the great races, prisoners in the Praetorium, the central police station, were stationed below the seats of the Green Faction. When the Emperor ordered their presence, at the celebration of a triumph, prisoners of war also stood there in chains.

In Justinian's time, the Grand Chamberlain, who was closely connected with the races, sat in the Kathisma during the contests. The Emperor directed him to give the instructions for the events. Attended by the Cubiculum, the Praepositus, as the Master of the Ceremonies, with all the

Silentiaries, proceeded to a point where all the competitors and the Decani awaited him. He was then approached by the Demarchs and Actuarius who made their obeisance to him.

On Sunday 11 January 532 a dispute arose between the Green faction and the Emperor. It concerned an official named Calopodius who may have been Grand Chamberlain at the time. The prelude to the celebrated insurrection since known as 'Nika' had begun, and a middle-aged Armenian eunuch named Narses was to perform his first historical, and possibly martial, mission.

Chapter III

'Nika'

> 'Now the watch-word which the populace passed around to one another was Nika [i.e. 'Conquer'] and the insurrection has been called by the name up to the present time.'
>
> Procopius[1]

The scene was set during the opening heats of races being run on Sunday January 11 532. There was a packed Hippodrome with the Emperor Justinian in his royal box of the Kathisma.

Some action on the part of the eunuch Calopodius had excited the anger of the Green Faction but their first complaints were modest and made in respectful tones. Obtaining no satisfaction from the throne in the Kathisma, the Greens, as the oppressed party, aired their grievances with violent invective. There ensued what Gibbon called 'the most singular dialogue that ever passed between a prince and his subjects.'[2]

The Dialogue

Justinian, as Emperor, did not personally engage in speech with the Greens, but was spoken for by a mandator, or herald. Confronting him was a spokesman for the Green Faction, or demes, surrounded by an organized body-guard.

Talking effectively across the Hippodrome was not a job for amateurs; it required professional voice-production in which both the Imperial mandator and the Green spokesman had special training. Furthermore, their speech obeyed metric laws, based on the number of syllables, and the accentuation of the last word in each clause.[3] To speak in a rhythmic chant presupposed special training in improvisation.

The opening words of the Greens were recorded in the Paschal Chronical (*c.*630). They were possibly set down by an 'exceptor' or a short-hand writer for the 'Acta', an official record, or even preserved in the archives of the Green Faction. A 'dialogue' was inserted in the ninth century chronicle of Theophanes, 'The Confessor' (*c.*758–817). This followed a short summary of Nika to which he had prefixed a detailed narrative of its events. However, his 'dialogue' exhibits no connection with the actual causes of that outbreak, and may record another incident that occurred during some other period of Justinian's reign. At best, it gives the popular language, as well as the manners of Constantinople in the sixth century; but it is a Greek mingled with many strange and barbarous words.[4]

The spokesman for the Greens, after wishing Justinian a long life, stated that the members of his faction were oppressed but feared to name the oppressor, lest he would grow stronger and they would endanger themselves. The mandator, speaking for the Emperor, replied that it was not known who was meant. The spokesman, possibly making a pun on the name of Calopodius (Kalopodios – 'pretty foot'), remarked that the oppressor was to be found in the shoemakers quarters or shops. The mandator still answered that his identity was unknown. The Green then came right out and named Calopodius ('the spathar'). The mandator asserted that Calopodius had nothing to do with him. The Green Faction next asked a question about the murder of a timber merchant at the Zeugma (a part of the shore, outside the Gates, where lumber was stored).

At this point the Blue Faction interposed with angry denials, and the 'Dialogue' degenerated into a slanging match. The Blues accused the Greens alone of committing all the murders on the racecourse; the Greens countered that when the Blues murdered they ran away. The Blues repeated that it was only the Greens who committed murder on the racecourse, and that they then threw everything into confusion. At this, the Green Faction left the Hippodrome in a body which was most likely meant as an insult to the Emperor Justinian himself.

None of this may have had any connection with the actual causes of Nika, but it gives a general idea of the sort of thing that took place in the Hippodrome on that Sunday afternoon.

Sunday Evening

The real cause of Nika occurred afterwards, on Sunday evening, and concerned the Prefect of the City, Eudaimon. He was the head of its police with the duty of preserving law and order; all of the trades were also under his control. His official quarters were in the Praetorium, the chief prison of the City, located in the Mesé, the main street of Constantinople. He had condemned seven of the Blue and Green Partisans to death for their part in causing a riot resulting in deaths.

The prisoners were taken to the place of execution, in the suburb of Pera, where four were to be beheaded and three to be hung. The sword had done its work effectively, but the rope of the gallows had broken and two of the condemned men remained alive. It so chanced that one was a Blue and the other a Green. Monks from the Church of St Conon rescued the two rioters from the further efforts of the clumsy executioner. They were carried by boat back across the Golden Horn for sanctuary to the Church of St Laurentius (since the Mosque of Pourkouyou). Eudaimon countered by throwing a cordon of police around the Church.

The Following Week

The next day, Monday, the 12th, was a quiet one, on which those in the background of the ensuing events must have made their preparations. An ominous sign was the many impoverished provincials within the walls of the city. On Tuesday, the 13th, the finals of the races run on Sunday were held.

According to custom races were held in the Hippodrome on the Ides of January, which fell on the 13th.[5] This time both factions appealed to the royal box for clemency for the two men in the Church of St Laurentius. As no answer was accorded, at the 22nd race of the day was heard the cry: 'Long live the humane Blue-Greens'. This implied that the two long-feuding parties would now co-operate with each other. The united cut-throat factions were to be known as the 'Prasino-venetoi' (Green-Blues) and their password was to be 'Nika' – 'Conquer'.

Fletcher Pratt, in a chapter of his book *The Battles That Changed History*, entitled 'Fighting in the Streets and the Future of Order', made graphic observations on the strife and violence that erupted on this day and continued for the following five. He commented on the 'excellent tactical sense' shown by whoever stage-managed this affair.[6] The mob that assembled to demand the fate of the two refugees still in St Laurentius did not march to the Church, as would have been expected; instead it went to the Praetorium, the central police headquarters.

Once there, the mob broke open the doors of the station, releasing all of its prisoners. They then beat up and even killed some of the officials on duty and drove the rest into hiding, including the Praefect Eudaimon himself. The station was then set fire to and partly burnt; thus was Constantinople's police force scattered and deprived of its leadership. This event has been fictionally referred to as a sort of Byzantine storming of the Bastille.

The mob, growing in numbers and in fury, next poured eastwards down the main street, the Mesé, towards the Imperial Palaces. At its terminus, they started smashing and burning the Augusteum (known also as the Forum of Constantine), the great marble paved forum built in honour of Helena. They set on fire the doubled-doored Royal Gate, and 'The Chalke' (so-called from its dome of brass), the main entrances to the Imperial Palaces. The flames spread back to the Bouleuterion, or Senate House, and the re-built version of Constantine's Church of St Sophia, which indicates a strong north-east wind. The fires burned throughout most of the night, probably because many of the public buildings were of wood.

The following morning, Wednesday, the 14th, the mob began anew, setting fire to the Thermae, or baths of Zeuxippus below the Senate House, off the South Portico of the Augusteum. Fires were also set in the Tetrastoon, a public square between the north end of the Augusteum and the subsequent site of Santa Sophia.

On this same day, Justinian ordered the races in the Hippodrome to be renewed. There, demands were made to three high officials of the State in the Kathisma; Basilides, Mundus and Constantiolus.[7] They had most likely come up from the Palace area to the Royal Box via the 'Cochlias', a broad winding marble stairway covered from view as it went past the north side of the Augusteum.

They had come to ask the multitude in the arena what they wanted. Not only did they want the dismissal of Eudaimon, but the Blues and Greens were united in demanding the dismissals of Tribonian and John the Cappadocian as well.[8]

Tribonian, when the magister officiorum, or head of the Imperial Secretariat, had probably also been the director of the Empire's Secret Service. In 529 he had been nominated and promoted as quaestor sacri palatii, the Quaestor of the Sacred Palace (the greatest judicial and legal officer). John the Cappadocian, the Praetorian Prefect in the East, was a notorious gatherer of taxes and had been invested the previous year, 531. When these demands were reported back to Justinian, he yielded to them at once; he appointed Tryphron the Prefect of the City, Basilides as Quaestor and Phocas as the Praetorian Prefect.

Meanwhile the mob had been hunting out the three nephews of the dead Emperor Anastasius. Two, Hypatius and Pompeius, happened to be in the Palace with Justinian; the third, Probus, was not at his residence which stood beside the harbour. The mob first searched the house for arms, and then set it on fire.

The strength of the Imperial Bodyguards of the Palace, who had their quarters behind the Chalke, was 3,500 men. They were divided into three classes; the Scholares, the Domestics and the Excubitors. However, if they were used to clear the streets of rioters, they had so many relatives and

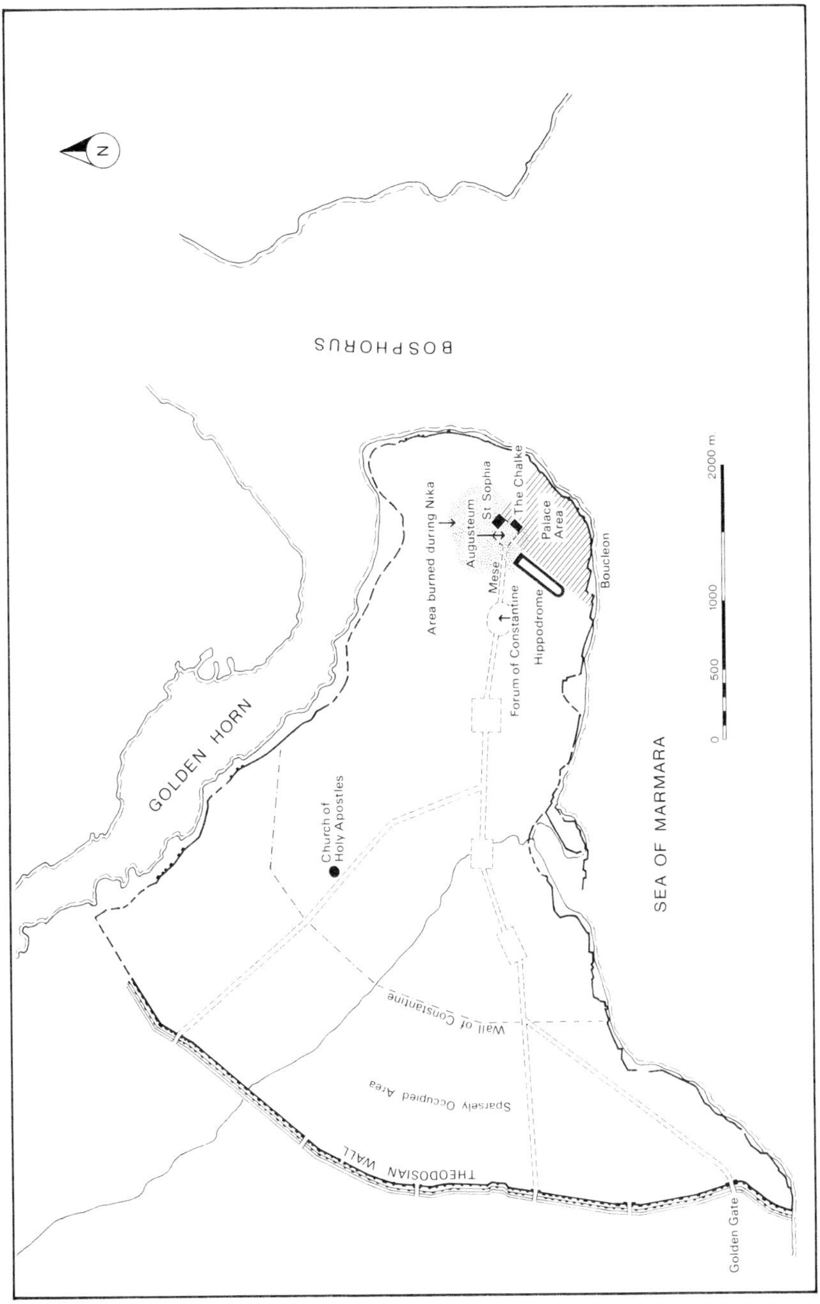

Fig. 2. Constantinople showing the area damaged during the Nika riots.

friends in the city, that they would be more likely to join the rising than suppress it.[9] It so happened that besides the two nephews of Anastasius, Belisarius himself was in the Palace at this time; having been recalled from the East. With him was his 'comitatus', (personal body-guard) composed of barbarian Goths. Also present was Mundus, recently appointed General of Illyricum, with a body of the even more barbaric tribesmen, the Eruli (Heruli). These were all the soldiers that Justinian could count on (*c.*1,500) to fight the city mob, although he could, presumably, have drawn upon the garrison of the Cyclobion (Castrum Rotundum) for more troops.

By Thursday, the 15th, Belisarius and Mundus at the head of their Goths and Heruls had already fought a battle in the Augusteum, the large forum outside the Hippodrome. They had killed many of the rioters, but their guards were too few in number to win a decisive victory. They had also been hampered by an incident when the clergy intervened between the combatants, and by the fact that their men were unwilling to attack the women who were taking part in the disorders.

Next, the barbarian mercenaries, loyal mainly to their commanders, found that they were no longer fighting a mere mob, but the armed retainers and bodyguards of the great landlords. This was the first indication that aristocrats may have been promoting the agitation; the force behind Nika was not only the Prasino-Venetoi, or 'humane Blue-Greens'. The original inspiration could have been religious, coming from the Monophysite party, with the aim of elevating a new emperor from the house of Anastasius.

A further purpose might well have been to prevent the projected African War. Whatever its reasons the revolt was now political and no longer merely concerned the fate of the two condemned rioters.

The Senators even had reasons of their own for discontent. They distrusted Justinian, and feared his policies. Now they too joined forces with the people of the streets. The Government may have behaved like a tyranny, but not like an effective one.

On Friday morning, the 16th, Belisarius and his men began anew to the north of the area of St Sophia, where the rebels had their base, around the Brassmarket. The mob countered by setting fire once more to the offices of the Praefect in the Praetorium, which was partly damaged.

Fire was also set to the Baths of Alexander, with a strong wind blowing the flames away from the Praetorium and into the faces of Belisarius' men. The same ill-wind carried the fires to the neighbourhood of the Church of St Irene (standing for two centuries, since the time of Constantine) north of the Augusteum and St Sophia. The Hospice of Eubulus was only partly burnt, but the Hospice of Samson was destroyed along with its patients. This was the Hospital in between St Sophia and St Irene's.[10]

That same evening, ships arrived with soldiers from the neighbouring cities of Hebdomon and Rhegium and further attacks on the insurgents were planned.

The very next morning, Saturday the 17th, Belisarius tried to get at their base in the Brassmarket, east of the previous line of advance. This was up a group of streets leading northward from the Mesé to the Basilica, or law court, and the quarter of Chalkopraeteia. The mob assembled in the Augusteum, intending an assault on the Imperial Palaces.

The insurgents occupied the Octagon, probably a public library, close to the Basilica. Some of the soldiers besieged them there, but being unable to expel the entrenched rebels, set fire to the building. A north wind blew its flames southward to the Church of St Theodore Sphoracius and the Palace of Lausus. Fires also raged along the Mesé in the direction of the Church of St Aquilana and the Augusteum which had its colonnades destroyed.

That Saturday night, Justinian sent away everyone in the Palace not of his immediate Court, including Hypatius and Pompeius. In their case, he may have suspected them of plotting, for Procopius informs that already in the late afternoon he had given them orders to 'go home'.[11]

By sunrise on Sunday, the 18th, the mob knew that the two nephews of Anastasius had quit the Palace. It made for the residence of Hypatius where he was found with his wife Mary.

Procopius described Mary as a 'discreet woman' with a reputation for prudence, who would not let go of her husband, certain that the people would be leading him to his death. But as the throng overpowered her, she had to unwillingly release him. Clothed in the white chlamys (official dress cloak), Hypatius was carried in triumph, though by no will of his own, to the great forum, or Augusteum. Once there, he was summoned to the throne, but the crowd did not have a diadem or any other customary object for crowning royalty. Therefore they placed a golden chain, or necklace, upon his head to proclaim Hypatius 'Emperor of the Romans'.[12]

Meanwhile, just over in the Hippodrome, Justinian appeared in the Kathisma, carrying a copy of the Gospels, to swear to peace and an amnesty. After he returned to the Palace, the new 'emperor' Hypatius was brought up into his vacated Royal Box.

Justinian was keeping quiet in the Palace with the nobles of his Court assembled there, according to custom, for the Ides of January. He may have been expecting the insurrection to wear itself out, with perhaps the Blues and Greens ultimately falling out among themselves. In any event, the fact remained that whoever held the Palace area still held Constantinople and the Empire.

The Imperial Palaces

This Imperial Palace area (built under Constantine) was a series of private apartments and palaces; throne rooms, banqueting and council halls; gates and guard houses with the quarters of the bodyguards; chapels and churches; baths, pavilions and terraces, etc. It was grouped mainly into three divisions:

1. The Chalke
   (The Prefect of the Palace, or Grand Chamberlain, had a residence in this area)
2. Daphne
   (The Private Palace)
3. The Sacred, or God-Guarded Palace

It was the seat of the Imperial Secretariat and the chief ministries of the State; the Treasure of the Empire was kept in its vaults. Narses was soon to draw on its resources.

Origenes, a member of the Senate, made a speech to the mob against attacking these Palaces; the mob went instead into the Hippodrome. There had been a report by Ephraim, an Imperial Guard, serving as a messenger from Hypatius to Justinian, that the latter and his Court had fled to Asia. This was a premature rumour; Justinian was actually in the midst of a council, discussing whether to stay on or to take flight on ships that were in the harbour of Boucleon. His Empire 'seemed on the verge of its fall'.

Besides Belisarius, Narses the eunuch and Theodora the Empress were present at this council. All appeared to be lost to Justinian; all except the spirit of Theodora. Gibbon remarked that the prostitute he had raised from the theatre now renounced the timidity, as well as the virtues, of her sex. Or, as a more charitable way of putting it, the Empress might not have been blue-blooded, but she knew the heroes of the arena.

Theodora's Speech

Theodora suddenly rose up violently, disagreeing with the proposed flight. With a power of diction and gesture from her acquaintance with the theatre, the effect can well be imagined. A version of her speech has been given by Procopius who, as the secretary of Belisarius, may have been present at the scene. He obviously composed his own speeches, conveying the substance of what was said, or bringing out the points of a situation. In this instance, Procopius used Thucydides as his model, but even in this garb it has an authentic ring.[13]

Theodora protested that the present time was inopportune for flight, it being impossible for an emperor to be a fugitive. As for herself, she would never be separated from the 'purple' or live to see the day when those who greeted her did not address her as 'Mistress'. She pointed out that flight was easy, gesturing to the harbour and ships, but asked Justinian, as an emperor, to consider if death was not preferable to safety. She concluded dramatically by recalling an 'ancient saying' that 'royalty is a good burial-shroud'.[14]

As it turned out, there was no need for burial shrouds for Justinian and Theodora, or even for their flight; their next move, involving Narses, was to break the back of the Nika insurrection.

Narses' Mission to the Blues

Theodora herself may have suggested, or even ordered Narses' involvement, and Justinian furnished the funds necessary for Narses to leave the Palace and bribe the leaders of the Blue Faction.

On his mission to the Blues, Narses appealed to their party loyalty, insinuating that like his uncle, a favourer of Monophysites, Hypatius would protect the Greens. His money was convincing enough, but his words must have been equally so; his warnings moved as swiftly as the fires. One version has Narses already distributing the money and distracting the factions before Theodora's speech.

Massacre In The Hippodrome

After Theodora's speech, however, Justinian was aroused sufficiently to send Belisarius at the head of his comitatus to arrest Hypatius up in the Kathisma. Belisarius, however, was balked in his first attempt to go straight up into the Royal Box by a small locked door held by neutralist guards. He returned to Justinian in the Palace, declaring the day to be lost. He had probably attempted going directly from the Palace to the Royal Box by way of the Cochlias. He was now told to go to the Bronze Gate (the inner pair of doors to the Royal Gate being of bronze) and a vestibule leading over to the Augusteum. In the deserted, burnt-out forum, Belisarius met Mundus and his Heruls, who may have come out through the gate called the 'Snail', so-called because of a circling descent (this could have been the gate below the Royal Gate, behind the Senate House).

Mundus stood outside the northeast corner of the Hippodrome by the 'Gate of the Dead'; a gate in imitation of the Roman porta mortua, by which dead bodies were removed. Belisarius ascended into the Hippodrome itself, reaching the Blue Colonnade, or Gate of the Blues, on the right side (east) of the Kathisma. He was able to pass unobserved, without suspicion, by the mob in the stands because of the lofty benches, and because all the other gates were closed.

By this time, the leaders of the Blues, who had received the bribes of Narses, were beginning to shout 'Justiniane Auguste, tu vincas'.[15] Giving out his war-cry, Belisarius led his men against the mob standing packed in a dense mass. Mundus, hearing the outcry, joined in, charging through the Gate of Death. The mob attacked in front, and in the rear, could not escape; friends outside could not make their way in to help. Before the massacre was over, cousins or nephews of Justinian, Boraides and Justus (the brothers of Germanus) dragged Hypatius from the throne on the Imperial Stand, and handed him over, together with Pompeius, for judgement.

In the meantime, Narses himself may have taken part in the action. Robert Browning has him leading a detachment of armed palace guards to an exit where he slaughtered any fugitives who came out.[16] Historical fiction accounts of these events describe him leading Belisarius into the Hippodrome and then arming hordes of the suburban Blue demes-men who broke into the arena to assist in the massacre.

And an appalling massacre it was; piles of dead bodies were left lying in the Hippodrome when Justinian finally ordered an end to the slaughter. Computations of the carnage range from *c.*30,000 up to 80,000. Since the seating capacity of the Hippodrome was 60,000, and on this occasion there must have been a standing-room only crowd, perhaps an estimate of 50,000 would be in order.[17]

On the morning following that sanguinary Sunday of 18 January 532, there were at least two more victims. Hypatius and Pompeius were put to death by order of Theodora, according to Zachariah of Mitylene. With them, and all of the dead bodies of the Green Faction in the Hippodrome, perished the Monophysite Revolt. It has also been seen as the triumph of Byzantine autocracy over the civil freedoms of the demes.[18]

The Aftermath of Nika

This whole episode established Justinian's power more firmly than before, and his punishment of the Senators was less severe than might have been expected, only exiling those who had actually sided with Hypatius.

Psalm XV, with slight modifications, was used to commemorate his triumph over the Factions; 'a chant of the unshakeable security of the faithful worshipper'. In effect, the righteous man shall not be overthrown.

The Hippodrome, however, continued to be the scene of troubles, demonstrations, burnings and riots, with fresh outbursts in 539, 541, 542, 544, 547, 548 and 551. In May 556 the Factions fought for two days. They also clashed in 562 and 563, and there were many undated clashes.[19]

Thomas Hodgkin commented on the end of the celebrated sedition of the Nika; its chief interest being to bring forth the two men who were to gather great fame in Italy, namely Belisarius and Narses. The general was only twenty-seven years old, the court eunuch fifty-four.

Belisarius was to be given a 'Triumph' almost three years later (1 January 535) on his return from Africa following his conquest of the Vandals, Procopius relating that it was in the 'ancient manner'. He went on foot from his own house, along the great street (the Mesé) to the Hippodrome, and then from the barriers to the Imperial throne in the Kathisma.[20]

Narses was to have his own 'Triumph' almost two decades later (in 554) but not in the 'New Rome' of Constantinople. His was to be in the ancient capital on the Tiber, where he celebrated the last Triumph held in the City of Rome.

Chapter IV

The First Command of Narses

'From the domestic service of the palace and the administration of the private revenue, Narses the eunuch was suddenly exalted to the head of an army; and the spirit of an hero, who afterwards equalled the merit and glory of Belisarius, served only to perplex the operations of the Gothic war.'
Gibbon[1]

The Background of the Gothic War (535–53)

As part of Justinian's great scheme to re-establish the boundaries of the Roman Empire, Belisarius embarked from Constantinople on 22 June 533 at the head of 15–16,000 soldiers. 20,000 sailors were needed to man the 500 transport ships, guarded by 92 war vessels. His conquest of the Kingdom of the Vandals in Africa, together with Sardinia and Corsica, was relatively rapid and easy; Gelimer, the Vandal King (530–34), surrendering about nine months later in March 534.

Then during the autumn of the year of his consulship, 535, Belisarius invaded Sicily with an army of 8,000 men. The murder of Amalasuntha, Theodoric's daughter, contrived by her cousin and co-ruler, Theodatus (Theodahad), was the 'causus belli' for attacking the Ostrogothic Kingdom of Italy. After landing at Catania, the Imperialists laid siege to Palermo. On the last day of his consulship, 31 December, Belisarius entered Syracuse.

Meanwhile, Mundus, the other hero of Nika, had occupied Salones (Salona) on the Adriatic coast of Dalmatia (modern Yugoslavia), but the Ostrogoths sent a large army to recover the area. This they accomplished temporarily, after the death of Mundus; he was mortally wounded while pursuing the Goths who had killed his son, Maurice, during a skirmish in the neighbourhood of Salona.

In April 536 Belisarius had to return to Carthage to put down a rebellion that had erupted there. This had begun on Easter Sunday with an assassination plot against the military governor, Solomon the Eunuch, whom Belisarius had left behind in charge. Together with another general, Martin, and Procopius himself, Solomon escaped in a small sail boat to reach Belisarius at Syracuse.

After defeating the rebels at the Battle of Membresa, Belisarius had to return to Sicily in May because of a mutiny in his own army. It was, therefore, not until the end of June 536 that he was ready to invade Italy itself crossing from Sicily over to Reggio di Calabria, and marching up to besiege Naples.

Justinian's first attempt at the conquest of the Italian mainland bears an historical similarity to the campaign of the Allies against the Axis Powers (1943–45). Then, Winston Churchill's 'soft underbelly' strategical approach to the same goal by using Sicily as a 'springboard' was applied.

A further historical coincidence is that invasion resulted in an overthrow of leadership. Benito Mussolini was deposed by the Fascist Grand Council on the night of 24–25 July, 1943, and then later placed under arrest. The Goths also deposed their King, Theodatus (534–36), who was unsteady, unreliable and a coward; he was later to be killed by one Optarius, soon after the fall of Naples.

Meeting in counsel at Regata in the Pomptine marshes, near Terracina, about half way up the coast between Naples and Rome, the Ostrogoths elevated Witigis (Vitigis) as the new ruler of their nation in November 536.

By 10 December 536, Belisarius had entered Rome, reclaiming the ancient capital for the Empire; however, he had to withstand a siege of over a year (3 March 537–12 March 538). This was led by Vitigis in person with an estimated 100,000–150,000 Gothic warriors.

In December 537 some 5,300 in reinforcements reached the outmanned Imperial forces in Italy; with them as a general was John, a nephew of Vitalian, and a personal friend of Narses. On the 21st of this same month, some breathing time was also gained for Belisarius and his beleagured forces by a truce of three months.

Before hostilities resumed, Belisarius ordered John with 2,000 picked Isaurian highlanders, 'the Swiss of the Eastern Empire', to move into Picenum (the Marches). He was supposed to raid the country around the Adriatic end of the Via Flaminia. John, however, disobeyed orders, not attempting to reduce Urbinus (Urbino) and Auximum (Osimo) which were too strong to be taken by direct assult. He instead pressed on to Rimini which he captured at the first assault.

After hearing that an Imperial army was occupying Picenum, and other soldiers of the Empire had been asked to seize Milan at the request of Datius, its Archbishop, Vitigis raised his siege of Rome and retired north eastwards towards Ravenna on 12 March 538. Belisarius, perhaps sensing

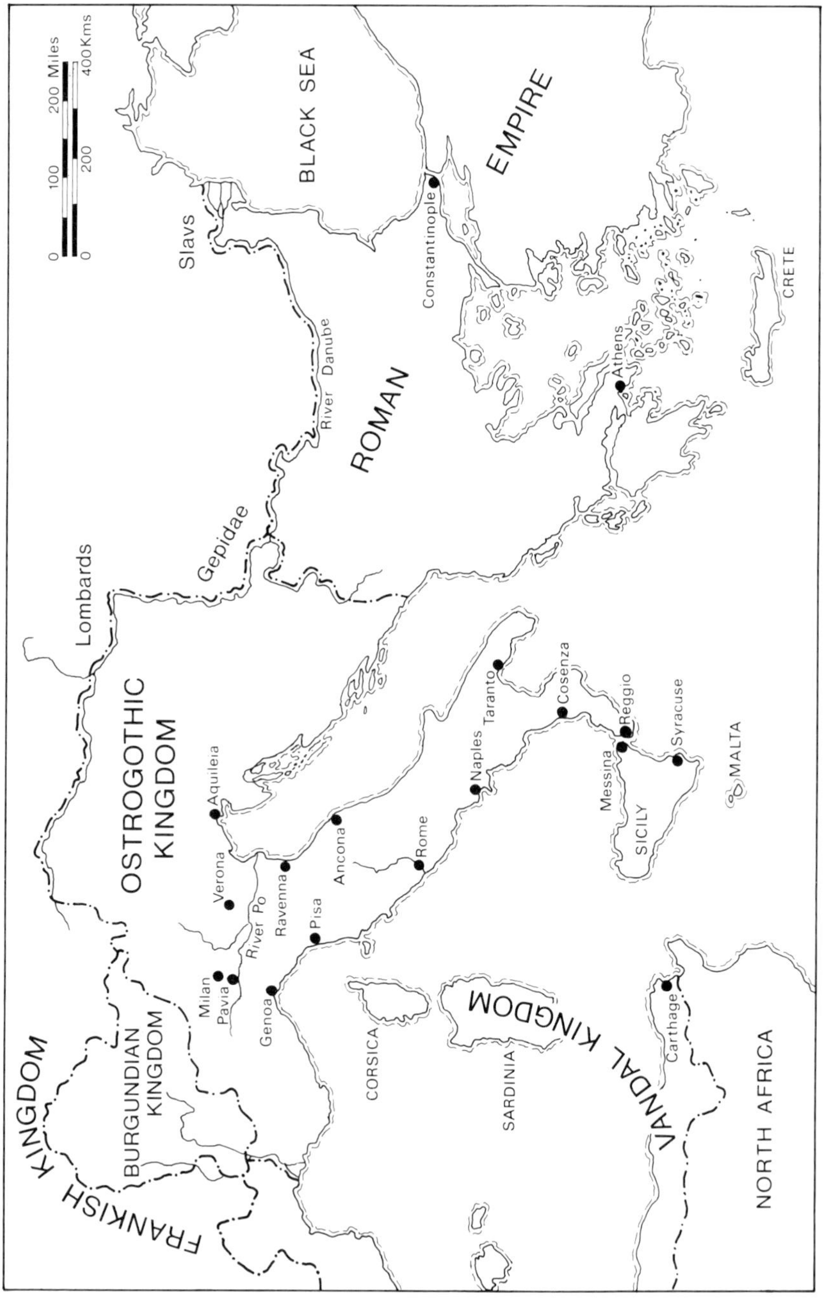

Fig. 3. The Kingdom of the Ostrogoths.

this as a 'retreat', sent part of his forces, about 1,000 men, by sea up the west coast to Genoa. The force consisted of Isaurians under Ennes, and Thracians under Paulus, with Mundilas in overall command. They occupied most of Liguria, and Milan as well. There was a battle at Pavia resulting in a victory, but the city itself was unconquered and the followers of Mundilas were reduced to 300 men.

Meanwhile, Belisarius had ordered John to withdraw from Rimini; John refused, which resulted in tension. Vitigis exploited this by moving in on the town and investing it in April 538. By May or June Belisarius, with a mere 3,000 men, advanced from Rome over to the east coast. He reduced two fortresses west of the Apennines, Clusium (Chiusi), and Tuder (Todi), but Urbs Vetus (Orvieto) remained unreduced. He also dispatched 1,000 men under Ildiger and Martin to recall John from Rimini.

Once again John refused to obey orders; apparently because he knew something that Belisarius did not; that further reinforcements were being sent by Justinian. He had also received an offer of marriage from Matasuntha, the daughter of Amalasuntha and sister of Athalaric (thus consequently a granddaughter of Theodoric the Great). Matasuntha had married Vitigis against her will; in revenge she would betray Ravenna, and was even suspected of burning its grain stores.

Then, in June, the execution of all of Belisarius' plans was disarranged by the report of the arrival of a 'great army' in Picenum, and by the surprising news that it was under the command of Narses the Eunuch.

The 'Aulic Councillor'

This army, which arrived on 21 June 538, probably at Ancona (held by Conon) consisted of *c*.5,000 soldiers of various barbarian nationalities. With Narses were Justin (the General of Illyricum) and Narses[2]. Also following him were Aluith, Phanitheus and Visandus with 2,000 Heruls, bringing the grand total up to about 7,000 much-needed men.

Belisarius marched over to Picenum to confer with Narses in order to arrange the future conduct of the war. A further complication for him was the question of why this new general was furnished with full powers as a commander-in-chief; did Justinian suspect the loyalty of Belisarius?

If this were the case, it would hardly be surprising. Belisarius had a large following of men-at-arms, his comitatus, who owed no oath of allegiance to anyone but himself. These long-term professional soldiers had served him loyally, in three wars; in Asia, Africa and now in Italy. Besides the fame of his exploits, he had been gorged with plunder and riches from these campaigns. Now there were rumours that he intended to seize the throne of Italy for himself.

Conversely there were many reasons why Justinian should feel that he could trust his loyal courtier. Narses was a eunuch advanced in age, already in his sixtieth year in 538 (if 478 is accepted as the date of his birth) and as such not a candidate for any kind of crown. He had proved himself a trusty councillor in the intrigues of the Cabinet, as well as the domestic matters of the Court, and had otherwise been deeply involved in the Imperial service. Therefore, as a matter of course, he was a colleague who would place the interests of his master above his own. Furthermore, he may have given some indication of military talents to Justinian and Theodora during Nika.

Procopius, in commenting on Narses' arrival in Italy, referred to him as a eunuch and as a keeper of the royal treasures 'but for the rest keen and more energetic then would be expected of a eunuch.'[2]

He may have even been sent as a sort of spy; not only to keep an eye on Belisarius himself, but possibly also on Antonina, Belisarius' wife, who travelled in his train. Finally, Narses has been likened to a sort of 'Aulic Councillor'. (The Emperor Maximilian, in 1497, established the Aulic Council, as a legislative and executive body to assist in governing the Holy Roman Empire.)

Council of War

Belisarius and Narses met at Firmum (Fermo) where a council of war was held. Besides the two commanding generals, it consisted of Martin and Ildiger, Justin, the brothers Aratius and Narses[2], Aluith, Phanitheus, Visandus, et al. The most pressing question to be decided was whether John up at Rimini was to be relieved, or left to his fate.

The younger officers blurted out invectives against John. Procopius, who may have been present, reports that the majority were hostile towards him, and made their speeches accordingly.[3] They accused him of 'unreasoning daring', with a desire to gain riches and going against Belisarius' prescribed operations for the war. Apparently, Belisarius, whose methods of warfare required exact obedience from subordinates, was not quite able to appreciate a man like John who possessed initiative of his own. Narses, however, 'who loved John above all other men', saw that his seizure of Rimini was strategically correct and was fearful that Belisarius would give way to the others and treat Rimini as of secondary importance.[4]

This grey-headed old man arose grave and elegant, and after some preliminary remarks admitting his own inexperience in war, pointed out the extraordinary circumstances at this time. He addressed the young hot-heads as 'fellow officers' who were not debating a customary question at all. In his speech, as reported by Procopius, he stated that John had already been punished for his 'insolence', and that if the disheartened Goths captured him with his whole army and the city, their fortunes and spirits would revive, turning the tide of the war.[5]

At this point, a soldier who had escaped from the besieged town, by slipping through the enemy lines, entered the camp with a message from John himself. The gist of it was that his provisions were almost exhausted and therefore he would have to surrender in the next seven days. This was a moment when the conduct, or the plan, of the war seemed to fall into the hands of Narses.

But Belisarius was still uncertain, and he hesitated. For one thing, he was worried about the Gothic garrison at Auximum (Osimo) in his rear. It was finally decided to leave Aratius with 1,000 men to keep watch over Osimo.

The words and will of Narses had prevailed at this, his first general staff meeting; John and Rimini were to be relieved.

The Relief of Rimini

Once the decision to relieve John was made, the combined Imperial forces moved rapidly. Ildiger led the main force, by sea, to Rimini; subordinate officers were Narses[2], Herodian and Uliaris. Martin led a second force along the coast via Ancona up into the 'great highway' or Via Flaminia, past Fano and Pesaro, keeping near the ships.

Together, Belisarius and Narses led a 'flying column' by way of an inland mountainous route, via Urbs Salvia or Urvisalia (Urbesaglia) to descend on Rimini from the northwest. They fell in with a small party of Goths passing the same way, a day's journey from Rimini, attacking and wounding some of them. This was all to the good, as these Goths spread panic-bearing reports to the besieging army of Vitigis.

Theoretically, all three Imperial armies should have arrived before Rimini at about the same time. (Ildiger was not to disembark until Martin arrived.) But, as it turned out, it was Ildiger and his men who were the first to enter the enemy's camp.

If John's besieged soldiers had had some daring or strength left in them they could have sallied forth from the town and killed a great number of the retreating Goths. As it was, they were prevented by their 'great fear' and weakness due to the lack of provisions.[6]

Belisarius and Narses with the rest of the armies arrived on the scene around noon on the following day. On seeing the physical condition of John's small garrison, Belisarius remarked that a debt of gratitude was owed to Ildiger. John replied that his obligations, as such, were to Narses, and not to Ildiger; the implication being that he knew Belisarius had not relieved him willingly but only because of the persuasion by Narses.

Procopius, who should have been in a position to know, comments: 'And from that time both these men [Belisarius and Narses] began to regard each other with great suspicion.'[7] Later historians go so far as to speculate that jealousy may have already originated at the time of Nika.

The Divided Command

While the relief of Rimini gave fresh proof of the military capacity of Belisarius, it was actually a 'moral victory' for Narses. It also served to greatly strengthen his partisans at the council-tables of the Imperial generals. For now friends and supporters gathered around Narses, and flattered by these subordinates he began to block the projects of Belisarius. He may have hinted to the generals who had accompanied the reinforcements to thwart them as well.

In any event, he could rely on his intimate relations with Justinian to take an independent line. And he may not have been there in the first place to co-operate with Belisarius, but to hamper his movements. Belisarius was soon made to feel that he might advise, but not command, the eunuch-general fresh from the Sacred Bed-Chamber.

Therefore during the autumn and winter months of 538–39, the Imperial Army was divided into two parties, and in reality two separate armies; those of Belisarius and Narses.[8]

Narses actually had the larger army, said to be no less than 10,000 men. Not only did he command the forces that came with Justin and Narses[2], his own guards and spearmen and the Herulian contingent, but those of Aratius and John as well.

Belisarius, with what was left of his own troops, kept watch over Vitigis up in Ravenna, while planning to mop-up the various fortresses back towards Rome. Evidently, the generals in the other camp, who had influence at Court, were inclined to seek easier and wealthier objectives.

Peranius (an Iberian prince, the son of King Gourgenus/Gurgen) was sent to besiege Orvieto again by Belisarius, while he personally undertook the reduction of Urbinus (Urbino). Narses and his army followed, but encamped apart; on the west of this hill town, with Belisarius on the east. However, Narses soon abandoned its siege, going back north to Rimini. At about the time of the winter solstice (21 December) its one spring of water gave out and Urbino had to surrender.[9]

Narses, who had remained quietly in Rimini all during the autumn of 538, is said to have been filled with both astonishment and dejection on hearing of its capture. He ordered John to an unsuccessful assault on the fortress of Caesena (Cesena) north west of Rimini, where Phanitheus, the leader of the Heruls, fell. Their command was assumed by Philemuth. John, together with Justin, nevertheless did capture Forum Cornelii, or Forocornelius (Imola) and recovered the rest of Aemilia.[10]

The Letter

It must have been at this time that the famous episode of 'The Letter' occurred. Justinian, back in Constantinople, must have heard of the divisions within his Army, and dictated a letter to a confidential secretary at the Court. As Procopius was Belisarius' own private secretary, he should have been in a position to know the contents of this letter, and he did give a quotation from it:

> 'We have not sent our steward Narses to Italy in order to command the army; for we wish Belisarius alone to command the whole army in whatever manner seems to him to be best, and it is the duty of all of you to follow him in the interest of our state.'[11]

The last six words, historians have seen as a questionable, or debatable phrase, and even an unique 'limiting clause'.

Narses, particularly in the fictional accounts of this historical episode, is made to take hold of these final words and use his bureaucratic mind to twist 'meaning' from them. Doubtless from years of intrigue back at the Court, it must have been second nature for him to turn Belisarius' new trump card by having him appear to renege. He informed all and sundry that Belisarius, at that time, was laying plans contrary to 'the interests of the state', and therefore it was not their duty to follow him. Once again Narses must have carried the day, as there still remained a divided command over two separate armies. The compromises and half-measures that followed led to the disaster of Milan.

The Fall of Milan

During the winter and spring months of 538–39, Milan was besieged by the Goths under Uraias, a nephew of Vitigis, together with 10,000 Burgundian allies, or 'volunteers' from Theodebert, the King of Austrasia. Belisarius now busy besieging Orvieto, ordered Martin and Wilihari (Uliaris) to the relief of the city; however, they remained idle on the south bank of the Po one day's journey distant from Milan. Martin wrote back asking for assistance from John and Justin. These two, over at Padua, refused to obey any orders except those of Narses who was still back in Rimini. He was asked by Belisarius to give them the necessary orders; he did consent; but, many weeks, if not actual months, were wasted in all of these discussions.

Not only time, but long distances were also involved; there were messengers moving back and forth from the Po to Orvieto, to Padua, back down to Orvieto, then up to Rimini, etc. To add to the delays, John had caught malaria fever.

The end result of all this was that Milan was surrendered by its starving garrison to the barbarians towards the end of March 539. Mundilas and his 300 men were allowed to live, but the city itself was given up to destruction. Out of a total population said to number half a million, 300,000 males of all ages lost their lives and its women were given as slaves to the Burgundians.[12] Reparatus, the Praetorian Prefect, (a brother of the future Pope Vigilius) is reputed to have been cut into pieces and thrown to the dogs. The Goths also took other cities with Imperial garrisons, thus gaining control over the whole of Liguria.

Belisarius duly reported the disaster back to Constantinople as the unavoidable result of a divided command. Justinian also received a graphic eye-witness report from Vergentinus (Cerventinus), a Roman senator (and another brother of Vigilius) who had escaped from the horrors of Milan. As a result, the emperor recalled Narses from Italy, and formally proclaimed Belisarius the sole commander-in-chief.

Narses' Recall

So Narses was recalled, but not in disgrace. He returned to his domestic duties in the Palace much as if nothing had happened. Procopius commented that Justinian treated no one with severity as a result of the events in Italy, and Narses was even allowed to retain some of his loyal barbarian guardsmen.[13]

Meanwhile, back in Italy, even after his recall, Narses left wounds for Belisarius to try and heal. The Heruli refused to remain after his departure, although Belisarius promised them many benefits from himself, and Justinian, if they remained. Instead they departed from Italy, but being the barbarians they were, looting on their way out. They first went to Liguria to sell slaves and booty to the army of Uraias, the conqueror of Milan. Then, over in Venetia, they repented and went on to Constantinople.

Despite these problems, however, Belisarius was initially successful. He captured Osimo and Fisula (Fiesole) then laid siege to Ravenna, the Ostrogothic Capital itself. He was offered the crown of their kingdom by Vitigis. He accepted the offer, and after 'treacheous negotiations', entered Ravenna in May 540. There, refusing the crown to be a Western Emperor, Belisarius had Vitigis seized and sent as a prisoner to Constantinople.

To regard this, however, as the end of the Ostrogothic Kingdom in Italy would be a premature judgement; the Goths were to have four more rulers in the next thirteen years (540–53). (See Appendix 2)

After the capture of his uncle, Uraias refused the kingship and eventually was put to death by the next ruler Ildibad (Hildibad).

Ildibad was a nephew of Theudis, the Visigothic King in Spain, and the uncle of Baduila (Totila), the future adversary of Belisarius, and then Narses. Because he gave the intended bride of a Gepid in his royal guards to another man, he was assassinated while reclining at a banquet, by the wronged suitor. The Goths considered this a just retribution for the murder of Uraias.

After Ildabad's short reign (540–41) Eraric, a Rugian, became the King of the Ostrogoths, but only for about four to five months (May–September/October 541). He was put to death for being involved in treacherous negotiations with Justinian.

During the autumn of 541, Baduila succeeded to the throne, one of his conditions being that Eraric be slain. Generally known as Totila, he was to reign until the year 552, after successfully frustrating all Belisarius' later operations.

Chapter V

After the Recall

> 'It would be but natural to suppose that Narses was punished in some manner for his marked insubordination, but this was not the case. He seems to have lost none of his favour at court, but to have remained the most trusted servant and minister of the Emperor and his consort.'
>
> James E. Dunlap[1]

During the next twelve years, i.e. 539–51, there is little historical mention of his name, but Narses continued to exercise his influence behind the scenes at the Courts of the Emperor Justinian and also the Empress Theodora.

In 539, the King of the Austrasian Franks, Theodebert, led an army of 100,000 men into Northern Italy attacking both the troops of Belisarius and those of his erstwhile Gothic allies. This turned out to be little more than a king-sized raid, but it was a foreboding of events in Narses' future career.

During the following year, 540, when Belisarius had apparently ended the Gothic War by entering Ravenna, there was an invasion of Illyricum by a large army of Huns from over the Danube. They are said to have captured 32 fortresses, and plundered as close as the suburbs of Constantinople itself. The Bulgars also over-ran the Balkan provinces.

One reason Justinian may have recalled his future Grand Chamberlain from the 'field' was to have his much-needed counsel at the Imperial Councils of State to deal with the insolence of the Persian ruler Khosrau (Chosroes). During the spring season of 540, the Great King broke the peace and invaded Syria. This event was to lead to the return of Belisarius himself from Italy to fight on the eastern Persian front for the next three years (541–44). This in turn explains the presence of his wife, Antonina, at the Court of the Empress Theodora in the year 541, for the plotting that led to the downfall of John the Cappadocian.

The Overthrow of John the Cappadocian

It is clear that the events in Italy had done little, or nothing, to impair the regal trust in the ability and loyalty of Narses. He was to be deeply involved in securing the evidence against John the Cappadocian (Justinian's chief tax-gatherer) that led to his loss of office, acquired wealth, and then imprisonment and exile.

This is the self-same John, who, appointed as the Praetorian Prefect of the East in the year 530 (invested in 531) was removed from his post, along with Eudaimon and Tribonian, at the demand of the mob, during Nika, in January 532. He was restored to his office before June 533.

By all accounts he was a ruthless but very efficient and capable tax-collector for the ever-needy coffers of Justinian's Empire. In common with most people of his day and age, including an educated historian such as Procopius, he was superstitious enough to believe in prophecies and omens. John had visions that he was destined someday for the royal power itself, because of a prediction that he would be clothed in 'the garments of Augustus'. Otherwise, for such an unattractive and unscrupulous character, his one redeeming feature was his devotion to his daughter, and only child, Euphemia.

Sometime during April or May 541 and for reasons best known to themselves, the Empress Theodora and her long-time friend, Antonina, conspired John's destruction. There may have been a smouldering animosity or enmity through the years between the Empress and John. Then again, she may have heard of the prophecies and been superstitious enough herself to try and head them off.

In any event, Theodora and Antonina went to attack John through the only soft spot in his tough hide, his daughter Euphemia. By means of conversation with the innocent, unsuspecting girl they hinted at plans and projects that would lead to the great future in store for her father. Euphemia dutifully brought back the whole matter to John, who was pleased at the news, jumping to the conclusion that a way was being offered to him to fulfil the prophecies of royal power.

He wanted an immediate meeting with Antonina, but she shrewdly advised caution to avoid any suspicions arising which might hamper proceedings. As her husband, Belisarius, was already fighting on the Persian front, she was intending to depart from Constantinople to join him in the East. Therefore, when she left the city and reached 'Rufinianum', the private country house of Belisarius in the suburbs, John should come as if to see her off on the journey; there they could confer on important matters of State.

John, unsuspecting, agreed to this, and a time and date was set to carry out the plan. Antonina reported back to Theodora, who approved of all the proceedings. On the appointed day, Antonina departed to spend the night in the house at Rufinianae, near Chalcedon, thus to begin her journey to the East the following day.

Theodora, meanwhile, had gone to Justinian and denounced John as a traitor. She, knowing it would be essential to have any treasonable conversation overheard by reliable witnesses, whom Justinian would have to believe, sent Marcellus, a Captain of the Guard, and Narses to the rendezvous. Justinian got wind of the plot, and sent a friend of John's to forbid him to meet Antonina secretly under any circumstances. To Procopius, 'it was fated that he should fare ill' for John, disregarding the warning, went to the clandestine meeting.[2]

He arrived on the prepared scene at about midnight, into an 'ambuscade of guards and eunuchs'; this was Marcellus and Narses stationed behind a nearby wall with Spartharii (sword-bearers). John himself happened to be one of the very few civilians authorized to possess a comitatus or body-guard (it actually consisted of several thousand men) and some of them were by his side. If his person was guarded, his tongue was not; he began by asserting to the plans of the baited trap. He of all people, who must have known the value of promises, was binding himself with the most dreadful oaths.

Having heard enough, Narses and Marcellus emerged from behind the wall and set upon him. In the ensuing struggle, Marcellus was wounded by John's guards and John was able to escape. Procopius believes that if John had gone straightaway to Justinian, he would have suffered no harm from the hand of the Emperor.[3]

Instead, he fled for refuge to a sanctuary giving Theodora the time and opportunity to work her will against him at her pleasure. A sentence of confiscation and degradation was passed on John, and he was banished to a suburb of Cyzicus, called Artace. He was forcibly ordained a cleric, a 'presbyter', under the Gospel name of Peter; but, presumably through Justinian's intervention, 'Peter' was able to retain enough of his ill-gotten fortune to live in luxurious retirement. The ill-will of Theodora still pursued him, however, and later he was imprisoned for the murder of the Bishop Eusebius, to whom he had been hostile.

The end result was that 'Peter' was stripped of what remained of his worldly goods, even his very clothes, and clad only in a single cloak, put aboard a ship bound for Antinous in Egypt.[4] The chastised Cappadocian was to turn up some seven or eight years later back in Constantinople. He returned at the summons of Justinian sometime after the death of Theodora, between the end of June 548 and 1 April 549.

Unable to recover any of his former power or dignities, he had to continue being a priest against his will. Nonetheless, John's vision of royalty also continued in his belief in the prediction that he was yet to wear the garment of Augustus. Ironically, Procopius tells of a certain priest, Augustus by name, who guarded the treasures of the 'temple of Sophia' (Santa Sophia?) and how when John was returned to priesthood by force, he was compelled to put on the cloak and the tunic of this Augustus.[5]

The Plague (542–43)

In the year following the banishment of John (Peter), 542, plague began to spread across the countries of the Eastern Mediterranean and by the middle of the spring of 543 it had reached Constantinople itself; Procopius, who was in the Capital, was able to observe first-hand its course over a period of four months. There were 5,000 to 10,000 dead each day and not a citizen wearing the chlamys.[6]

Tribonian, the ex-magister officiorum, may have died of the disease at this time; Justinian himself developed one of its symptoms, a swelling of the 'boubon' or groin.[7] Other symptoms were a 'languid fever' and bubonic swelling, not only of the groin, but also under the armpits, beside the ears and parts of the thighs ('buboes' meaning inflamed lymph nodes). Otherwise, victims either fell into a deep coma or a violent delirium coupled with insomnia. It was even reported that the Emperor had died.[8]

Besides nursing Justinian through his illness during the summer of 543, the Empress Theodora must have had to make decisions for the Empire; e.g. considering recalling Belisarius from the East to return to Italy to fight against Totila. If true, she would have consulted Narses on such matters, including the decision to grant the command of the Army of the East to Martin.

Justinian recovered, but the plague moved on, spreading eastwards to Persia and westwards over into Italy, reaching Gaul by the year 546. It was to take a large toll of the Imperial Army in Africa at the very same time that the Moors were threatening fresh troubles. There would be a second outbreak in Constantinople, much the 'same' as in 543, fifteen years later during the Spring of 558. It was to claim an estimated 100 million lives in all during the sixth century.[9]

Mission to the Heruli

By the early summer of 544 Belisarius was back in Italy to fight a frustrating, futile five-year war against the Goths under Totila. Always short of men and money, he wrote requesting both, sending a letter back to the Capital with John in 545.

That general, delayed until the following year, married Justina the daughter of the Patrician Germanus who was either a cousin or nephew of Justinian. If the latter, the bride would have been a grand-niece to the Emperor. The bridegroom, and thus possibly grand-nephew by marriage, was sent with Isaac, the Persarmenian deserter, to Durrazzo, in order to form a new army for Italy.

As part of this operation, Justinian sent Narses to the rulers of the Heruli, in 545, to recruit troops for the campaigns of the following spring (546). Evidently, Narses was still popular with this barbarian nation as he was followed by a large number into Thrace. He was also accompanied by a 'capable warrior' known as John the Glutton.[10]

Also during the year 545, Thrace was invaded by another barbaric nation, the Sclavs, or Sclaveni; there, they were thoroughly defeated by Narses and the Heruls he had engaged under the command of Philemuth.

The Pretender Chilbudius

It was at this time that an incident occurred which can be used to show both the complexities of life on the borders of Justinian's empire and the value of Narses as a trusted councillor of long standing.

Back in the year 531, a certain Khilbud (Chilbudius) of Justinian's own household had been appointed magister militum, or the Master of Soldiers, of Thrace to watch the Slavs over the Danube. He was killed in action in 534 while attempting to repel the Slavs and Bulgars.

Later in a battle between his former tribe, the Antae, and the Sclaveni (the opponents of Narses' Heruls) a young Antic, also named Chilbudius, was taken captive by a Sclaveni and made a slave. Back in the home-land of the Sclaveni, this 'vigorous warrior', wearing his first beard, served his master loyally and well; even saving his life by endangering his own.[11]

The Antae, as Eastern Slavs, were not averse to slavery themselves, for they raided Thrace bringing back many 'Roman' natives, i.e. loyal citizens of the Empire, as captives. It so happened that chance brought a rascally captive into the hands of a kind and gentle Antic master. In order to return to the territory of the Empire, this rogue went to his master, taking him into his confidence with a scheme for collecting a large reward.

The master was informed that the former Imperial general Chilbudius was now among the Sclaveni unknown as a slave. By purchasing him and returning him to the Empire, a fair amount of fame, and no little fortune, could be acquired as the Emperor would pay an enormous ransom.

The two, master and captive, set out for the land of the Sclaveni, for the Antae who had the same language, and even appearance, were mingling with that tribe once more. A large sum of gold was paid out for such a loyal and brave slave. After returning to the land of the Antae, the purchaser naturally inquired if the slave really was Chilbudius the General.

The man told the truth about being only an Antic tribesman captured in battle but went on to add that according to the law, once back in his native land, he was a free man. The master was vexed at this but his own rascally captive, to controvert the truth, reassured him that the man was afraid to reveal his true identity while still among barbarians.[12]

Eventually, rumours began to spread among the entire Antae nation that the General Chilbudius was in their midst. According to their customs, a general assembly was held to determine if this man was really the Imperial commander.

Also, at this time, Justinian sent envoys to the Antae, offering them the ancient city of Turris, built by Trajan (98–117), and its adjacent lands, to settle in and garrison against the Huns. They agreed, provided that Chilbudius was restored as an Imperial general and assisted them in establishing their city.[13] By now, the tribesman had begun to claim to one and all that he was that Chilbudius. Accordingly he was sent to Constantinople in order to see the Emperor Justinian.

On the way, Narses came upon him and was able to expose the fraud, even though the imposter was playing his part to the hilt; speaking Latin and even assuming some of the personal peculiarities of the general. Unfortunately for him, Narses had personally known the former Khilbud. The pseudo-Khilbud was thrown into prison and compelled to confess that he was only the pretender Chilbudius; he was then brought back to Constantinople in Narses' own train.[14]

The Death of Theodora

In the meantime, events were occurring that were to have a profound influence on the later career of Narses. During the next five to six years, many characters shuffled on to and off the stage; and, while he is scarcely mentioned, if at all, he was waiting in the wings, so to speak, ready to make his grand entrance.

Justinian's 'reconquista' of Italy was going badly. In 546, Totila had Rome under siege once again and during the siege Isaac, the youngest of the Persarmenian deserters, was killed. He had disobeyed the orders of Belisarius by attacking from Portus (Porto) and after winning a local success, had been taken prisoner by the Goths. During Isaac's attack,

Ròderic, a favourite attendant of Totila's, was wounded and died two days later. Totila, in a rage, had Isaac deliberately put to death.

Back during the Plague Year of 543, Isaac had carried his older brother, Narses[2], mortally wounded from before a mountain fortress near the village of Anglôn within Persarmenia.

Totila eventually captured Rome on the night of 17 December 546 after some Isaurian soldiers let him in through the fatal Asinarian Gate. But Belisarius had reoccupied the deserted city in April 547. The gates and walls pulled down by Totila were quickly repaired by Belisarius in time for Rome to be besieged for yet a third time by the Goths.

His under-supported command must, however, eventually have caused even Belisarius to despair of success in this luckless campaign against Totila. He sent Antonina, most likely in sheer desperation, back to the Court to exert her inflúence with the Empress herself. But before Antonina completed her journey, Theodora had reached 'the term of her life', having died from a 'loathsome and incurable disease' (in all probability a virulent type of cancer).

The day of Theodora's death in the year 548 has been variously given as 27, 28, 29 June and even 1 July. Likewise, her exact age has been given different estimates, ranging from forty-five to fifty-one years. At any rate, Justinian was now sixty-six years old and even though he may have been anywhere from fifteen to twenty-one years older than his consort, he was to live another seventeen years (until 565).

Narses was older still; if actually born in 478, he would have been in his 70th year. As the Praepositus, he probably helped to organize the burial ceremonies. Theodora was buried in her tomb at the Church of the Holy Apostles, begun by her in the year 536 and consecrated on 28 June 550.

The Armenian Conspirators

Without his capable and cunning consort, the Emperor Justinian, to all appearances, sank into a dotty old age. Flavius Cresconius Corippus, a Carthagean school-master, commented:

> 'The old man no longer cared for anything; his spirit was in heaven.'[15]

To his subjects, he must have appeared more a grey-bearded theologian than a ruler.[16] Instead of attending to affairs of State, e.g. the loss of Italy to the Ostrogothic King Totila, his thrills of battle came from theological debate with bishops and monks. Instead of checking the returns of his new tax-gatherer, Peter Barsymes, made by Theodora the successor to John the Cappadocian, he burnt the Imperial midnight oil over rolls of Scripture, or

Commentaries on them. Victory in a subtle 'Greek' dispute, known as the 'Three Chapters', was far more important than the loss of Rome.[17]

Yet there may have been a method to his theological madness; Justinian's zeal to reform the Christian Church could have been based on his belief that God's favour alone determined victory for his armies in battle.

Soon after Theodora's death a conspiracy occurred involving the Persarmenian general Artabanes, together with his fellow countrymen Arsaces and Chanaranges. Also involved 'indirectly' were Germanus (John's father-in-law) and his elder son Justin.

While still an enemy of the Empire, Artabanes is credited with the killing of Theodora's brother-in-law, Sittas, the husband of her older sister Comita. Artabanes himself had had a wife of his own since childhood; a relative he had repudiated long before.[18] He was to come into contact with the woman he wished to marry after being sent with his Armenians to Africa (Libya).

This was Praejecta, the daughter of Justinian's sister Vigilantia, and the sister of Justin and Marcellus; thus, a niece of the Emperor himself (see Genealogical table, p.67). She had married a member of the old nobility, the Senator Areobindus, who was sent to Africa, as magister militum, to replace Sergius, the incompetent nephew of Solomon the Eunuch.[19] Solomon, deserted by his own troops at the Battle of Cillium (Kasrin), had been overcome and slain by the united Moorish tribes in 544.

In March 546, Areobindus was treacherously murdered by Gontharis, dux of Numidia, who had been a bodyguard of Solomon. This tyrant then seized Praejecta, hoping to force her into a marriage with him. By May, Artabanes had avenged the murder of Areobindus by assassinating Gontharis, when saturated with wine, at a banquet. He also wished to marry Praejecta, who had rewarded him with 'great sums of money';[20] she consented to the match out of a debt of gratitude.

The long-forgotten wife now appeared as a supplicant to the Empress Theodora who not only refused Artabanes a divorce, but forced him to take back his wife.[21] The ambitious, or amorous, Armenian deeply resented this.

After Theodora's death in 548, he put away his wife again, but Praejecta was now given in marriage to John, a nephew of Hypatius (the nephew of Anastasius I). Outraged and resentful, Artabanes was incited by another Armenian, a blood relative named Arsaces, to plot against Justinian.

This Arsaces had his own axe to grind as earlier he had been detected in treasonable negotiations with Chosroes and the Persians. He had got off lightly, being only mildly punished by the standards of the day; a few blows on his back and being set up on a camel. He had not suffered exile, or even loss of property, but Arsaces still resented his humiliations.[22]

When he saw that Artabanes was weakening, Arsaces brought yet another Persarmenian, one Chanaranges, into the plot. He also promised that the Emperor's relatives, Germanus and his sons, would be made parties to the undertaking. It was held that Germanus was irritated at Justinian for over-turning the will of his late brother Boraides, restoring the estate to the daughter.

An approach was made to Justin, the elder son, who, however, refused flatly, both for himself and his father, to be involved. Justin reported the matter back to Germanus, who in his turn conferred with Marcellus. Possibly as the result of his experiences with Narses in the affair of Cappadocian John, Marcellus advised against reporting the conspiracy to Justinian until there was more evidence.

Therefore, a meeting was arranged between Germanus and Chanaranges where Marcellus had a jurisconsult, Leontius, a man who could be trusted to speak the truth, planted behind a curtain to overhear their conversation.[23] It turned out that the conspiracy involved not only the killing of an emperor turned theologian, but of Belisarius and Marcellus as well. In spite of hearing of his own death warrant, Marcellus still did not report such 'evidence' to the Emperor, but Germanus revealed 'everything' to his military colleagues, Bouzes (Buzes) and Constantianus.[24]

Bouzes was a general who had succeeded Sittas in Armenia and had treacherously slain John, the father of Artabanes. He was arbitrarily imprisoned by Theodora, during the illness of Justinian in 543; being thrown into a pit in the Palace and 'forgotten' for a period of two years and four months. He had suffered weak sight and ill-health ever since. Constantianus was the commander of the Royal Grooms.

Later, hearing that Belisarius himself was returning from Italy, Marcellus finally saw fit to report the whole affair to Justinian, who ordered Artabanes and his Armenian associates arrested. A session of the Senate was called which cleared Germanus and his son Justin of any offence against the state.[25]

The upshoot of this latest conspiracy, with all of its many and varied characters, may have been that Justinian was at last aroused from his absorption in theology to attend to the war in Italy, unless it was due to the entreaties made by Pope Vigilius and the Italian clergy. For not only Germanus and Justin were spared, but even Artabanes himself was only placed under Palace arrest; it being said that they all were needed for the supreme effort to reconquer Italy.[26]

Early in 549, Belisarius returned from the peninsula, his military career, for all practical purposes, at an end. Thus, by this year, the careers of the inner-circle of Theodora, Tribonian, John the Cappadocian and now Belisarius were over. Like the Empress herself, Tribonian's had been ended by death. John, and now even Belisarius were in disgrace, but for Narses a new career was about to begin.

Plate 1. The walls of Constantinople, built by the Emperor Theodosius II in 413. The landward towers were repaired in 447, after an earthquake. Behind these walls Constantinople was able to withstand all attacks until the thirteenth century, when the Frankish 'Crusaders' and the Venetians took the city by storm.

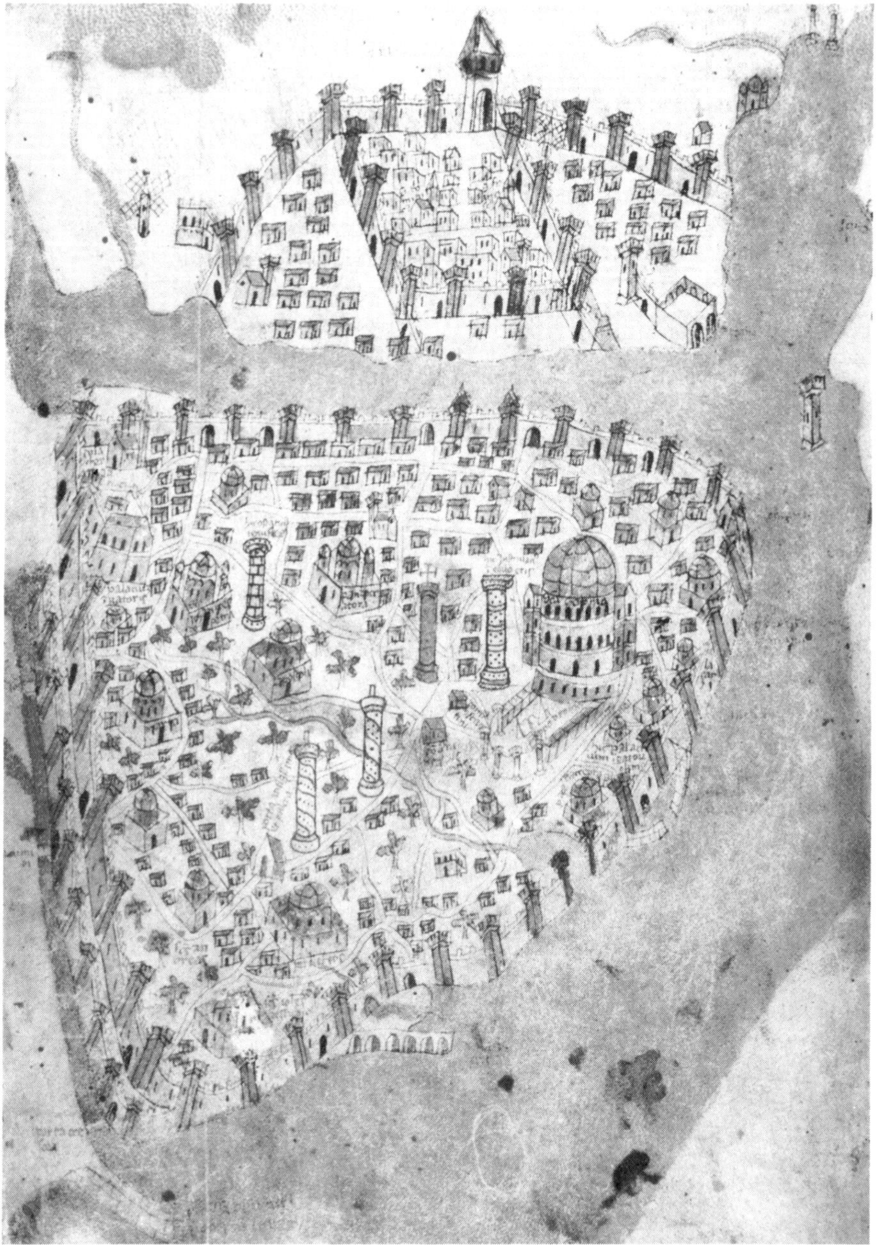

Plate 2. A map of Constantinople (Istanbul) dated 1422, showing the city still dominated by the church of St Sophia (by then a mosque), the ruins of the Hippodrome immediately below St Sophia's, and Roman monumental columns.

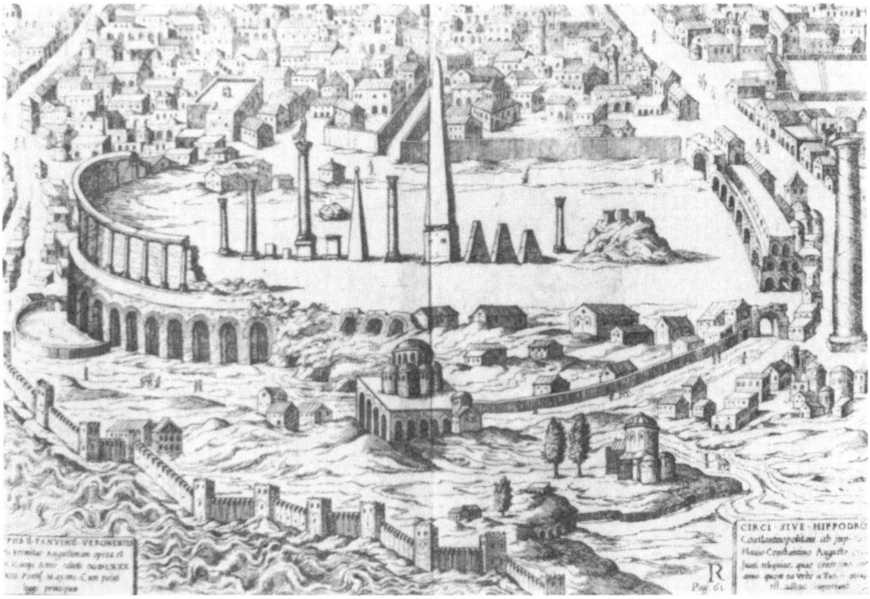

Plate 3a. The ruins of the Hippodrome from a late-fifteenth century engraving, showing the monuments still standing on the *Spina*.

Plate 3b. The church of St Sophia from the west, depicted in a late-nineteenth century lithograph. The minarets were added when the church was converted to a mosque.

Plate 4. (left) A leaf of a consular dyptych from Rome dated 530. It shows the consul Rufus Gennadius Probus Orestes. The two figures flanking the cross at the top of the panel are the Gothic Queen Amalasuntha and her son Athalaric.
(right) A leaf of a consular dyptych from Constantinople dated 517, showing the consul Flavius Anastasius presiding in the *Kathisma* of the Hippodrome. Below him are scenes from the circus.

Plate 5. (above) Gold medallion of Justinian I.
(below) A silver coin (twice life size) of Teias (Theia), showing the head of the Emperor Anastasius on the obverse even though the coin was minted during the reign of Justinian.

Plate 6a. The Porta San Sebastiano (Porta Appia) Rome, restored by Belisarius and Narses.

Plate 6b. The Bay of Naples showing Vesuvius on the left and, in the background, the *Mons Lactarius* into which the Goths were driven by Narses and the imperial forces.

Plate 7. The Bridge of Narses (Ponte Salario), from Piranesi's *Vedute di Roma*. The tower is a later feature.

Plate 8. The mosaic of Justinian and his court in San Vitale, Ravenna. Could the man behind Justinian's left shoulder be Narses?

Part II
The Victories of Narses

Chapter VI

The Supreme Command of Narses

'After the loss of Germanus, the nations were provoked to smile by the strange intelligence that the command of the Roman armies was given to a eunuch.'
Gibbon[1]

Justinian may have finally made up his mind to reconquer Italy for his restored Roman Empire, but he was subject to vacillation in the choices of his commanders. He was to make at least five changes in generals to oppose Totila after the recall of Belisarius in 549. There was never any question of his being sent back. The ultimate choice was made two years later in 551, this being Narses the Eunuch.

During all that time at least four other generals were in and out of command. They were Germanus, Liberius, Artabanes (the late conspirator) and John the nephew of Vitalian.

There is some question as to whether or not Justinian actually appointed Germanus first, or merely thought of doing so. He did appoint Liberius, early in 549, to command the fleet in Sicily, but cancelled the appointment before the latter had even started out. It is not certain whether Germanus now had a go, but a few months later Liberius was appointed again, and this time did sail to Sicily, temporarily relieving Syracuse.

The Career of Liberius

Petrus Marcellinus Felix Liberius was an extremely old civilian with little or no military experience; if the 'modified military command' he held while the Praetorian Prefect of Ligurian Gaul be discounted. (As a 'Roman' he was debarred from a military command under the Ostrogoths.) Otherwise, he had served in civil capacities under the barbarian rulers in Italy, first loyally serving Odovacar (Odoacer), then transferring his services to Theodoric.

Under the government of the first Ostrogothic King in Italy, Liberius became its first Praetorian Prefect, holding office for seven years (493–500). He was also a Roman Senator, and was later promoted by Theodoric to be a Patrician. He is known to have founded a monastery in Campania, at Alatri, south-east of Rome, before the year 534.

In 534, Theodoric's successor, his grandson, Athalaric, died at the age of sixteen. Theodoric's daughter, Amalasuntha, who had been acting as a regent for her son, now sought to strengthen her position by taking in as a partner her cousin Theodahad. He was the son of Amalafrida, a sister of Theodoric, and Trasamund, a King of the Vandals in Africa.

There soon developed a correspondence with Justinian concerning the transfer of the Ostrogothic Kingdom to the Eastern Empire. Amalasuntha herself wished to desert Ravenna and to be received in Constantinople. Meanwhile, the new King, Theodahad (and his wife, Gudelin) wanted to turn over his vast Tuscan estates for a large sum of money, the rank of senator and permission to live in the Eastern Capital.

Peter the Illyrian, a Patrician and ex-counsul, travelled back and forth on the Via Egnatia, linking 'Asia' and Italy, to conduct secret negotiations in person for Justinian. Theodahad, for his part, had Amalasuntha imprisoned on Martana, an island in the Lake of Bolsena, in Lazio, north of Rome and Viterbo and southwest of Orvieto. This may have been a part of his 'Tuscan estates'.

Liberius and another Senator, Opilio, were sent as envoys to Constantinople bearing letters that Amalasuntha was suffering no wrong. They met Peter waiting at the port of Aulon (Valona) for passage over to Italy; he was informed of Amalasuntha's captivity. While Opilio sought to defend Theodahad and his actions, Liberius came out with the whole truth, that her life was in danger. And he was proved correct for, presumably with Theodahad's consent, she was strangled in her bath (30 April 535) by the relatives of three Goths whom she had had executed.

For his candour, Liberius was to be accorded in Constantinople the same honours as were due to a Praetorian Prefect of the East. Shortly afterwards he passed into the service of the Emperor Justinian.

Procopius in his regular History may have been deliberately vague as to time and events.[2] In his Secret History however, he further explained that Theodora herself actually instigated the murder of a 'very comely' and dangerous rival. She had given Peter secret instructions to persuade Theodahad to dispatch the contriving Amalasuntha after his arrival in Italy. For this deed, she was to later reward Peter with the rank of Magister Officiorum (Commander of the Palace Troops).[3]

The Empress Theodora was also to avail herself of the services of Liberius. This occurred during her investigation of the conduct of Paul, the Patriarch of Alexandria, who had deprived her own candidate, Theodosius, of the see in 536. Liberius was appointed to succeed Rhodon as the Augusta Prefect, or Magistrate of Alexandria; sent out with him was a clerical commission that included the Archdeacon of Rome, Pelagius (the future Pope).

Theodora also dispatched an army of 6,000 men to reinstate Theodosius, under the command of a Narses. It is possible that this was Narses^{2}, as it is known that the Persarmenian deserter was stationed in Upper Egypt at about this time. In *c*.540 he was the commander of the troops at Philae, a fortress on an island in the Nile near Elephantine. In the quest for orthodoxy, Justinian ordered him to destroy the temple there of the cult of Osirus and Isis which still had worshippers in two tribes up-river, the Blemyes and Nobadae. Narses^{2} destroyed their sanctuaries, put the priest under arrest and sent the 'divine' images to Constantinople.[4]

It is, however, possible that it was Narses the Eunuch who was sent to Alexandria in 537, and this could help to explain his emergence as a general in Italy in 538.[5]

Liberius in the year 550 was an octogenarian (at least ten years older than Narses) trying to defend Sicily against Totila with a small armament. Sailing from Syracuse to Palermo he learnt that his appointment was once again cancelled by the vacillating Emperor, who was sending Artabanes to relieve him.

Historians have since commented that Liberius' appointment to so important a command was 'curious'; even Procopius remarked on his being 'an extremely old man.'[6] One possible reason for the appointment in the first place may have been that as an Italian, he would inspire confidence in the Italians themselves. As for his lack of military experience in the field, making him unfit for command, perhaps his later career in Spain justified Justinian's judgement.

Liberius was next the commander of an expedition to Spain where the dynastic disputes of the heretical Arian Visigoths, in the midst of a hostile Spanish-Roman Catholic population, enabled Justinian to gain a toe-hold. Agila, the successor to Theudegesil, who was assassinated in 549, attempted to conquer the territories of the independent Spanish-Roman nobles; he was defeated by the Andalusians before Cordova.

A Visigothic noble, Athanagild (secretly a Catholic) having designs on the crown, solicited the support of Justinian, who ordered Liberius out directly from Sicily.

The 'inexperienced' octogenarian patrician proceeded to take important towns in the east and south, i.e. the districts round Valencia, Murcia and Andalusia. Liberius, combining forces with Athanagild, helped defeat Agila east of Badajoz. Agila withdrew to Merida where he was assassinated by his own followers. Athanagild was acknowledged as King *c.*554, and made a treaty with Justinian; most likely rewarding him with territory.

Liberius, however, was to encroach on the agreed-upon boundaries causing Athanagild to declare war on this 'treachery'; a war that lasted until the end of his reign (567). He transferred the Capital from Tarragona to Toledo, in order to put as much distance as possible between himself and the Eastern Romans in possession of the old province of Bactica with the cities of Cartagena, Cordoba, Malaga and Seville.

As for Liberius, sometime after the year 554 he died in his native Italy, and was buried at Rimini.

Germanus

Artabanes, who had supplanted Liberius as possibly Justinian's fourth or fifth appointment in his revocations of generals, was to meet disaster at sea. Sailing for Sicily in 550, he was personally wrecked at the island of Melita (Meleda) and had all his other ships caught in a storm off the coast of Calabria and driven back to Greece.[7] Justinian, without cancelling Artabanes' appointment, then once more proposed sending Germanus, with a large army to Italy itself, as the commander-in-chief against Totila.

There is some confusion as to the exact family relationship between Germanus and the Emperor, Procopius calling him a nephew, while historians such as Bury and Hodgkin refer to him as a cousin. Justin I may have had a brother, or another sister, who had three sons, Germanus, Justus and Boraides.

Nonetheless, early in the year 550, Germanus, then fifty years of age, married for a second time. His first wife was Passara, of the noble western Roman Anicii family, the mother of his two sons, Justin and Justinian, and the daughter, Justina. Upon her death, he married the Amal princess, Matasuntha, the young widow of the Gothic king Vitigis.

Now, soon after the marriage, Justinian decided to send Germanus out to reconquer Italy; he had already held commands in Thrace, Africa (as Military Governor) and in Syria. He planned to have his new wife with the Army, calculating that the Goths might be reluctant to take up arms against her as she was the granddaughter of Theodoric the Great. Incidently, Matasuntha was now the mother-in-law of John whom she had wished to marry back in 538.

Thus, in the sixteenth year of the Gothic War, Germanus assembled his forces at Serdica (the present day Sofia). Before starting out, he was ordered to drive back an incursion of the Sclaveni into the province of

GENEALOGICAL TABLE OF THE HOUSE OF JUSTIN

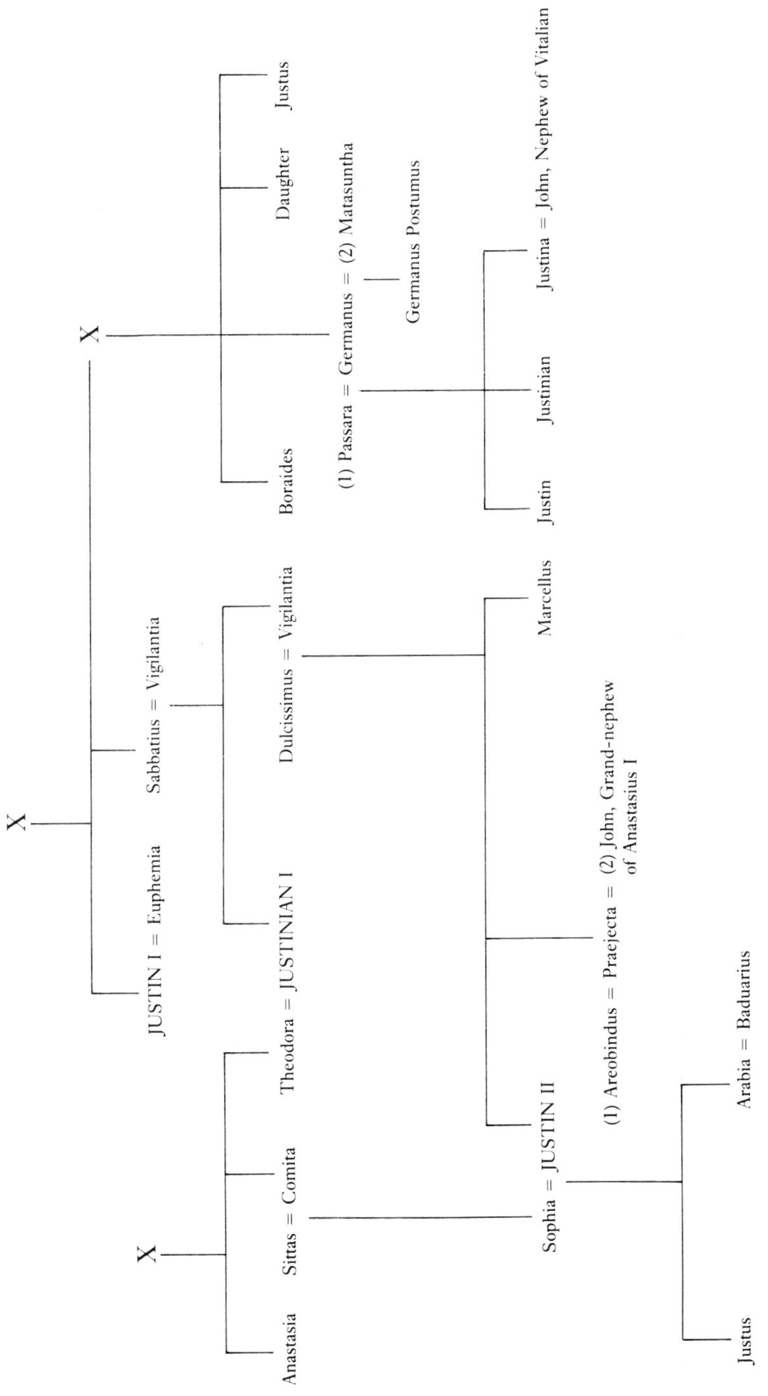

Illyricum; they retired at his approach. But, in September 550, Germanus fell ill; and, in the curt statement of Procopius, 'abruptly reached the term of life'.[8] Fever, and even poison, have been hinted at as the cause. His brothers, Justus and Boraides, had already died in 545 and 547 respectively.

His name was not to be a famous one in history; fewer have heard of him than even of Narses. The fate of Germanus was oblivion, and yet he could be said to rank as a splendid might-have-been.[9] After his death, Matasuntha, a widow once more, bore a son named Germanus Postumus. He was to carry on the family name by taking a prominent part in affairs during the reign of the tyrant Phocas (602–10). His daughter married Theodosius the elder son of the Emperor Maurice.

With the loss of Germanus to the Empire, his younger son, Justinian, was appointed as a joint commander of the army now to be assembled at Salona on the Adriatic (near the present day Split). The other appointee was John, the General of the forces in Illyricum. This, by virtue of John's marriage with Justina, made the joint leaders brothers-in-law. John must have been the stronger personality of the two, for in the following events he is mentioned as the responsible general.

Totila, the reason for all these appointments, was meanwhile unchecked in Sicily. He decided at this time to winter back in Italy, with the intention of later returning to Sicily. John wintered at Salona, possibly because there was not a sufficient supply of ships to transport the army assembled there. The Imperial forces already in Italy were inactive, awaiting his coming.

The Tuscan Prophecy

With the beginning of the following year, 551, John intended to depart from Salona, and lead 'his' army as quickly as possible against Totila and the Goths. However, the Emperor prevented this, ordering him to remain until Narses should arrive.

Totila, about to re-invade Sicily, wanted first to make a peace proposal to the Empire; even offering to resign his claim to the island and Dalmatia. His envoys were not even admitted into the presence of Justinian, who had at long last decided on the final appointment for the successor of Belisarius as commander-in-chief for the Gothic War.

It is said that the very name of the Goths was hateful to him, and although having conducted the war against them very negligently, he now decided on one last great effort to exterminate them once and for all. Therefore, in April 551, the seventeenth year of the Gothic War, and the twenty-fifth of his reign, Justinian appointed Narses the Eunuch to the supreme command.

One reason given for John's dismissal from the leadership of the army at Salona was that the other generals, including perhaps his brother-in-law, were unwilling to take orders from him, not consenting to be his inferiors in rank.[10] The other, put forward by Procopius, is that of the 'Tuscan prophecy'.

He repeats the tale of a Roman Senator who told of a herd of cattle entering Rome during the time of Athalaric (526–34) and of a steer leaving the herd to mount a bronze bull standing by an ancient fountain before the Forum of Peace, or Vespasian. This statue originally stood in the market place of Athens, and was reputed to be by Pheidias, or Lysippus. By chance, a very rustic man of Tuscan birth passed by, and taking in the scene being acted out, was able to explain the significance of the steer's action. The Tuscans throughout antiquity were credited with having the gift of prophecy, and this one prophesied that the 'Ruler of Rome' would one day be overthrown by a eunuch.[11]

As for the eunuch in question, evidently he lacked his emperor's possible acquaintance with prophecies, not to mention John the Cappadocian's faith in them, for just before his appointment to the supreme command, Narses, (now in his seventies) had built a church and monastery in Cappadocia to which he intended to retire for his remaining years.[12]

And now, twelve years after returning from his first controversial command in Italy, Narses was appointed to accomplish what Belisarius, the greatest of the Imperial generals, had left undone; the overthrow of Totila and the Ostrogothic Kingdom.

A 'Strange' Appointment?

This final appointment of Justinian's has been controversial, and debatable to historians ever since he first made it. If they found that of Liberius to be 'curious', the term generally used in connection with that of Narses is 'strange'. If the former was an octogenarian patrician, the latter was a septuagenarian eunuch. He is generally referred to as being seventy-six years of age when chosen, but even if born as early as the year 478 he would have been seventy-three in 551.

Much the same reasons have been advanced for his nomination and full support by Justinian as were given for his original command thirteen years previously (in 538) when he was only sixty years old. As a eunuch, even more advanced in age, Narses could never rebel and hope to wear the Imperial crown. If still chiefly a creature of courts and committees, because of his high position and influence with the emperor he was implicitly trusted. Furthermore he had conducted a successful military operation in

545, with the Heruls against the Sclaveni. His very fidelity assured him the great authority and powers of a general-in-chief whom all would obey, and who could secure united action in the War.

Narses' conduct in Italy during 538–39 evidently was not held against him, and possibly he could have been credited with having gained a practical knowledge of the country and its people. In camp, he had proven his popularity with persons as different in temper and tradition as Persian deserters, erratic Heruls and intractable Thracians. In addition, the ascendancy he had acquired over his fellow-officers, and over the soldiers themselves, must have increased the good opinion that Justinian already had of him. It has been claimed that Narses handled men as though he had been born and bred in a camp.[13]

As for his having been only a guardian of the royal treasures, perhaps this was his ultimate qualification and strength. As the Imperial Treasurer he held in his hands the key to open up the main impediment in all the previous campaigns; that which had stinted even Belisarius, the need of funds.

Coupled with his financial resources as the Emperor's Treasurer, was the reputation Narses had as a man of 'princely generosity'. Furthermore, he was free from being reproached for avarice or perculation; all during his tenure at Court he was well-known for his liberality, being more than eager to help those in actual want. It can be inferred that Narses had used his power wisely, not only in his sovereign's interest but also in his own.

Many military leaders and their followers, having known his generosity in the past, would naturally flock to serve under him; some to repay past favours, others in the expectation of future rewards. His habitual liberality would ensure that every soldier of fortune throughout the Empire would be anxious to join his expedition. In Narses' recruiting operations among the barbarian tribes and nations, he had treated them 'especially well'; the Heruls in particular being well disposed towards him.[14]

Yet some historians accuse Narses of parting with the treasures of his master, and himself, not from generosity as such, but with the motive of hoping to gain the richer rewards and spoils of Italy. He was not only extremely liberal to his barbarian recruits, but almost shamelessly appealed to their cupidity. Hodgkin[15] and Dunlap[16] explain the motley army of 'discordant nationalities' that he led to the reconquest of Italy as being united in a passion for plunder.

Then again, a nineteenth century Scots minister, the Rev. James White, asserted that it was not cupidity or spoils, but religious fervour that assembled such a 'motley' crusade. To him, it was the religious piety and orthodoxy of Narses, a believer in the decrees of the Council of Nicaea (325) that won him the following of all the orthodox barbarians, e.g. the

Heruls. With them, Narses formed an army of 'infuriated missionaries' who would fight with all their accustomed barbaric fierceness against the heretical Arian Ostrogoths.[17] In any event, as history has shown, crusades and spoils are not mutually exclusive.

In common with Liberius, Narses was to show that Justinian's appointments of civilians with little or no previous military experience were not freaks of folly or the height of madness. Once again, the Emperor's choice turned out to be a wise selection, showing his deep knowledge of men and character when he set his mind to it.

Even the orders to John, the dismissed general at Salona, to await the new leader assuming the command of the troops, initially raised by Germanus, showed logic and method. Although Narses had already shown the qualities of a born leader, any deficiencies in actual military matters could be remedied by John acting as his right-hand man. Indeed, this Thracian lieutenant was to give valuable advice when Narses was initially attempting to get his whole army around the 'road-block' of the Franks.

Nevertheless, this eunuch, one of the very few generals starting a career at such a mature age, was to develop a 'great latent military genius' under the pressure of sheer necessity.[18]

From the very beginning of his appointment, Narses, instead of being overwhelmed by the honour, showed that he had the ambition befitting a general. While recognizing the urgency for a fresh expedition to Italy, he declared that under no circumstances would he accept the command unless he could lead a force adequate for the undertaking.

By taking this position, Procopius affirms that he not only obtained the money, but the men and arms in numbers 'worthy of the Roman Empire'.[19] In re-kindling the Gothic War from its ashes, Narses showed himself to be in full vigour displaying an almost tireless enthusiasm, and by his diligence assembled what he thought an adequate army. Evidently, the forces awaiting him at Salona were considered insufficient.

With the key to the Empire's treasury, he paid off the arrears of pay which had accumulated among the soldiers in Italy; even tempting back some of the deserters and fugitives still there.

B.H. Liddell Hart holds that Narses had been a long-time amateur of war, keenly studying its theoretical aspects, and thus welcomed the chance to prove his practical skills.[20] If so, he could be placed in the company of generals such as Benedict Arnold and Henry Knox during the American Revolution: the former an apothecary and book seller in New Haven, studying books on warfare; the latter, on becoming the owner of his own book store in Boston, having the leisure to read about soldiering.

An Ironic Delay

Eager to reach his awaiting army at Salona, over on the Adriatic coast in Illyria, Narses set out from Constantinople in June 551. It is an irony of history (or a 'satire' on Justinian's policies) that he was not to reach his destination until the autumn. He was held up about 300 miles from the Capital, at Philippopolis in Thrace (the present day Plovdiv, the second city of Bulgaria) which is about 80 miles or 128 km south-east of Sofia and which commanded the main road from Macedonia to the Black Sea.

The delay was caused by an irruption from across the Danube by the Kotrigurs, a remnant of the Huns who had established themselves along the northern coast of the Black Sea, between the mouths of the Dneiper and the Don. Together with the Sclaveni they made for an unsettled state of affairs in the Empire's Danubian provinces, which were continually being invaded and plundered.

There had been two invasions by the Sclaveni in 550, said to have been hired by Totila to harass Justinian's plans for Italy. Needless to say, very little persuasion was required. Germanus brushed back the first incursion after assembling his army at Serdica, but after his death there was another, more serious, irruption. An Imperial army with his elder son, Justin, and also Aratius, Constantian, John Phagus ('the Glutton') and Nazares, all under the supreme command of another Palace eunuch, Scholasticus (otherwise unknown) suffered a defeat by these Sclavini near Hadrianople.[21] Apparently their soldiers had forced the leaders to give battle, against their better judgement, and the Sclaveni gained a bloody victory. They were to approach to within little more than a day's march of Constantinople itself, to winter inside the Empire, and then retire with most of their spoils in the spring of 551.

As the Sclaveni retired, the Kotrigurs swept down to ravage Illyria, perhaps incited by the Gepids. Narses, with his reinforcements, established a camp at Philippopolis to wait it out until the combined diplomacy and force of the Empire should clear his path. Evidently it was not his duty to tackle these intruders, but that of Imperial policy.

Justinian's rebuttal policy was to have Sandichl, the King of the Utigurs, invade the homeland of the Kotrigurs. The Utigurs, crossing over the Don, routed the few remaining tribesmen there, and carried the women and children away into slavery. Next, Aratius, the surviving brother of Narses[2] and Isaac, was sent to the Kotrigurs to inform them of the latest tidings from home. They were also offered a large sum of money to evacuate Imperial territory.

However, before they decided whether to accept the bribe or not, the Hunnish host split into two separate streams; the first towards Constantinople, the second to the south-west, towards Thessalonica. Narses, adroitly seizing the opening between the two currents of Kotrigurs, set his army in motion westwards across Macedonia, leading it to join up with the one at Salona.

There, he was to spend the rest of the year (551) organizing his combined forces for the grand expedition to Italy. However, in spite of all the preparations he had made for this expedition, Narses found that he was unable to convey his whole army directly across the Adriatic to Classis (the port of Ravenna).

It appears that Justinian's Empire of the East just did not have enough ships to transport such a multitude of men, not to mention their horses. Although not hampered by a lack of money, the shipping was simply unobtainable; Narses was to take more than a year (from the time of his appointment) to reach Italy. He had to inflict upon himself, and his entire army, a long land march up from Dalmatian Salona along the coast of the Adriatic Sea, around the Gulf of Tergeste (Trieste) and into the really difficult country lying between its head and Ravenna.

The Naval Battle of Sena Gallica

Another complicating circumstance for Narses was that in the initial stages of his operation, Totila actually controlled the sea approaches to eastern Italy. He had gradually built up his naval forces over the past several years, and was able to send a fleet of some 300 small vessels to raid the coasts of Greece (the Island of Corfu, and Epirus). Not only that, but he intercepted transports carrying supplies to the army of Narses still waiting at Salona. In addition, during the summer of 551, a fleet of 47 Gothic ships blockaded Ancona.

Totila also had the naval power off the western coast of Italy to occupy Corsica and Sardinia. John the Troglite, as the Master of Soldiers in Africa, sent an army which was defeated near Caranalis (Cagliari) during the autumn.

The theory has been advanced that these wars in the West were not decided on the land at all, but on the water. Archibald R. Lewis sees the ultimate victories of Justinian as due to his naval command of the sea. His sure instinct chose the Vandals in Africa, the only real naval power in the West, as the first adversary. Once their power was broken, his armies could proceed into Italy and Spain.[22]

Lewis holds that Totila came to understand this naval factor; thus building up the Gothic fleet, then sending it out to furnish real opposition to the plans of Justinian. It came close to destroying them by making communications between the East and the Western coasts of Italy nearly impossible.[23] Totila also realized that the Eastern Emperor was now making a supreme effort to destroy him, hence his aggressive naval policy in the Adriatic.

The Empire may not have had sufficient transports for its men and horses, but it was able to dispatch 50 naval vessels to relieve Ancona. John from Salona led 38 ships up the coast to Scardon (Scardona), while Valerian, stationed at Ravenna, sailed over with 12 more. Together they met a Gothic fleet at Sena Gallica (Senigallia), above Ancona, halfway up the coast to Fano, under the command of Gibal and Gundulf (Indulf, a former guard of Belisarius, who had deserted to Totila).

The number of vessels on each side was nearly equal; 50 Imperial opposed to 47 for the Goths. Procopius graphically described this naval battle which resembled a battle on land.

The usual exhortations were made on both sides before the engagement; then the opposing ships met head on, with their bows up against each other. There were arrows being discharged and fighting at close quarters with sword and spear, just as on a battle field.[24]

The Goths began to show their lack of experience in sea-fighting during the later stages of the conflict, and fought in great disorder. Some of their stragglers were rammed singly by the Imperial vessels; the rest crowded together in such large groups that their decks appeared to be woven into a mat.[25] Justinian's 'admirals' won an overwhelming victory off Sena Gallica; 36 of the Gothic ships were sunk, Gibal was captured; Gundulf (Indulf) escaped with the remaining 11, but burnt them on reaching Ancona. Although the Empire may not have had enough vessels to ferry Narses' army across the Adriatic Sea, it had enough fighting ships to control it.

While Narses was engaged in rounding the head of the Adriatic by land, Artabanes, reinforced after his ship wreck (in 550), reconquered Sicily.

Lewis had to qualify his sea-power theory when he pointed out that this naval menace to Justinian had ceased. He was to complete the reconquest of Italy, besides taking 'rich cities' over in Spain, but only after the overthrow of Totila by Narses in a land battle.[26]

Chapter VII

The Italian Expeditionary Force

> 'It was a powerful army; but it was not an ancient Roman army. It was such an army as that with which Agamemnon set out to conquer Ilium: an army of gods and fighting men. For the time being Europe had sunk back into the heroic age from which it sprang.'
>
> G.P. Baker[1]

The army collected by Germanus and his sons in 550 had been a new one; not made up of drafts from the regular Imperial armies. It had been raised from volunteers to serve with Germanus, many professional fighting men resigning their posts with lesser generals.

This Army of Illyricum, equal to four Imperial divisions, was comprised of the comitatus of Germanus himself and also the followers of John. In addition to some regular regiments from Thrace, there were new recruits of 'stalwart highlanders' raised in Thrace and Illyricum, besides Philemuth and his Heruli.

Among the other barbarians recruited was a Lombard contingent of 1,000 men sent by their King Audoin (Edwin), but even with this catalogue of cohorts, the army of Germanus did not seem sufficient to Narses. He personally raised additional forces that included a large body of regular troops from Constantinople, plus many more men from Thrace and Illyricum. However, it was barbarians that he chiefly engaged; Narses seems to have had a decided predilection for the fiercest tribes, and to have been very successful in handling them.

Now, he engaged additional warriors of a barbaric nation whose name was to become significant geographically as well as historically: the Lombards. Having heard of their fierceness and fighting qualities in battle he sent messengers to King Audoin asking for further assistance against the Goths. A chosen band of 2,500 warriors accompanied by a retinue of their retainers of some 3,000 other armed men were sent down into Italy in support of the Empire.[2] They were not sent to Salona, as were Germanus' initial 1,000 men, but joined up with Narses when he reached the lagoons of Venetia. It may be surmised that only he could have brought them into battle against the Goths in the first place.

Besides two divisions of regular cavalry, there were already more than 3,000 Heruli horsemen under Philemuth and other leaders. Dagisthaeus was restored to favour by being released from prison to lead his followers. Also engaged were a great number of Huns (some 2,000), besides two small free-lance bands of Heruls and Gepids. The former were led by the 'Romanized' Aruth (he had married a granddaughter of Mundus); the latter, numbering only around 400 men, were under Asbad, a 'young man' who was the eventual slayer of Totila. Significantly there was a corps of 4,000 Persian deserters under Kobad (Cavades) who was a nephew of Chosroes and a real, or reputed, grandson of the late Shaninshah. Cavades is supposed to be the authority from whom Procopius derived his knowledge of Persian history. But the historian also gave vent to suspicions that this fugitive was an imposter; the real claimant most likely having been killed. Last, but certainly not least, there was John the Glutton, heading 'a large force of able Roman soldiers'.[3]

As for the entire strength of the army that Narses was to lead on his grand expedition, Procopius gave no word as to its final size, except that it was 'an extraordinarily large one'.[4] In any case, it was the first time that a proper force had been sent for the reconquest of Italy, and quite possibly the largest army that Justinian ever sent on a single campaign. Its numbers have been estimated to have been from 20,000 to 35,000 men; a fair estimate of the force that Narses led into battle against Totila might be *c.*25,000. For this particular period of history, and in this part of the world, this could indeed be considered an 'extraordinarily' large army, if the hordes of half-armed, half-clad, free-booting barbarians be discounted.

Its size alone was not its only, or even main, strength; it was a memorable gathering of warriors. To the casual eye the final assembled expeditionary force at Salona may have appeared as a conglomoration of strange allies from the far-flung corners of the Empire, and even beyond. Narses, however, was to rely not only on quantity but on quality as well, in his forthcoming battles.

The Great March of Narses

If the first stage of Narses' march up the Dalmatian coast of the Adriatic Sea from Salona to Aquileia at its head was fairly long and difficult, it was to assume even greater difficulties once it entered Venetia. As he could not use the regular invasion route into Italy, the 'Pear Tree' pass, his movements were very slow.

The distance between Aquileia and his initial destination of Ravenna was close to 300 kilometres (about 180 miles) with Padua (Padova) being about half way, where his route would turn southwards. It is in this region that the whole drainage system of the southern side of the Alps, from the mountains of Dauphine in the west, to the Julian Alps in the east, discharges itself into the Adriatic. Back in the time of the Emperor Augustus (27 BC–AD 14) this whole area had been an impenetrable tract of woods, lakes and morasses. Among the difficulties involved in moving an army through this region were its many rivers and their mouths; below Padova were the Adige and the Po, each of which would take a large army several days to cross.

Further obstacles were made for Narses by Totila who dispatched his lieutenant, Teias, based in Verona, to effect delaying tactics. Merely by cutting breaches in the dykes and destroying any bridges that had been built in the past 500 years, Teias could bring this entire area back into its original impenetrable condition.[5]

In addition to these geographical problems, Narses had political problems to contend with. At this time, the Empire held the coastal towns of Venetia while the Goths still had a few fortresses left; but it was the Franks who had the greater part of the province under their sway, including all of the main roads. Furthermore they, and Narses' allies, the Lombards, were deadly enemies.

The Franks, who usually played a waiting game in this war between the Empire and the Goths, now used the pretext of not allowing any army that included Lombards to pass through their territory. Narses having no desire to compound his difficulties, and perhaps Justinian's, by fighting the Franks, hugged the coast controlled by the Empire. This was not an easy choice, what with the region's bays, lagoons and numerous river-mouths; but under the circumstances it was the only one.

Procopius states that Narses was 'completely bewildered', but that John, being familiar with this part of Italy, advised him on how to proceed.[6] There were evidently some ships of the Imperial fleet accompanying the march of the army along the coast, perhaps ferrying supplies, but not enough to transport it from the mouth of the Isonzo (below Monfalcone) to Classis. However, the inhabitants of this region were subjects of the Empire who possessed many small flat boats used in their daily lives and they were now to come to the aid of Narses' army.

Whenever the army came to a river, a bridge (ponti de barche) was made of all these accompanying boats set against the current, thus rendering a comparatively easy crossing.[7] Narses, by adopting the advice of John, not only turned the flank of the Franks, but in this way got his whole army to Ravenna unopposed.

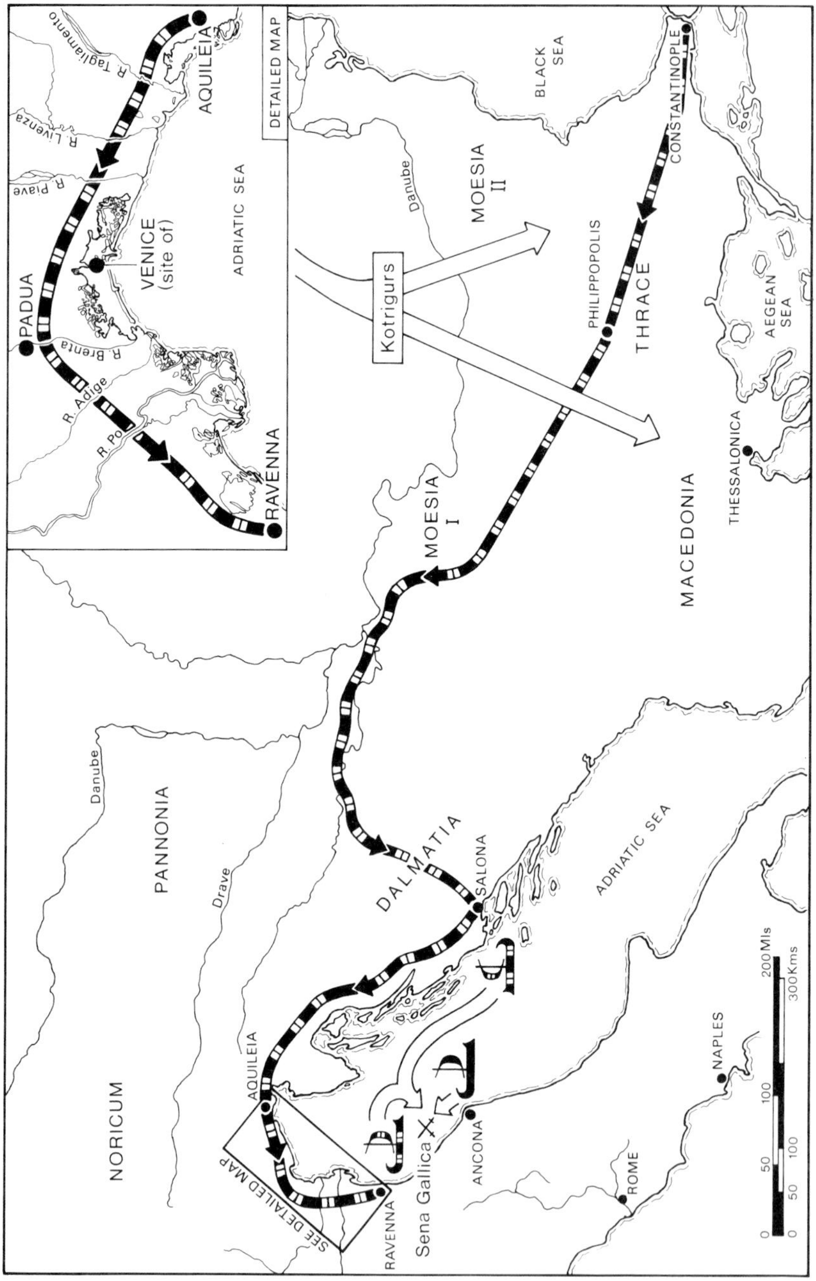

Fig. 4. The Great March to Italy, with a detail showing the area around Venice at the head of the Adriatic.

These salt-workers and seamen, dwellers of the lagoons, beginning to emerge into history as the 'Venetians', also used their vessels to help transport supplies and cargo for Narses, including his Lombard mercenaries. The second batch of these barbarians, numbering over 5,000 men, had been held up on entering Italy by a flood at Aquileia. Narses, wishing to effect a junction with them, was given further timely aid by the 'Venetians', beginning their career as 'middle-men', who transported this valuable cargo to its destination. They may have rendered their assistance to the Imperial cause either from friendship or plain policy; but, in any event, Narses was to show his gratitude after his great campaign was over.

His 'incredible march' may have been aided by Totila's belief that an invasion would have to come by sea, as all previous ones had. Therefore, once he attempted the difficult coastal march, there was no active opposition except for the delaying tactics of Teias. Ravenna was thereby reached in safety. Time may have been lost initially, but all things considered, the progress of Narses had been unexpectedly rapid.

Narses at Ravenna

Once the army led by Narses had reached Ravenna, by the end of May or the first week of June 552, it was joined by the forces of the Empire in the area under Justin and Valerian.[8] The Eunuch-Generalissimo was to remain there for nine days, much like Julius Caesar before his memorable crossing of the Rubicon in 50 BC.

Of the two routes to Rome, Caesar had taken the longer, and less direct, one down the Adriatic coast. Narses was to take the shorter and more direct inland route; although he had to fight a major battle, and go through the formality of a siege, before entering Rome.

After nine days had been spent at Ravenna, an insulting challenge was delivered from Usdrilas, the commander of the Gothic garrison down at Rimini. Procopius refers to him as 'an exceptionally capable warrior'.

His insolent letter was actually addressed to Valerian.[9] In it, he taunted the Imperialists with being braggarts and assuming airs of more than mortal pride, imagining they would frighten the Goths in this way. But they were hiding in Ravenna, without showing their faces, as a way of protecting their pride.

He also mentioned the horde of barbarians with them being used in the ruin of a country which did not even belong to them. Usdrilas concluded his challenge by daring them to hurry out and show themselves by engaging in battle with the Goths, who had been waiting a long time for the chance.[10]

This letter was brought to Narses himself who, after reading it, laughed at the affrontery of the Gothic commander. He immediately prepared his army for departure, leaving Justin behind with a garrison at Ravenna.[11] Procopius did not specify which 'Justin'. The indexing of his works in the Loeb Classical Library lists the 'son of Germanus' (Volume V)[12] and 'the General of Illyricum' (Volume VII).[13]

The Skirmish with Usdrilas

Thundering down out of Ravenna, through Classis, on the Via Popillia to Rimini, Narses' march came to its end at the bridge over the river Marecchia. The Ponte Tiberio had been started under Augustus in AD 14 and finished by Tiberius in the year 21. It was held by Usdrilas and his Goths; the last of its five arches may have been destroyed and Narses' engineers had to set to work bridging the river. Today the bridge spans dry land above the canal lock of a small craft and fishing boat basin; the main branch of the river is now a half a mile to the north.

An engagement at the river between two scouting parties ensued, actually more of a skirmish, in which Usdrilas, the insolent Gothic commander, was killed by a Herul. His head was cut off and sent back to be displayed to Narses.[14] The eunuch commander was in such haste to seek out Totila's main army that he did not even bother to occupy Rimini. Instead, he marched through the town to Augustus' triumphal Arch (Arco d'Augusto) where the great north-south road, the Via Flaminia, started.

This famous white road of the Roman legions ran along the coast to Fano, where it made an almost ninety degree turn, leaving the Adriatic, to head into the hills. Then, it continued south-west above the north side of the River Metauro via Forum Sempronii (Fossombrone) through the Furlo pass to Acqualagna, where it turns almost due south. The Goths held control over this passage into the Apennines at the Passo del Furlo where there was a fortified tunnel, too strong to be easily, or quickly, taken. Consequently, during some stage of his great march, Narses would be compelled to leave the Via Flaminia in order to turn, or outflank, this obstacle in his path.

Petra Pertusa

The Romans had hewn the remarkable gallery, or tunnel, through the grey rock hemming in the Candigliano, a tributary of the Metauro, leaving just enough room for the Via Flaminia to pass through. They knew it as Petra

Pertusa, 'tunnelled rock'. Its current name is Gola del Furlo. According to an inscription cut into the rock this work was achieved under Vespasian in AD 76:

> 'IMP. CAESAR. AUG. VESPASIANUS. PONT. MAX. TRIB. POT. VII. IMP.XVII. P. P. COS. VII. CENSOR. FACIUND. CURAVIT.'[15]

This tunnel was 38 metres long, 5.5 metres wide and 4.5 metres high. The name of the pass it held, the Furlo, was derived from the Forulus, or perforations.[16] In its neighbourhood occurred the battle between the Carthaginians and the Romans in which Hannibal's brother, Hasdrubal, lost his life (207 BC). Some 745 years later, in 538, Petra Pertusa itself had been the scene of an engagement during this Gothic War.

When Belisarius had sent Ildiger and Martin from Rome to order John's withdrawal from Rimini, the pass had been held by a Gothic garrison which had closed the tunnel itself by means of gates at each end. This garrison also had their families with them, living in block-houses on the far, or Adriatic, side of the tunnel. The 1,000 men on this mission, failing against the entrance to the passage, sent some of their number to the top of the cliff to dislodge boulders on the 'houses' below. Concern for their women and children caused the Goths to surrender on this particular occasion.[17] Ildiger and Martin left a garrison behind and continued on through to Fano, down to Ancona, and then back up the coast to John at Rimini. Totila had re-captured Petra before marching south to besiege Naples.

John, who had been in command for a long time, while being besieged at Rimini, had a good knowledge of this entire region. Doubtless, he was now able to give Narses further valuable advice as to just where to leave the Via Flaminia. This would be in order to turn completely this road block, called by Gibbon 'an obstacle of art and nature'.

The Routes To Battle

After Narses had broken Usdrilas and crossed the river at Rimini, his route was not precisely indicated by Procopius. This has led to confusion, not to mention misunderstandings, among latter-day historians attempting to trace his movements.

Closely connected is the further problem as to the exact site of the field where Totila, marching up from Rome, engaged the eunuch in battle. Procopius called it 'Busta Gallorum',[18] from the final encampment of Narses' army, but this battle, which went a long way towards deciding the fate of the Ostrogoths in Italy, is generally referred to as Taginae.[19]

Thomas Hodgkin (1831–1913), a banker turned historian, had Narses leading his army on the Via Flaminia past Fano (where it turns inland) south to a point above Sena Gallica (Senigallia). There Hodgkin suggests that Narses made a sharp turn to his right near the mouth of the river Sena (Cesano) between the modern seaside resorts of Marotta and Cesano, to ascend the valley of that river. He could then have marched along a road on the near or northern bank of the Cesano up through the minor pass at Ad Pirum (Pergola) on to Ad Calem (Cagli), to rejoin the Via Flaminia having completely out-flanked the fortress of Petra Pertusa.[20]

Marching south on the Via Flaminia once more, it would have been an upward hike to the Roman posting station at the crest of the pass of Statio ad Ensem (Scheggia). This would have been between Monte Petrano (1,162 metres) and Monte Catria (1,701 metres) through narrow defiles and over narrow bridges, crossing and re-crossing the torrent of the Burano.

An attack by the enemy along this part of the route might easily have thrown the entire army into disorder; at the very least, Narses would not have been able to bring his full force to bear on the foe. He did, however, get through without mishap and Hodgkin had him encamping initially in the neighbourhood of Scheggia.[21]

The Anglo-Irish historian John Bagnell Bury (1861–1927) wrote a four page Appendix objecting to this route given by Hodgkin as a misunderstanding of a sentence in the original Greek of Procopius.

> 'From there [Rimini] he left the Flaminian Way and went to the left.'[22]

Bury then proceeded to trace the alternative routes that Narses could have taken to turn Petra Pertusa and reach his final camping place. If he had left the coast below Fano, Narses would have had the inland section of the Via Flaminia on his right, but Procopius plainly stated the exact opposite. In order to have this highway on his left, he would have had to turn inland between Rimini and Fano.

It is implied that Procopius supposed Narses to have diverged inland close to Rimini itself, passing behind Monte Titano (San Marino), following a road to Pievadi S. Stefano. After crossing the watershed of the Apennines he would have reached Tifernum Tiberinum (Citta di Castello). This would represent a deviation almost as far as Arretium (Arezzo). Then he could have either back-tracked up to Urbania, and on over to Acqualagna, or gone down to Iguvium (Gubbio), and over to Aesis (Scheggia).[23]

Bury gave two more alternatives to Narses; to proceed along the coast as far as Pisaurum (Pesaro) which Procopius' informant might not have mentioned, there to take a road to Urbino; or to take a side road running from Rimini to Urbinum (Urbino), and then around to Acqualagna by way of Fermignano.[24].

By any of these various routes Narses could have returned to the Via Flaminia, beyond the 'tunnelled rock', bypassing its garrison either from the north or south.

The Camp Of Narses

The identity, and situation, of the place where Narses' army finally encamped is as controversial as the actual route taken to reach it. Procopius referred to it as Busta Gallorum – Sepulchres of the Gauls – a commemorative name for the site near Sentinum (close to the present Sassoferrato) where, in 295 BC, the consuls Decius and Fabius had defeated the Gauls and their Samnite allies.[25]

G. Colucci, in volume vii of his Antichita Picene (1790), discussed at great length (in over sixty pages) the questions of where the Roman consuls defeated the Gauls, and Narses defeated the Goths. He identified Busta Gallorum with the castle called Bastia, and came to the conclusion that Narses fought in the plain south of Sassoferrato (Piano della Croce) and Fabius and Decius still further to the south, near Fabriano.[26]

Hodgkin originally placed Narses' camp in the neighbourhood of Scheggia because of Procopius' supposedly accurate description of its exact situation.[27] However, he corrected himself with the aid of his friend, James Bryce (1838–1922) and a local antiquary, S. Ulpiano Garofoli, of Sigillo. He saw Scheggia as being too confined, and moved the encampment further south to where the Valley of the River Chiascio (a tributary of the Tiber) is 'somewhat broader'. Hodgkin disregarded altogether Procopius' Busta Gallorum, and ruled out the ground near Sassoferrato.[28]

Bury presented three objections to all of this 'reconstruction' by Hodgkin. First, from Procopius' description of the battle, the ground even below Scheggia was unsuitable. Second, Procopius' informants, who knew the scene well, did not mention Scheggia, Helvillum (Sigillo) or even the Via Flaminia to him. Lastly the name Busta Gallorum was not taken into account.[29]

Instead, once Narses had reached Acqualagna, Bury had him marching on the Via Flaminia only as far as Cagli. There, he diverged south-eastwards through Frontone and Sassoferrato to the valley of the 'Bono' (the Torrente Sentino).[30]

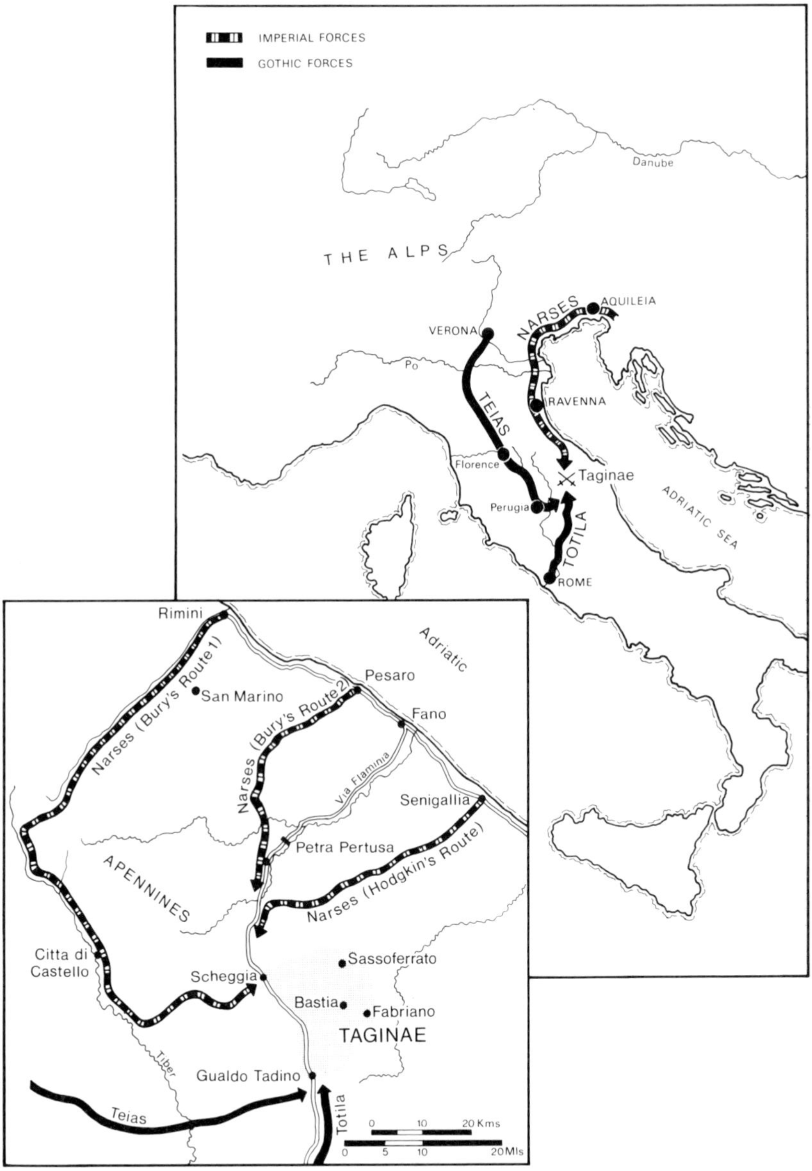

Fig. 5. The route to Taginae. The detail shows three different routes by which Narses could have bypassed the fortified tunnel on the Via Flaminia at Petra Pertusa. The most likely area for the battle of Taginae is indicated by a stipple.

The Movements Of Totila

The last leg of Narses' long journey to seek out his enemy naturally depended on the movements of Totila, who was initially in Rome. There, he heard that Narses had evaded the Franks altogether, and had overcome the obstacles created by Teias, reaching Ravenna intact. Teias, back up in Verona, was summoned to join him with all available troops, for the successful occupations of Corsica and Sardinia had reduced his own forces in Italy. Yet he eventually left Rome before Teias and his 2,000 troops arrived, after hearing of the death of Usdrilas before Rimini.[31]

Totila would not, however, have been unduly concerned for he would naturally have assumed that Narses' large army could advance only on the Via Flaminia, and that it would be held up, if not stopped, at the almost impregnable position of Petra Pertusa. His mistake was in failing to guard all the passes, or possible outlets, and in not keeping a more careful watch over the movements of his assailant.[32]

Totila led his army northwards up to Umbria on the Via Flaminia, which crossed the Tiber out of Rome on the famous Ponte Milvio (Milvian Bridge). Narses, in effect, once he had turned the position of Petra Pertusa, would be marching south on the same road. Thus, the two armies were on a collision course, the only question remaining being which one would first reach the best place on or off the road to give battle.

As it turned out, Totila reached a point just about halfway between Rome and Ravenna, the small town of Tadinum (Gualdo Tadino).[33] It is here that he is generally said to have encamped; his position may have depended on the route taken by Teias from Verona. The latter would come by way of Bologna, down through Tuscany and Umbria, via Florence, Arezzo and Perugia. Gualdo Tadino would have been a convenient place on the Via Flaminia for an army waiting for reinforcements coming over from Perugia.

It is possible that Totila arrived in the valley, less than fifteen miles below the pass at Scheggia, about the same time that Narses was gaining the crest of the pass.[34] He may have had time to seize the outlets of the valley, and draw up his army so as to compel Narses either to fight, or make a perilous retreat back over the difficult pass.[35] On the other hand, his smaller force would have been compelled to fight the entire army of Narses in the more open valley above Gualdo Tadino.[36]

Bury reasoned that Narses, hearing of the movements of Totila and the Goths, decided to choose the battle ground himself. He proposed that the camp of Totila was actually further to the north at Fossato (Fossato di Vico). From there Totila could have reached Narses' defensive position by marching over and up to Melano, in between Bastia and Fabriano.[37]

A reasonable conclusion to be drawn from all of this is that the subsequent Battle of Taginae was fought in the Apennine area of Umbria, on the borders of Umbria proper and transapennine Umbria, i.e. the Marche. The field of Taginae could be said to have been either below Sassoferrato, or south of Scheggia somewhere in the area bounded to the south by Gualdo Tadino, to the west by Sigillo and to the east by Fabriano.

The engagement probably took place on a small upland plain with just enough breadth of ground suitable for the movement of cavalry. Both commanders, the daring, rash Totila, and crafty, subtle Narses most likely welcomed this scene, for different reasons.

Chapter VIII

The Battle of Taginae

'The decision of three decades of war was now to
be reached in an open battle at last.'
John W. Barker[1]

Narses won three great victories in battle over the western barbarians, the Ostrogoths, and the Franks with their Alamanni allies. The background and preparations leading up to the first of these full-scale battles should be sufficient evidence as to his capacity to command and manoeuvre large armies. It is also evident that no matter which route he may have taken past Rimini, he had strategically out-manoeuvred his opponent, Totila, by out-flanking the fortified position at Petra Pertusa. Only the battlefield tactical abilities of Narses remain to be seen.

Actually, in the decades of open warfare between the Gothic and Imperialist armies in Italy, there had been numerous blockades and sieges, marches and counter-marches, but very few pitched battles. The very first tactic employed by Narses showed his knowledge of barbarians and their ways. He sent trusted officers to the camp of the Gothic king offering him a chance to surrender, or if he was determined to fight, to give the day for battle.

In making such an apparently simple proposal, Narses knew exactly what he was doing; among the northern tribes and nations, this was a familiar practice. Over 650 years earlier, Boiorix, the leader of the Cimbri, appointed the day and place for the battle with Marius on the Raudine Plain (101 BC).[2] Far more recently there had been the case of Clovis and Syagrius, the last Roman commander in Gaul (Battle of Soissons, 486).

As for Totila, Procopius quoted his answer to the envoys of Narses: 'At the end of eight days let us match our strength.'[3]

Once again, Narses showed his insight into the barbarian mind, for he reacted accordingly when informed of the words of the Gothic leader. He had no illusions as to the perfidious character of his enemy, and judged the purpose of the response correctly by taking the corresponding precautions. For on the very next day, Totila showed up 'self announced' with his army, and both forces immediately took up positions opposite each other not further apart than 'two bowshots'.[4]

The size of the army facing the one of Narses is unknown, except that it was 'considerably smaller'.[5] The strength of Totila's forces in relationship to those of the Empire has been estimated on a ratio basis, apparently as three to five.[6] In terms of numbers of men, this could have been something in the order of 15,000 against 25,000. The fact that cavalry seemed to have formed 'a good half' of his army is a clue as to the tactics that Totila purposed using in the coming battle.[7]

The Orders of Battle

Both armies stretched on a more or less equal front, on as level a piece of ground as was to be found in this region. Totila's lines were overlapped on each flank by the enemy's superior numbers. The chief factor, however, was to be the originality of Narses' tactical disposition of his forces before the beginning of the actual battle. The order of battle adopted by the eunuch-general was of his own invention, not having been used by any other general in the warfare of that time.[8]

Narses placed his Gepidae, Heruli and Lombard auxiliaries in his centre; but he dismounted these barbarian horse-men, and armed them with the lance. This was a cleverly baited trap for the Goths, who, with their instinctive offensiveness, would hold in contempt the idea of 'frail' infantry resisting a cavalry charge. By having his own barbarian cavalry dismounted, using lances on foot, to appear like infantry spearmen, Narses may have had political as well as military reasons. He could have had doubts about the fidelity of these mercenary contingents, 'of approved valour and doubtful faith', suspecting them of having sympathy, and even admiration, for Totila.[9] By placing them dismounted, to fight on foot, in the very centre of his army, he diminished the possibility of treachery driving them to flight.

On either side of his centre, Narses placed 4,000 of his regular foot-archers. This was contrary to the rule of Belisarius, who would have used horse-archers. The 'peculiarity' of this formation was in the combination of these flanking foot-archers with the dismounted cavalry, and all in the heavy mass of a close phalanx. Totila probably had no idea at all as to the strength of the tactics opposed to him.[10]

On either wing of this first line of 'foot' soldiers Narses arrayed his regular mounted cavalry, the Hippo-toxotai. The left wing was held by Narses himself, and John, with the 'the flower' of the Imperial army, near a small steep hill; on the right wing were John the Glutton, Valerian and

Dagisthaeus. In addition, he stationed two detached bodies of cavalry, picked forces of 1,000 and 500 men respectively, behind the hill on his extreme left flank.[11] Ordinarily the natural position for such detachments would have been behind the centre; however they were there not only to aid any part of the line hard pressed, but to deliver a surprise stroke on the rear of the Goths when they had become deeply engaged.[12]

These tactics of Narses, as a whole, showed 'an almost ostentatious disregard' for the fate of his centre.[13] He was determined to conquer with his wings, and that it should be Totila who made the attack; and, when he did, he would be out-flanked and surrounded by picked troops on both flanks. As B.H. Liddell Hart put it:

> '. . . having drawn his full profit from the strategic offensive, Narses preferred the tactical defensive on meeting Totila.'[14]

There are no particulars as to Totila's order of battle, but, while Narses had laid his plans with consummate skill, Totila, brave as he was, revealed at long last that he was not even a general. Although he had shown some strategical insights against Belisarius and the Empire, his long run of success did not mean that he possessed transcendent talents. Once Justinian made the supreme effort to end the war, an immediate change in the situation occurred, and all that Totila had achieved in nine years was to be undone by Narses in two.[15]

Now, in this, Totila's first large pitched battle (he had won victories at Faenza and Mugello over disorganized Imperial generals) he was to be in the phrase of Procopius 'out-generalled by his own folly'.[16] To begin with, he drew up his entire army in much the same array as the enemy's, although his was much the smaller; then, he permitted himself to be enticed by Narses into making the attack. Evidently it was the purpose of Totila to carry the day by a single cavalry charge: There was to be no skirmishing, or slow advance, only a sudden, unexpected, onslaught which hopefully would break through a centre, which, to all appearances, was only infantry. The object would be to get at the enemy as quickly as possible, avoiding the showers of arrows which were the main defence.[17] By making the Goths take the lead in attacking, Narses foreshadowed by more than 860 years the English tactics against the French chivalry at Agincourt.

As a final compounding error Totila gave orders to all of his troops that they should not use bows, nor any other weapon except the spear. This prompted Procopius' phrase about his 'folly': throwing his entire army against the enemy with inadequate arms, being out-flanked and in no respect a match for his antagonist.[18]

The Fight for the Hill

Part of the strength of Narses' defensive position was a small, steep and isolated hill. It was in front of the extreme left of his line, and would cover any attempt by the foe to outflank him and thus attack from the rear.

Narses had occupied this hill with a small force of about fifty infantry-men during the night, or early morning hours, before the day of battle. When Totila espied the situation, he sent a squadron of horse-men to seize the hill. The Imperial infantry, formed into a close phalanx, repulsed repeated attacks by these, and then other Gothic cavalry.[19]

Archer Jones comments on this action of closely packed infantry resisting heavy cavalry : 'This skirmish proved an accurate forecast of the outcome of the battle.'[20]

Procopius relates the heroism of Paulus and Ansilas in repelling the numerous attacks of the Goths up the steep path leading to the summit of the hill. These two left the shelter of the phalanx, and gave a display of valour surpassing all the others. They grounded their swords, and used the bow and arrow with telling effect against the enemy's men and horses.

After their quivers of arrows were empty, they continued to fight off the assailants from behind their swords and shields. Paulus, after his own sword was bent double, rendered useless from hacking away the heads of Gothic spears from their wooden shafts, seized the spears of the attackers with both of his bare hands. He continued to fight with at least four spears captured in this manner. In consequence of such heroism, Narses was to make Paulus a personal guard of his own.[21]

Eventually, Totila gave up the attempt to capture the hill. This was only an isolated engagement at the extremity of the lines, the main armies having not as yet joined battle. Instead, he went along his battle line to encourage his troops with 'voice and expression' on to greater boldness. Narses did the same, but by holding up bracelets, necklaces, golden bridles and other such 'incentives to bravery'.[22]

Display before Battle

The manner in which the battle itself began was typical of that day and age. A Gothic champion, an Imperial deserter named Coccas, rode up to the Imperial lines and challenged the enemy to single combat. Anzalas, an Armenian retainer and spearman of Narses, accepted the challenge, and the two champions met between both armies.

Coccas charged full-speed at his opponent but Anzalas swerved at the last moment, and dealt the Gothic champion a mortal blow in his left side.[23]

The next act, or scene, in this battlefield drama was to be provided by King Totila himself. He rode forth on a magnificent charger into the space between the two armies, arrayed in gold-plated armour with purple trappings, to give a display of his martial prowess.

He skilfully performed 'the dance under arms'. While wheeling about on his large war horse he tossed his javelin into the air and caught it again; fell back on his shoulders, spreading his legs and leaning from side to side.[24]

It must have been strange contrast between the lithe barbarian displaying his skill and strength (Totila was not yet thirty when he became King in 541), and the aged eunuch opposite, who probably kept his seat on horse-back only with difficulty.[25] Narses, however, may have only nodded his head and smiled at these theatrical antics. In spite of Totila's martial prowess, he knew far more of the deadly science of war, and his brain was already devising the overthrow of the athlete.[26]

Actually, it was probably the sheer necessity of delaying tactics that prompted Totila to such a 'chivalrous' display; the fact being that Teias and 2,000 of his horse-men had not yet arrived from Verona. Such numerical reinforcement, particularly of cavalry, would be crucial to Totila's plan of attack, outnumbered as he was.

After his display, but before knowing that Teias and his troops had arrived, Totila, wishing to prolong the postponement of the battle, sent word to the Imperialists that he wished to confer with them. Narses responded that he must be trifling. When he had been given the opportunity to make proposals, he had been set on fighting; now on reaching the field of battle, Totila wanted to parley.[27]

The Goths resorted to one further delay, or ruse, once the awaited horse-men from Verona had arrived. They broke their own array of battle to retire within their camp to eat. Totila must have been confident that Narses would not attack; he being determined to stay entrenched in his strong defensive position. There is the possibility that the Goths expected the other army would likewise break its ranks to eat, and a quick re-assembly would catch it unawares. Once again, however, Narses was not to be taken in by any such barbarian wiles; he had his troops take their repast standing in their ranks, fully armed.[28]

Meanwhile, Totila had changed his kingly trappings for the dress and equipment of a simple, private soldier; a transformation that was to prove fatal.

The Gothic Onslaught

It must have been getting well on into the mid-afternoon of a late June, or an early July day, when Totila's army returned to mount its long-delayed attack on Narses' position. In the morning its array had been much the same as that of the army of Narses. Now, however, Totila adopted an entirely different plan; he placed his entire cavalry, a good half of his army, in a single front line, and left his infantry, mostly archers, behind in a second.[29]

This has been compared to the same mistake which contributed to the defeat of the Emperor Valens (364–78) by the Visigoths under Fritigern, and the Ostrogothic cavalry led by Alatheus and Saphrax at Adrianople (Edirne) almost 174 years earlier (9 August 378).[30]

To meet Totila's new tactic the resourceful Narses made a slight, but what was to prove very significant, change in his own dispositions. The two bodies of foot-archers, originally facing full front, were turned half round and moved forward to form crescents facing each other.[31] This created an enclosed empty space in front of the dismounted centre; pushed forward as they were, they could enfilade any assault there. These foot-men must have been on elevated ground above the plain, so as not to have been in a position to have been swept away by the Gothic cavalry.[32]

As it was, Totila left the wings of archers alone, falling into Narses' cleverly baited trap by having his cavalry charge with 'reckless impetuosity' the apparently unreliable 'infantry' in the centre.[33] The Goths, chafing for hand-to-hand encounter with their spears, or great javelins, suffered badly in their onslaught from a converging hail of arrows on their flanks. Their initial charge failed to break the firm stand of the dismounted lancers and it was checked, losing any impact it may have had.[34]

For a long afternoon the Gothic cavalry rode again and again into the Imperial formation, but all of their furious charges were to no avail. As they went into the semi-circle formed by Narses' formation, trying to reach its centre, they began to fall by the hundreds from the converging fire on their flanks. They ultimately became so disorganized – what with their heavy losses and the plunging and swerving of hundreds of wounded or riderless horses in their midst – that their charges slackened altogether.[35]

The Gothic infantry, who should have supported their cavalry by engaging the enemy's foot-archers, hesitated to advance far enough to be effective; consequently, they took no part in the fighting. They feared to expose themselves to being attacked in their own rear by the detached horse-men behind the flanking hill.

Narses' own foot-archers had by now closed in on the flanks of the Gothic cavalry who were increasingly galled by their actions. They discharged their arrows, impetuously dashed in, wheeled about feigning flight, then sent more arrows at the horse-men who advanced too eagerly. In fact, they were using 'Persian' tactics to win a 'Roman' victory.[36]

Battle's End

The Gothic cavalry, after continuing their vain efforts for some time, became disheartened. By the evening, after one final effort, they found themselves gradually being pressed back onto their own infantry in the second line.

As they began to give way, retiring to their rear, Narses charged with his own fresh cavalry that had been held in reserve.[37] The Gothic horses ran over their own infantry, who instead of opening their ranks to let them pass through, and then facing the enemy themselves, turned and joined the general retreat.[38] This soon became a rout, the Goths even killing one another in the darkness: 6,000 perished on the field of battle, the chief casualty being their king, Totila himself. The survivors scattered into the hills. They had fought fiercely and with their usual courage, but being out-numbered and out-manoeuvred, only darkness saved them from annihilation.

Large numbers surrendered; the Imperialists initially making prisoners of them, but later on showing no quarter and slaying them. A contributing factor to this apparent cruelty was the great numbers of the old Imperial soldiers in their ranks (German mercenaries), who had earlier deserted.[39] A number of warriors were still left to the Gothic cause however; those who had succeeded in hiding out in the hills, or escaping completely from the neighbourhood. Out of a presumed total of 15,000 men that went into the battle, 6,000 were killed; the number of prisoners taken, and also those executed as deserters, is not known. Therefore, the number of survivors that eventually fled northwards with Teias to the Po is completely unknown.

The Death of Totila

Procopius presented more than one version of the death prophesied for Totila less than a decade earlier by Saint Benedict (*c.*480–*c.*547). During the campaign at Naples (543) Totila visited the Saint, in disguise, and was told that after capturing Rome for a second time, he would die within ten years.

Procopius' shorter version is that the Ostrogothic King was mortally wounded at the very beginning of the battle, during the first great onslaught.

He was struck by an arrow from a bowman who did not even recognize his target; consequently, his army fought leaderless all afternoon.[40] This could explain the whole conduct of the battle by the Gothic side as being so unworthy of his previous reputation.

The first version given by Procopius, in greater detail, is more generally accepted by historians, possibly because it has more picturesque details. In it, Totila, surviving the actual battle, was accompanied by not more than five faithful followers as he was leaving the field in the darkness afterwards. Asbad, the leader of the Gepids, with four of his own men, overtook the small party, and not recognizing the Gothic leader made ready to strike at him. Whereupon, an accompanying Gothic youth cried out:

> 'What is this, you dog?
> Are you rushing to smite your own master?'

At this, Asbad drove his spear with all his might into Totila's body, and was wounded in the foot by Scipuar (a Gothic commander), who was wounded in turn by one of the pursuers. The small band of fugitives carried their wounded king 84 stades, or 12 Roman miles (18km) to the village of Caprae, (Caprara) west of the Via Flaminia, where he expired and was hastily buried.[41] It is not known how far Totila had fled from the battle before being wounded.

Later, an old Gothic woman revealed the location of the grave to the Imperialists. The body was exhumed, gazed upon for a long time, and positively identified.

Totila's blood-stained garments and the cap he had worn, which was adorned with gems, were taken to Narses, who sent them on to Constantinople. There, in August 552, they were laid at the feet of Justinian as visible proof that the enemy who had defied his power for so long was no more.[42]

Tributes to Totila

Baduila, or Totila (so-styled on his coins), was to be the first of opposing barbarian leaders to lose his life in offering battle to Narses. The career of this romantic Teutonic hero, one of the great figures of the German heroic age, had finally been brought to a close.

He had waged a long fight, in a not ignoble cause, only to have a sudden reversal of fortune and an adverse fate bring failure in the end. His revival of the Gothic cause, with only 5,000 men at the start, led to an almost unbroken string of successes and the reconquest of Italy save for four towns (Ravenna, Ancona, Crotone and Otranto). Such a career had just the elements of tragedy in it to arouse the sympathies; and appeal to the imaginations of even his enemies.[43]

During his career, Totila had attracted deserters from the Imperial forces and made efforts to conciliate the native Italians, even gaining a good reputation by his treatment of the Neapolitans after capturing their city in 543.[44] At the very least, his actions have been seen as being dictated by 'good policy'. His initial fame, however, was gained chiefly through his enemies' mistakes and weakness; and he himself was capable of political, as well as military, blunders (e.g. the abandonment of Rome).

Notwithstanding, by the late nineteenth century, Totila became an heroic figure of romance; a 'very perfite gentil knight'. He was distinguished from his fellow barbarians by chivalrous sentiments, noble behaviour towards foes and overall with gentle and humane instincts. [45] He came to be considered, even more that Theodoric the Great himself, the noblest representative of the Ostrogothic nation.

It was claimed that if he had originally occupied the position of Athalaric, or of Vitigis, then Totila would have assuredly made a world-famous name for himself in history. If only his Ostrogothic Kingdom in Italy had continued to exist, he would have held the same exalted place in its annals as Englishmen accord to Alfred the Great, Frenchmen to Charlemagne, and Germans to Barbarossa.[46] Otherwise, Theodoric has been referred to as the Alfred of Gothic history, while Totila was its King Harold.[47] In other words, Taginae was Totila's Hastings.

If Totila could have put into the field the 100,000 or so men that Vitigis had when besieging Rome, the outcome of the battle might have been very different.[48] Alternatively, the slaughter might have been that much worse. Narses was to show in future battles with barbarian hosts (e.g. the Alamanni-Franks), that he was not to be overwhelmed by sheer numbers.

In the final analysis, Narses personally did not have any illusions as to Totila's character, not imagining him to be a 'pure chevalier'. He knew Totila to be 'an ordinary perfidious barbarian', and consequently took the 'corresponding precautions'.[49]

Narses' Victory

The Battle of Taginae had presented the strange spectacle of the struggle of a hero with a eunuch. Fortune may have indeed wearied of Totila at long last, but the victor Narses had displayed military talents not inferior to those of the great Belisarius. His victory was all the more striking as the Goths were not led by a Vitigis, but by a leader credited with thoroughly knowing the methods and tactics of the Imperialists.

Narses fully deserved his victory. He had brought his enemy to battle and then devised tactics which were original,[50] differing entirely from those used by Belisarius in his Persian campaigns. The description of this battle comes from Procopius, who in turn relied on an eye witness report, possibly from John, and therefore it is deficient in some details. First, the exact numbers of the two armies engaged are unknown; as is the behaviour of Totila and his ablest lieutenant, Teias, during the course of the action. Further, it is not clear whether Narses' centre, or his wings, were the more heavily engaged. None the less, it can be established that the generalship of Totila was deficient, and that he could have made better use of his forces, inferior in numbers as he was.

It is also clear that the tactics of Narses had ended in complete success; the first experiment in 'modern' history of combining the pike with the bow.[51] His barbarian auxiliaries did what the Roman Infantry had failed to do at the Battle of Adrianople, stand up to the shock of Gothic cavalry. His bowmen disorganized and demoralized the Ostrogothic horse-men at Taginae before his own cavalry charged to annihilate them.[52]

Some historians and military analysts see these decisive counter-strokes as sealing the fate of the battle. It was ultimately to the bow that Narses trusted, and it won him a complete victory.[53]

Procopius himself ignored any distinctions between mounted and unmounted troops when it came to their common enthusiasm, energy, valour and vigour in repulsing the enemy's assault. His admiration for all the branches of Narses's army was equal. Furthermore, he points out that the 'Romans' had used all weapons; bows, spears, swords, or any other convenient suitable arms.[54]

A naval historian, William Ledyard Rodgers, compared the tactics of this battle up in the hills with those of the sea fight off the coast, to the northeast, at Sena Gallica. There, the Goths, after an initial charge, fell into a huddle through their lack of skill. In both cases, the Imperialists used their archers to shake the confused foe, and then charged to destroy him.[55]

An interesting point to consider is that both John and Valerian were commanders in the two engagements.

Afterglow of Taginae

The pious, victorious eunuch was overjoyed at the outcome of his first great battle, and could not cease attributing everything to God. Yet, at the same time, he attended to 'all urgent matters'.[56] One of the very first of these was to dismiss his Lombard allies from the territory of the Empire.

The behaviour and general lawlessness of these valiant savages left much to be desired even by barbarian standards.

The Lombards devoted themselves to 'the congenial occupations of arson and rape'.[57] They were continuously setting fire to any buildings and villages they chanced upon, and forcefully violated the women, matrons and virgins, even when they had taken sanctuary at the altar.

Narses accordingly propitiated them with large sums of gold, releasing them to return to their current home in Pannonia. He assigned Valerian and his nephew, Damianus, with their soldiers to escort their march as far as the limits of Imperial territory.[58]

The Lombard historian, Paul the Deacon, varied in emphasis from Procopius in his account of their dismissal; he stated that they returned to their country as victors, honoured with many gifts.[59] Be that as it may, Italy had not seen the last of these savage warriors; they and the name of Narses were to be interwoven into a tangled saga.

Now, however, in the afterglow of his first epic victory, Narses had yet more pressing matters to attend to; the resistance of the Goths to the Imperial forces was not yet over. In the words of Gibbon: 'The Gothic war was yet alive.'[60]

Chapter IX

The Destruction of the Ostrogothic Nation

'There is not a place name in Italy today of Gothic origin; nor is there a single word in the Italian language of Gothic derivation.'
Warren O. Ault[1]

The remnant of the Gothic forces which succeeded in escaping from the field of Taginae fled north-westwards all the way across the Po into Ticinum (Pavia) which they occupied, together with its adjacent territory.[2] Before taking his troops to meet Narses, Totila had left a garrison in that town to guard a large treasure prudently deposited there.

Teias

A new ruler of the Ostrogoths was now acclaimed, 'the bravest of Totila's generals' who had survived the battle – Teias. Agathias gave the name of his father as Fritigern. From his coins it is known that his name was also spelt Teia, Theia, Thela and Thila. In all probability he was still a young man, or in his early middle age.[3] Teias found the treasure hoard left by Totila at Pavia intact, with which he hoped to get the Goths back together again, organizing them into some sort of order. He also purposed to bring the Franks into an alliance.[4]

Narses, hearing of all this, sent orders to Valerian to march to the Po, near Pavia, and guard the movements of the Goths. Valerian, after performing the task of escorting the Lombards out of Italy, had moved over to Verona. There, he entered into negotiations with its Gothic garrison to surrender, but these fell through because of intervention by the Franks, who were still strongly entrenched in Venetia.[5]

Teias himself gained nothing from the 'faithless Franks' except a promise of neutrality. It would naturally suit them to adopt the attitude of being spectators, waiting quietly until the rivals were exhausted and then attacking the victor on their own account. As for Narses, after the great battle in the Apennines, he marched southward towards Rome, occupying Narnia and Spoleto on the way, while sending a detachment to capture Perugia.[6]

Narses Captures Rome

On reaching Rome, Narses actually had to conduct a short siege of the once mighty city. Totila had left behind a small garrison; too small in fact to guard the still quite extensive circuit of walls. He had enclosed the small part of the city around Hadrian's Tomb with a new short wall; by connecting this with an earlier external wall, he had made a sort of fortress.[7] The 'Mausoleo', begun by Hadrian in AD 139, had been turned into a prison by Theodoric, and was later to be converted into the fortress Castel S. Angelo.

Small though the Gothic garrison was, they made some attempt to defend the walls wherever the enemy attacked. Narses himself attacked on one side with a large force of archers, while John and his followers made an assault at another part of the walls, and Philemuth with the Heruls at yet another point.[8] However, it was only a question of time, a few days at most, before a detachment under Dagisthaeus succeeded in scaling an unguarded sector with ladders and opening the gates.[9] Narses advanced in full force against the inner fortress on the river, and the surrender of its garrison was soon arranged.

Procopius saw this event as yet one more example of the strange sport that fortune makes of human affairs. Four years earlier (in 548) at the beginning of the Lazica War, Dagisthaeus had been sent with 7,000 Imperial troops and 1,000 Tzanic auxiliaries to recover the fortress of Petra. He succeeded in gaining a victory over the Persian general Chorianes by the river Hippis in Colchis. This was not enough however, to save him from being accused of misconducting the siege, through disloyalty, or culpable negligence, and being arrested by the order of Justinian.[10]

His replacement was none other than Bessas (an Ostrogoth of Thrace), whose reputation had suffered after losing Rome to Totila back in 546. That old warrior had proceeded to go on and capture Petra in 551. Now, in or about August 552, Dagisthaeus was instrumental in effecting the entry into Rome. Thus each man had reversed his role.

In any event, fateful or otherwise, in the eighteenth year of the Gothic War, and the twenty-sixth of Justinian's reign, Narses captured Rome for the fifth and final time during this conflict. In close to sixteen years as a battle ground of the Empire and the Goths, Rome had been entered, besieged, liberated, re-taken, betrayed, besieged again, betrayed yet again, even abandoned and deserted. Finally, Narses the general from the new capital marched into the ancient one, which he, as a pious Christian, had been taught to revere.[11] But he also immediately sent the keys of its gates back to his emperor.[12]

H. M. Gwatkin, in dealing with the chronological difficulty of where to begin 'Medieval History', maintains:

> 'The Rome which Belisarius delivered was still the Rome of the Caesars, while the Rome which Narses entered sixteen years later is already the Rome of the Popes.'[13]

In fact, the city experienced the profound transformation of emerging from its holocaust of sieges no longer ancient, but medieval Rome.[14] Narses was to remain in this transformed Rome putting it in order, but at the same time he began a war of extermination against the remaining Gothic warriors in Italy. The harbours of Porto, to which part of the garrison at Rome had fled, and Centumcellae (Civitavecchia) were invested, while detachments of his army were dispatched north and south.

During the spring of 552 Croton (Crotone) was hard pressed by a Gothic blockade. The mere appearance of an Imperial relief squadron in its harbour caused the besiegers to break camp and flee. This 'bloodless victory' had the effect of bringing the commanders of the Gothic garrisons at Acherontia (Acerenza) and Tarentum (Taranto) into negotiations for surrender.

The leader at Taranto was an upstart Hunnish adventurer named Ragnaris. Even the defeat and death of Totila did not hasten Ragnaris' surrender of his post as he possibly had some dim visions of wearing the Ostrogothic crown himself. Moreover, he believed that the Goths, allied with the Franks, could still turn the tide of the war. Eventually, however, he entered into negotiation and Pacurius, the Imperial commander at Hydruntum (Otranto), went in person to Justinian in Constantinople with the conditions of surrender. On his return, he sent fifty soldiers to conduct Ragnaris to Otranto and then on to Constantinople. Ragnaris seized the men of Pacurias as hostages and the latter marched over to give battle.[15] Before coming out to fight, the faithless foe murdered the hostages, and, later, Narses personally would almost be a victim of his treachery. Taranto was recovered for the Empire when Pacurius routed Ragnaris outside the town, forcing him to flee to Acerenza.[16]

The Treasure at Cumae

Although Totila had deposited a large hoard of treasure at Pavia, just below Milan, he had actually placed the bulk of the riches of the

Ostrogothic Kingdom well to the south, at Cumae, west of Naples. (He had also added 'great sums of money'[17] and his own personal loot.) These rich prizes were to strongly influence the strategy of both Narses and Teias.

Cumae (Cuma) was an ancient Greek colony on the peninsula above Capo Miseno (the ancient Elysian Fields) situated between Lago di Fusaro and Lago d'Averno. It was the only fortified place in Campania, except for Naples itself, during the Gothic Wars.[18] Both Procopius and Agathias testify to its strength; the former calling it 'an exceedingly strong fortress'[19] the latter declaring it 'very well fortified'.

It was actually an acropolis, 269 feet above sea level, lying barely 100 yards from a low sandy shore. This rocky hill was a mass of trachyte which had broken through the surrounding tufa, and was traversed by caves, with many branches, at three different levels, some of which may have once been quarries. These caverns were famous in legend as being the seat of the oracle of the Cumaean Sibyl.

If Procopius and Agathias were agreed as to Cumae's strength, there is a difference of opinion as to the status of Totila's appointee to command the garrison there – Aligern. Procopius gave the relationship to the late Totila as 'his own brother',[20] while Agathias, writing later, referred to him as 'the youngest brother of Teias'. Associated with Aligern in guarding the Gothic treasure was the former 'Roman' governor of Spoleto, Herodian. Procopius, in his Secret History, charges that he had been driven by the greed of Belisarius to surrender his post to Totila.[21]

Narses, in Rome, sent John and Philemuth northwards, to Tuscany, to watch the movements of Teias, while Valerian was sent over to Picenum, re-occupying Petra Pertusa.[22] At the same time, a considerable detachment of the Imperial army was sent southwards to Campania to besiege Cumae. The outcome of all these movements was that the war wound down into the attempt of one side to seize and, of the other, to defend the remainder of the Ostrogothic treasures.

Teias soon lost hope of reinforcement from the Franks, who had received most of the treasure at Pavia just to be propitiated. Learning that the greater treasure at Cumae was in danger, he decided to march southwards with the forces he had to help defend it. A German historian, O. Körbs, calculated that Teias' small army had about 814 kilometres (about 488 miles) to travel from Pavia to Campania; marching at least 30 kilometres a day, it would have reached its destination in about a month. The shortest route was via the roads of Tuscany, but Narses had already sent John with a force to guard them.

However, Teias, like Narses on his own march, did not take the shortest, or most direct, route. To avoid his enemies, he went by round-about and

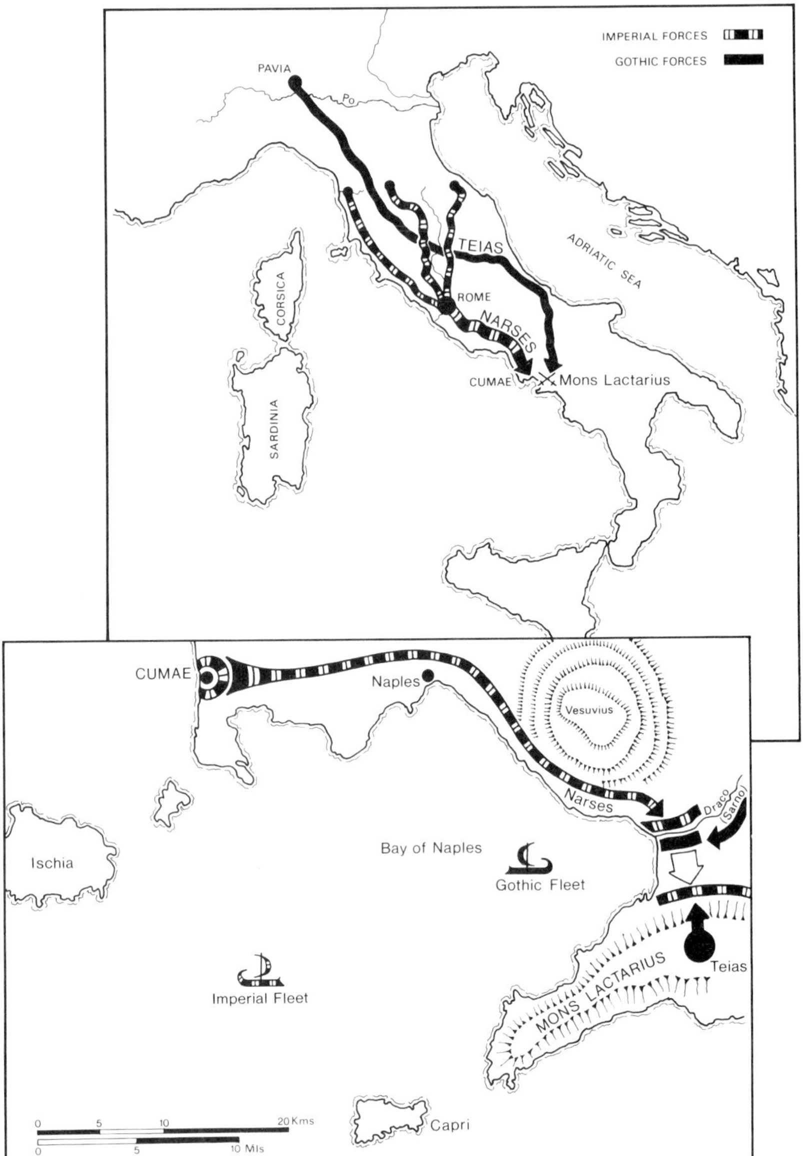

Fig. 6. The Battle of *Mons Lactarius.* The detail shows the Gothic forces of Teias initially confronting Narses across the River Draco (Sarno), before retreating to *Mons Lactarius*. Eventually, driven by starvation and desperation, the Goths came down from the mountains to fight a two-day battle. The result was their complete defeat.

devious ways. Going far to the east, he finally travelled the coast road of the Adriatic, then probably came back across the peninsula by way of Beneventum (Benevento). He would then have had the choice of proceeding via Capua, or Salerno, to the vicinity of Naples. Körbs reckoned that he started soon after the middle of July 552 and reached Campania after the middle of August.[23]

Narses, when he realised that Teias had eluded his generals in the north, summoned John, Philemuth and Valerian to join him in a great movement, with all his forces, southwards to Campania. The rapidity of the movements of all these commanders most likely frustrated Teias' plans to reach Cumae itself and effect a junction with Aligern.

Teias descended from the mountains, probably near Nuceria (known today as Nocera Inferiore), to the south-east of Mount Vesuvius. His objective was to the north-west, on the other side of the great volcano. He could expect the land approaches to Naples to be guarded, but the remainder of the Gothic fleet was assembled nearby in its Bay. As there was no enemy fleet to oppose him, he may well have planned to reach Cumae by sea, embarking his army towards Sorrento (possibly at the present day Castellammare di Stabia, or Castellammare Terme).

Teias at Bay

Narses' good intelligence service, and his vigilance, enabled him to foil this plan just in time by preventing Teias from reaching the southeast corner of the Bay of Naples. He found the Imperial army drawn up on the banks of the Draco (now the Sarno), a small, unimportant stream flowing into the Bay, north of the peninsula of Amalfi and Sorrento. Behind Teias and his Goths was the lofty range of mountains which fills up most of the peninsula; before them, the Draco with a view of the distant green mounds, which formed the grave of the vanished city of Pompeii, and the fertile plain reaching to the base of Vesuvius. Here, the small army of Teias stood at bay, skirmishing with the much larger force of Narses, for 'two months'.[24] If Teias reached Campania after the middle of August, Agnellus of Ravenna's dating of the battle commencing on the lst of October 552 would indicate the confrontation during the weeks of September. Otherwise, from the vague indications of time given by Procopius, the armies could have faced one another from December 552 through January 553, with the battle occurring in February. If, however, Procopius was reasonably accurate, then the date given by Agnellus is wrong.[25] Henry Fynes Clinton, in his Chronology, had the two armies opposed to each other for two months, from January on, coming to the conclusion that the battle was fought at the beginning of March 553.[26]

Initially, Teias may have been supplied by his fleet, but innumerable Imperial ships began to arrive, at first from Sicily, and then from all parts of the Empire. Not long afterwards, the Gothic commander treacherously surrendered his fleet. Narses, in the meantime, had erected wooden towers on his bank of the stream and succeeded in completely dampening the spirits of the Goths.[27]

After being deserted by his fleet, Teias and his army reluctantly retreated to the shelter of the long mountain overlooking the plain. It was called, in Latin, 'Mons Lactarius', i.e. 'Milk Mountain', and since the time of Galen (*c.*129–200) Roman physicians had sent their patients there for the benefits of its air and milk.[28] Today, it is named Monti Lattari, and butter is still made there. Nevertheless, it soon became apparent that in gaining safety from attack on its steep slopes, the Goths had stumbled on a worse fate – death from starvation (evidently there was little milk and honey on 'Milk Mountain' then). Once again, barbarian warriors had been out-manoeuvred and outwitted by the keener intelligence of Narses.

The Battle of Mons Lactarius

The Ostrogoths, in sheer desperation, came down from Mons Lactarius to launch a surprise attack on the enemy entrenched at the foot of the mountain. The sudden appearance of the barbarian warriors was so unexpected that the Imperial army did not have time to receive them in formed ranks. The Goths were on foot, advancing as a solid mass of infantry, formed into a 'deep phalanx'; the Imperialists, also unmounted, received them in an unformed mass. There has been much conjecture on the resulting battle between unmounted foes renowned for their cavalry prowess; Procopius himself not giving any explanations for the Goths advancing on foot, and the 'Romans' not mounting to meet them.[29]

Narses may have constructed fortifications, such as earthworks and ditches, to blockade the enemy, that could only be attacked and defended on foot. Consequently, the Goths were obliged to attack, and Narses' army to defend, in this manner.[30] The very nature of the ground at the foot of the Mountain may have been unsuitable for horses, rendering all tactics difficult, and cavalry tactics impossible. Since the Goths had been forced from their position by hunger, possibly their own horses were not in fit condition to go into battle, or could even have been eaten. Whatever their reasons for being horseless, the very suddenness of the Goth's attack could have prevented the enemy from mounting. A final conjecture is that the 'Romans', either from policy or generosity, also dismounted to fight in the same fashion or manner.[31]

The 'Homeric combat' that followed left no room for tactics; it was a sheer trial of personal bravery involving strength and skill alone.[32] As for the psychological implications of this sudden clashing of the two armies, it was a battle between despair and desperation on one side, and on the other, shame at the very thought of being attacked, much less beaten, by a mere handful of antagonists. Although there is no listing of the numbers involved, a possible estimate could be 7,000 for the army of Teias, and at least 15,000 for the forces of Narses.

The ground where the encounter took place appears to have been less than a mile (about a kilometre) south-west of the present town of Angri at the Pozzo dei Goti (Well of the Goths). According to local tradition (which had forgotten the battle itself) this was a large covered-in and bricked-up well once filled with the bones of Goths. At the present time, the main road passing this way to Sant Antonio Abate, and S. Maria La Carita, is the Via dei Goti.

The two-day battle that occurred was a valiant fight, more of a 'saga' than some of the other recorded deeds of the northern nations. In this, their last stand, the Ostrogoths fought bravely, almost down to the last man; but, they had no bard remaining to tell of their glorious end. At best, there is the narrative of Procopius giving an account of the heroism of a single individual, their leader, King Teias.

First Day of Battle

If there was no description of the behaviour of King Totila, or his 'ablest general', Teias, during the action at Taginae, the exploits of the latter at Mons Lactarius are given vividly. Procopius introduces this engagement by asserting that he will describe 'a battle of great note' and that the heroism displayed by one man, Teias, was not inferior to any of the heroes of legend.[33] Procopius personally did not witness the battle, he narrated from the descriptions of informants, who may not have been wholly reliable, but who were impressed by what they saw.

The last King of the Ostrogoths led the deep phalanx in the assault on the enemy, and this time there would be no question as to his identity. From the very onset he was a marked target for the Imperialists and their missiles, which he received from behind his great shields. As soon as one shield was covered with the barbs of the foe, he would turn to a man-at-arms in attendance and receive a new one. In this manner Teias is said to have fought for the third part of the day.[34] The exact time that the Goths began their surprise attack is unknown, but, considering their hunger, it may have occurred shortly after dawn.[35] Therefore Teias could have waged his heroic fight until the late hours of the morning, or even the early forenoon.

Finally growing weary at a point where twelve spears were stuck in his shield, Teias called for a fresh one, and was mortally wounded by a javelin in the brief moment his chest was exposed making the exchange. The enemy cut off his head, mounted it on a pole, and raised it above the battle to announce to the Goths the fate of their leader. The effect, however, was the opposite of the one intended.[36] The Goths, instead of being disheartened by the death of their king, fought on yet more fiercely in one of the most savage battles of all time.

The whole account of this first part of the battle gave a fanciful version of the heroism of Teias; he alone was on stage, with the deep Gothic phalanx apparently playing no part in the action.[37] Yet, even with Teias swept off centre stage by death, the long first act of this battlefield drama continued. His followers fought on for the remainder of the day to avenge his death, until with the darkness of night comrades could no longer be distinguished from the foe. The Goths, after this savage first day of battle with a vastly superior enemy, went to sleep with their weapons; the combat was to be renewed with the return of daylight.[38]

Second Day of Battle

This 'Homeric combat' resumed with the early dawn and continued unabated all through a second full day, until once again the sun had set. The second day of battle was much like the first, a stand-up fight of sheer physical prowess, with little or no organized tactics. The very fierceness of the fighting should have assured heavy losses on both sides.[39] In a battle of elimination however, the heavily outnumbered army would have little, if any, chance of victory. Once again, here is an example of 'barbarian' heroics falling before 'civilized' organization.

Procopius even alleges that the Goths came to feel that they were fighting against the power of God. Realizing at last that victory was impossible, they sent some of their notables to Narses, agreeing to surrender if they were allowed to keep their freedom and leave Italy forever. Narses, following the advice of John, accepted their offer, granting these terms. John's words were to the effect that victory was sufficient for the wise, but extravagant desires could perhaps turn out to one's disadvantage.[40]

Only a paltry number of Goths were left standing at arms, and Narses may have felt something of true admiration when he granted them permission to depart from Italy. A small column of the remnants of this once powerful nation passed through the Imperial lines with the dead Teias, on one of his shields, at its head. It is not known whether Narses restored the severed head to the body. In any event, the Gothic army as an entity had been destroyed and all that remained was for the strategical and political gifts of Narses to deal with the scattered garrisons remaining in the Peninsula. As a prime example there was still Aligern over at Cumae.

The Disappearance of the Ostrogoths

Whether his victory occurred in October 552, the following February, or in March 553, Narses had practically completed the reconquest begun by Belisarius back in 536. It had taken three days of fighting in two full-scale battles to make the Ostrogothic Kingdom only an historic memory after sixty years (see Appendix 2).

As for the fate of the surviving Gothic warriors, there has been as much speculation on their dispersal after their last battle as there was on why they went into it unmounted in the first place. The first conclusion generally drawn is that they shared the fate of the other barbaric nations overthrown in warfare; they would be mixed with, and ultimately submerged into, other tribes. The Heruls were to suffer this fate a decade later. The Goths may have marched northwards to the Alpine passes and out of Italy altogether, but one tradition has a number of them settling in the 'German' South Tirol (Alto Adige).[41]

Other traditions of the dispersal give such various destinations as the lands of their ancestors, i.e. Prussia and Lithuania;[42] Spain, to find a new home with the Visigoths; and even the Crimea.

Narses is said to have furnished them with vessels to leave Italy and its hostile natives; or to have transported a remnant to Constantinople, where they were soon lost and absorbed into the population of that cosmopolitan city.[43] Then again, it is reported that the mercy and generosity of Narses won over many of the surviving warriors to take service under him.[44]

Finally, Procopius informs us that a small but determined band of some 1,000 Goths refused to pledge themselves to the terms of the surrender. They broke away under the command of different men (among whom was Indulf, the late naval commander) and retreated all the way back to the walls of Pavia, and the country beyond the Po.[45]

In all of these accounts of the disappearance of an entire nation there has been no mention of women and children; even a warrior-kingdom must have had its share of camp followers. Furthermore, in sixty years of occupation there is likely to have been some inter-marriage with the native women, and the sireing of at least two (if not three) generations of offspring.

Be that as it may, Narses' destruction of the Ostrogoths has been compared with that of Rome's destruction of the Etruscans and Carthaginians. It was the same type of strange catastrophe, and all the more startling because the Goths were a people more nearly connected with modern concepts of government and organization. They had set up a relatively enlightened kingdom, and had been able to send 150,000 warriors into the field.[46] At the hands of Narses, they were all but annihilated and forgotten. A further tribute to his accomplishment in overthrowing this powerful barbarian kingdom, is the fact that the Ostrogoths were not a degenerate race like the Vandals in Africa, nor their government weak and corrupt like that of the Visigoths in Spain.[47]

Francis Marion Crawford contended that in his two great victories over the Goths there was no doubt but that Narses stemmed the stream of history at Taginae, and turned it at Mons Lactarius – 'and he deserves to be numbered among the world's great generals'.[48]

Any appreciation at all of his battlefield tactics, not to mention his overall strategy, should be convincing proof that Narses' victories were due to more than mere superiority in men, materials or money.

Events in Italy after Mons Lactarius

The battles of Taginae and Mons Lactarius may have destroyed the Ostrogothic nation in Italy, but Narses still had much strenuous campaigning before him, before Italy was to know a brief respite of peace. There were yet to be long marches, assaults, blockades, parleys, sieges, surrenders, skirmishes, even more battles – one of which, in the scale of its slaughter, was greater than Taginae and Mons Lactarius combined.

Even if there was an exodus of Goths following the surrender at Mons Lactarius, a considerable number still remained scattered about Italy. Some had hoped to merely escape unnoticed; others, refusing the offered terms, contrived to join the Franks. These barbarians they now urged to war on the Empire, the main argument being that since Narses had routed the Goths, he would hasten to drive the Franks out of their part of Italy.

Narses had first to deal with isolated bands and garrisons still remaining in strongholds and fortified cities. Towns up in Tuscany such as Pisa, Florence, Lucca, and Luna (on the border of Liguria) continued to hold out. Further north there were Pavia, with the 1,000 men said to have taken refuge there; Crema to the north-east; and finally Verona. Nearer at hand, Aligern and his garrison still faithfully guarded the royal treasure at Cumae.

The Siege of Cumae

The personal attention of Narses was next turned to besieging the fortified rock of Cumae, up above the far side of the Bay of Naples. He is said to have spent the 'winter months'[49] doing so, but due to discrepancies or vagueness in Procopius and Agathias it is difficult to determine which months.

If the Battle of Mons Lactarius did occur in the first two days of October 552, then Narses could have begun his supervision of the siege from that month on into March 553. If the battle did not actually take place until February or March, then there could not have been much in the way of 'winter months' left in this part of Italy.[50]

Further confusion has been generated by historians, who, giving March 553 for the twin events of the death of Teias and the battle, also tend to refer to the latter as 'Cumae'. Procopius himself, in the final words he wrote in his eight books of Histories, was ambiguous; in taking leave of the Battle of Mons Lactarius and the surrender of the Goths, he asserted: 'Thus the Romans captured Cumae and all that remained, and the eighteenth year as it closed, brought the end of this Gothic War, the history of which Procopius has written.'[51]

From this it could be concluded that not only did Narses destroy Teias and his army, but succeeded in taking Cumae and its treasure at the same time. Procopius has also hinted that, following their surrender, the surviving Goths received their own money from various fortresses in order to leave Italy.[52]

Agathias stated, however, that the siege of Cumae lasted 'above a year' (from the autumn of 552 into the winter of 553–4?) From this point on, he is the 'authority' who must be followed for the events in the next few years of Narses' career (552–58). Agathias was not an historian in the accepted sense of the word that Procopius was; but, as a contemporary, his unfinished work of five books on the reign of Justinian deals chiefly with the wars of Narses. It was Gibbon who remarked about relinquishing 'a statesman and soldier' as a guide, and having to follow in the footsteps of 'a poet and rhetorician',[53] Agathias being a rhetorician given to composing poetic epigrams.

Gibbon also paid tribute to Aligern and his spirited defence of Cumae and its treasure. Obviously accepting Agathias' version of his relationship to Teias, Gibbon stated that his spirit, as well as his situation, prompted Aligern to imitate rather than to bewail his brother. [54]

It was Aligern's personal bravery, as well as his military conduct, that was the backbone of the stout defence put up by the besieged garrison for over a year. As an example of his warlike prowess, it is claimed that such was the force of the arrows shot from his bow that even stones were broken into splinters. On one occasion, Palladius, a chief officer of Narses, led a storming party to the wall, and Aligern, taking careful aim from the ramparts, transfixed him with a single arrow which pierced both his shield and breastplate.

The industry of the besiegers scooped the Sibyl's cavern into a prodigious mine, and introduced combustible materials to consume its temporary props. The wall and gate of Cumae did sink into the cavern, but the resulting ruins 'formed a deep and inaccessible precipice'.[55]

Therefore, when all the assaults and devices of Narses failed, he was forced to fall back on the tedious process of starving the garrison into submission. He left a small investing force to blockade the now inaccessible citadel, and proceeded to march up into Central Italy. There, he had the various strongholds of diehard Gothic garrisons to deal with. He may have hoped to have completed their reduction before the summer months, but his plans were to be disconcerted by the appearance of a fresh and far more formidable foe.

It was probably the threat of a new incursion into Italy by the Franks that was the immediate cause of Narses breaking off his personal supervision of the siege of Cumae and heading north. Along the way, by granting terms to their garrisons, he obtained the surrender of Civitavecchia (invested after the fall of Rome), and the Tuscan towns of Florence, Pisa, Volterra (Volaterrae), north-west of Sienna, and Luna.[56] Only Lucca bargained for a delay with the impatient Narses; if no succour reached the garrison within thirty days, it promised to surrender then, and even gave up hostages for the fulfilment of this pledge.[57] Meanwhile Narses had already sent on the greater part of his forces, under John and Valerian, to the southern banks of the Po, to guard against the new invaders.

Evaluation of the Ostrogoths

Challenging to historians, as was the physical disappearance of the Ostrogothic Kingdom and nation to historians, equally so were the results of that disappearance. The all-conquering eunuch general who overthrew the Goths in battle sounds almost personally condemned by the assertion: 'It was a profound error to destroy them.'[58] Historians have looked to the Eastern, or 'Byzantine' administration in Italy, and the subsequent invasion of the Lombards (a tribe infinitely below the Gothic cultural level), and proposed that, with the Goths perished for centuries Italy's only hope for political union and freedom.

H.A.L. Fisher develops the case of cause and effects; if the Goths had been left in peace, there might not have been any Lombard invasion (or their spears would have deflected it into the Balkans); no revival of the (Roman) Empire in the West, and no papal state(s) in Italy. He contends that the political unification of Italy, achieved so painfully only as late as the reign of Queen Victoria, might have already been known by the reign of Ethelbert (King of Kent 560–616). Fisher also suggested that by crushing the Goths Narses affected the course of history for over a thousand years. The Lombards being deflected over into the Balkan Peninsula would have resulted in a largely Teutonic population there, and the 'eastern question' (*c.*1815–1914) would have assumed another, and perhaps easier, form.[59]

Along similar lines was the proposal by Hodgkin that the Goths, as 'brave Teutons', welded with the native Latins, would have produced a 'noble' people made to cultivate, and to defend, the Italian peninsula.[60]

Then there are others who see the Gothic War, and its after effects, not as an issue of race, but of two religions, the Arian and the Catholic. As Sidney Hook phrased it: 'Those who accept the theology of the Council of Nicaea [Constantine's ecumenical council in AD 325] call Justinian's crusade a blessing',[61] for the Vandals in Africa, and the Visigoths in Spain, were also heretical Arians. Consequently, to them, Narses, in defeating Totila and Teias, insured the continuance of Catholic civilization and culture for Europe. Even the Lombards were dismissed as mere heathens who could never have been as dangerous as heresy. Therefore, Narses saved not only Italy in concluding these 'unhappy campaigns', but the very soul of Europe.[62]

Fletcher Pratt (who described the Monophysite revolt during Nika) avows that sentimental regrets over the downfall of such 'noble barbarians' as the Goths and Vandals cannot alter the fact that they were 'peculiarly determined' to see the triumph of their own Arian sect.[63]

Nonetheless, the Goths at least were credited with an aptitude for receiving Roman, (i.e. Latin), civilization. Only later would their merits be forgotten; they would be spoken of as without laws or taste; the architecture and writing of the Middle Ages were to be condemned in the one word 'Gothic'.

In the final analysis, the historical event of Narses' destruction of the heretical Arian Ostrogoths can be seen as either an 'error' or a 'blessing'. Sidney Hook, in his book *The Hero in History*, remarked that whether this event should be called an 'error' depended on one's religious predilections. The philosopher sums up the destruction of the Ostrogoths by Narses the Eunuch in these words: 'But error or blessing the act was fateful for the history of Europe.'[64]

Chapter X

The Invasion of the Alamanni–Franks

'Then came Ammingus, leader of the Franks, and Buccillinus; they also in like manner wasted Italy. But with the help of the Lord they too were destroyed by Narses. And all Italy was joyful.'
Liber Pontificalis[1]

This possibly contemporary citation from the Book of the Popes sets forth an actual historical event in very broad and general terms. Actually, this invasion of Italy, from across the Alps, was by two Alamanni brothers, Buccellinus and Leutharis, sometime after the Battle of Mons Lactarius, during the year 553. Here, the name of a chieftain, Amingus, is linked with that of the more aggressive brother, Buccellinus, but he was removed from this event by at least a decade. Amingus will turn up later to confront Narses, around the year 561, but he may have originally entered Italy back in 539 with the King of the Franks, Theodebert.

Theodebert

In 539, after Narses' recall, Theodebert, son of Theodoric (Thierry) and a grandson of Clovis, King since 534, had lead an army of 100,000 men into Northern Italy, attacking both his Gothic allies and the troops of Belisarius. On this occasion, once the Franks were faced by a lack of proper food and the attendant evils of diarrhoea and dysentery, they hurriedly retreated back over the Alps with little more accomplished than a large scale profitable raid.

Later, when Totila was occupied in the South, and in Sicily, Theodebert made a provisional occupation of the province of the Cottian Alps, and the greater part of Venetia. When Narses marched along the coast of Venetia, he had to go to great lengths to avoid the Franks stationed there.

When master of Liguria, Venetia and Emilia, Theodebert was the first barbarian king to declare his formal independence of the Empire by minting coins with his own name and effigy, at Bologna.[2] The coins issued by the Ostrogothic Kings in Italy almost always had the head of an Eastern Roman emperor. Those of Teias, for example, had that of Anastasius.

Theodebert is said to have been so indignant at Justinian adding 'Francicus' to his titles that he considered raising an army with the object of marching through Thrace to Constantinople itself to place the imperial crown upon his own head.[3] Forestalling Justinian, he might have revived the Roman Empire with a grandeur that even Charlemagne himself never succeeded in endowing it with. All these fair schemes however, were put to an end by his premature death at the age of forty-three (547/48) while out hunting. According to Agathias a wild bull was the culprit.Procopius, however, proclaims that he was 'taken from the world by disease.'[4]

Among his many activities, Theodebert had carried on wars of conquest east of the Rhine; gradually absorbing Bavaria and the territories of the Alamanni in Raetia (Switzerland). Therefore, at Theodebert's death, his kingdom of Austrasia, with its capital at Metz, extended well into western Germany. The Austrasians were also to be known as the 'Oriental Franks'. The heir to these domains, including the recently absorbed Alamanni, was his fourteen year old son Theodebalt.

Theodebalt

Theodebalt, or, according to the old French historians, Thibault, was a youth feeble in body and possibly in mind.[5] He had lost the use of the lower part of his body after being struck by paralysis. Evidently he was already tottering to an early grave when he came under the influence of two Alamanni nobles, or tribal chieftains. These were the brothers Leuthar (Leutharis), or Lothaire, and Butilin (better known as Buccelin or Buccellinus).

When these 'Alamanni brethren' knew for certain that the power of the Ostrogoths in Italy was irretrievably broken, they affected to be moved by the pleas of a few refugees from that nation who had not been directly involved in the compact with Narses. They quickly levied an army generally estimated at 75,000 men, but what proportion of Alamanni to Franks is not known. It is assumed that it was made up of far more 'idolatrous Germans' than Franks.[6] The Frankish armies which descended upon Italy in the sixth century were composed principally of Burgundian warriors. This had been the case in 538, before the recall of Narses, when Theodebert had sent 10,000 of these 'volunteers' to assist the Goths, under Uraias, in besieging Milan.[7]

There are various opinions as to the official auspices under which this invasion by a host of 75,000 barbarians took place. With Narses tied down in besieging the remnants of the Goths in their various strongholds, the Franks themselves could have freely invaded Italy from Gaul. The feeble young King Theodebalt however, had no heart for daring enterprises. He may have also been intelligent enough to have had some idea of the strength of the Imperial forces and the ability of their commander.[8]

Even if Theodebalt was determined not to be directly involved himself, by merely turning a blind eye on the two adventurous brothers, he could have granted them a free hand to cross the Alps on their own account.[9]

If they were victorious, then Italy would be annexed to the already extensive Kingdom of Austrasia. If they succeeded in only starting a prolonged war, their original army could always receive reinforcements from Gaul. Finally, if they were initially defeated, Theodebalt could deny any responsibility for their act.[10]

French historians have seen the action of the two Alamanni chieftains as an independent expedition undertaken against the will of their King.[11] Whether or not Theodebalt, and the rest of Gaul, approved, Buccelin and Leutharis were confident they could overwhelm Narses, for whose military talents they professed supreme contempt.[12] Agathias avows that they actually marvelled at the Goths and their slackness which had allowed them to be conquered by 'such a delicate and womanish thing . . . such a mere shadow of a man'.[13]

Meanwhile the despised Narses was engaged in besieging and negotiating at Lucca, and had directed his other generals to guard the passages of the Po. They were not to risk a general engagement with the mighty host, but only to harass the enemy as much as possible by skirmishing warfare. The Imperial generals involved in these operations were Artabanes, John and Valerian.

The leader of the Heruls, Philemuth, whose name has been so often linked with theirs, had very recently died of disease, and the command of his 3,000 foederati had passed to his nephew, Phulcaris (Fulcaris). This bold Herulian was a brave soldier, but as events were shortly to prove, an unskilled commander.

All the remaining Goths in the Ligurian and Aemilian provinces had rallied to the 'Frankish' invaders, who were probably already in command at Pavia. Furthermore, Buccelin had advanced far enough south to have captured Parma.

The Defeat at Parma

Fulcaris headed the vanguard of the Imperial forces stationed below the Po, and apparently made some sort of an attempt to recover Parma from the invaders. He was evidently rash enough to conceive that personal bravery was the 'sole duty and merit of a commander'.[14] He was marching along the Via Emilia in disorder, and without taking due precautions, when an ambuscade of the invaders suddenly rose up from the amphitheatre of Parma, surprising and routing the troops under his command. Fulcaris personally refused to escape, declaring that death itself was less terrible than the 'countenance' or speech of Narses.[15]

This defeat, together with the loss of the latest leader of the Heruls, must have been the reason why John and Valerian retreated to Faventia (Faenza), on the Anemo (Lamone) river.

The reverse at Parma also had the effect of causing great alarm among the soldiers of Narses besieging Lucca; they feared being caught between two fires; being simultaneously attacked by the invaders on one side, and a sortie from the town's garrison on the other. At this late date Narses perhaps began to appreciate the predicament of Belisarius when he had the forces of Vitigis before him and the garrison of Osimo in the rear (538).

Nevertheless, Narses was to behave with such admirable firmness that he would not only revive the courage of his own troops, but ultimately induce Lucca to open its gates to him. In order to present his determination at this point, Hodgkin harkens back to a classical quotation to illustrate the natural inclination of the 'little withered eunuch' to follow the advice given by the Sibyl of Cumae to Aeneas: 'quam tua te Fortuna sinet, tu ne cede malis, sed contra audentior ito' – 'The mightier ills thy course oppose, press the more boldly on thy foes' (Virgil, The Aeneid, vi.95–6).[16]

Narses and Lucca

Narses was determined to capture Lucca, and prosecuted his siege of it with vigour. The town would have surrendered sooner, but Frankish officers had succeeded in entering it to stiffen the defence. It was during this siege that an example of the renowned magnanimity of Narses occurred.

After the specified thirty days passed, the garrison, most likely encouraged by the appearance of the invaders on the scene, refused to honour the agreement to surrender. Some of Narses' officers, indignant at this breach of faith, were for putting all of the hostages to death. Narses however, was not a barbarian, and would not commit the injustice of killing innocent men.[17] His humanity, or perhaps prudence, would not permit him to exact the forfeited lives of these hostages from the repeatedly perfidious Luccans.[18]

Instead, he hit upon the stratagem of fitting up the hostages with blocks of wood wrapped in cloth on the backs of their necks. He had them led up to within sight of the walls of Lucca and proclaimed that they would be executed on the spot if the town did not immediately surrender.[19] When the garrison still failed to yield, the guards of the hostages brought down their swords on the protected necks of the intended victims, who feigned death.

Among the spectators on the town's walls viewing this performance were the relatives and loved ones of the 'victims'. Howls and wails went up, and there was a universal cry of shame on the heartless cruelty of Narses. He answered the townspeople by sending a herald with a message to the effect that they had only themselves to blame by the shameless violations of their oaths. Yet, if they would come to their senses, all would still go well for them; their men would return to life, and nobody would suffer any harm.[20]

The Goths had no doubts but that he was deceiving them, but they swore that if he showed the hostages alive again, they would capitulate at once. Then Narses commanded all of the 'dead' to stand up together and show themselves safe and sound to their friends, who were divided between joy and incredulity. It was incredulity that finally prevailed, and Narses with well calculated magnanimity set the hostages free to return to their own people in the town. So, after a siege that had lasted in all three months, the grateful zeal of the hostages, or the will of the majority of the citizens, prevailed, and the Luccans opened their gates and received the army of Narses, who agreed not to punish them for their ill faith.[21]

Towards the end of autumn, Narses headed over to Ravenna to arrange for the disposition of his troops in fortified towns for the approaching Winter of 553–54. He would in effect be surrendering the open countryside to the ravages of the invaders, but this was a lesser evil to him than keeping his own soldiers shivering through the winter in open fields while the barbarians from across the Alps would suffer little hardship or inconvenience.[22]

Due to the vagueness of Agathias, there is some confusion as to the time of the year in 553 that these latest visitors entered Italy. If it is assumed that Narses spent the winter months of 552–53 besieging Cumae, and then marching north because of impending invasion, then the traditional spring incursion from over the Alps could be inferred.[23]

This would have given Buccelin and Leutharis a full 'season' to plunder Italy, unless they did not begin their expedition until the autumn. In any event, they were still confined to the North late in the year.[24] This in itself may hint at a lack of motivation on their part to move further south into the peninsula. Perhaps it is an indication of the scale of loot and plunder they had already indulged in.

The 'Victory' at Rimini

On his way to Ravenna, Narses stopped over in Rimini, with his train of household troops, in order to receive a military oath from a newly succeeded King of the Warni. This was a tribe from the far distant Elbe who were allies of the Empire. Their new ruler was the son of Waker, a chieftain in the Imperial army who had held a sort of 'wandering royalty'. Simultaneously with the administration of the oath, the young king received presents in the Emperor Justinian's name. Considering the past generosity of Narses, possibly all the tribesmen who followed his standard received a donative as well. In any case, the bond, which lacks a suitable name, uniting this German tribe and the Empire was renewed and strengthened.[25]

It was while still quartered at Rimini that Narses personally first came into contact with the invaders in a skirmish. A band of 2,000 of the invaders, cavalry and infantry combined, had marched into the neighbourhood and began plundering the nearby countryside. From the chamber at the top of his quarters, Narses personally saw their licentious rapine; ravaging the fields, driving off the oxen, and carrying away the spoils of hamlet and villa. He was indignant at this hateful sight, and was unable to endure it. Mounting his war-horse, he rode out at the head of his household followers, only 300 in number, to chastize the marauders.

These barbarians however, were too wise in warfare to be vanquished by a mere troop of horsemen. They therefore formed into a compact mass, with the infantry in the centre, resting on a dense wood or forest, and the cavalry covering the wings. Narses, seeing that this cleverly posted force was too strong to be attacked by his followers, gave them orders to feign panic and flight. The enemy, seeing this as an opportunity to end the war at one stroke by capturing Narses, came out of the wood in pursuit.[26]

When he saw that his pursuers were sufficiently separated and disordered, Narses gave his men the signal to wheel about and return to the attack. By his skill and valour, this large band of barbarians were routed by the eunuch and his horsemen. Their own cavalry did manage to make good their escape back into the wood, but 900 of the infantry were left dead on the field; the rest escaped, disheartened, back to the camp of their leaders.[27]

In spite of this slight success, or 'victory', Narses lacked the man-power to oppose the invading horde, and he continued on to the shelter of Ravenna. Besides the military reasons for going to this impregnable capital in the marshes, he may have had political ones as well. Antiochus had been appointed Prefect of Italy, and under his feeble rule things may have gone wrong that had to be set in order.[28]

It was while Narses was at Ravenna, or to be exact, at its port, Classis, that an important event occurred; the surrender of the fortress and fortune at Cumae by Aligern in person in early 554.[29]

Aligern had been shut up on his acropolis rock for many long months still unshaken. He had also had much time to survey the hopeless condition of his nation, and to meditate on the course of future events. The nature of the new allies who had 'answered their prayers' would soon have become apparent to even the most stubborn of the Goths. These latest barbarian invaders were incapable of organizing a government, or any other kind of administration. The only course they could pursue was to indulge in rapine, and to occupy the land as brigands, not as civilized conquerors. The Goths came to realize that the bulk of the invading army was composed of German tribes who had not been converted to any form of Christianity, and that they therefore had nothing to hope for from such 'allies'.

It must have become obvious to Aligern that the invaders were not in Italy to restore the Goths to power, least of all to allow him to succeed to the vacant throne. As custodian of the Ostrogothic royal treasure he was faced with the necessity of ultimately surrendering it to the plundering Alamanni-Franks or to the civilized power of the Empire. He came to the conclusion that he had less to gain from 'Frankish aid' than by capitulating to the Imperialists; judging it far more honourable to gain the friendship of Narses than to become a slave to the Franks.[30]

Aligern thus decided to go in person on the journey northward, from Campania to Classis, where he presented himself before Narses. With the keys of Cumae in his hand, he made his submission to Justinian's commander in Italy. Not only that, but from that time forth, Aligern became a faithful soldier of the Empire, fighting valiantly in its cause.[31]

Narses Winters At Rome

The cause of the Empire was to be best served during the winter of 553–54 not in the Ravennate region, but further south at Rome. If the number of invaders that originally streamed over the Alps came anywhere near the 75,000 generally ascribed to them, Narses just would not have had the necessary man-power to deal with such a 'deluge' of barbarians. As we have seen, the most generous estimates of his own expeditionary force that set out to conquer Italy two years previously run to only 25–30,000 men. During those two years, he had fought two major battles with the Goths in which losses must have occurred; at Mons Lactarius they could have been fairly heavy. In addition, there had been minor skirmishes and some major sieges (e.g. Cumae and Lucca), which even if the actual casualties were light, would still have tied down large bodies of men. Furthermore, he had seen fit to dismiss a number of his barbarian allies, the 5,000 or more Lombards being a case in point.

With his forces thus considerably reduced, Narses had to bow to the storm and keep them within fortified cities and towns.[32] Initially these were the ones held by the Imperialists in northern, or 'Lesser Italy', for it was here that the first year of the invasion was confined. Since their plundering was taking place so comparatively close to home, it is quite possible that the invaders were constantly receiving fresh recruits who would be only too pleased to come and help pillage these fertile districts.[33]

Perhaps it was this preoccupation with rapine that decided Narses' next move. He noticed that the invaders only ravaged the open countryside and un-walled towns as they streamed on, and shirked fortified places.[34] He abandoned the Adriatic provinces with Tuscany and Umbria to the enemy, and withdrew with his army to quarters at Rome.

There is some difference of opinion among historians as to how Narses spent this winter of 553–54. It could have been in 'humiliating inactivity', or in patiently and systematically drilling his own troops. Drawing from the original Greek of Agathias, Hodgkin waxes most elegantly in descriptions of this latter activity.

The cavalry received special attention, the horsemen being trained to spring nimbly onto their mounts, and wheel them to the left and right. The heavy-armed infantry were taught the 'pyrrhic dance'; and horsemen and foot-men alike, in unison, raised a proudly ascending war-song, the 'barritus', to the martial notes of the trumpet.[35]

The other forces of Narses were kept shut up as garrisons in fortresses, while the invaders were quartered for the winter among a defenceless population. This exposure of innocent civilians to the tender mercies of near-savages by a humane person like Narses can perhaps be explained by his desire to ultimately bring the enemy to a definite action. The worst prospect by far would have been a long, dragged-out war; any expedient would be justified if it brought about a swift development and a decided end.

With the coming of spring, and the campaigning season, he issued orders for the concentration of his forces at Rome. His field army thus collected and reunited, Narses was ready to begin his overall strategy of forcing the enemy into a decisive engagement. Although he had to wait for the fulfilment of his plans, in the end he attained them.

The Second Year Of The Invasion

At the first flush of spring in the fateful second year of their invasion, the barbarian brethren led their huge army from Cesena southwards into central Italy. They moved slowly, down into the bulk of 'Greater Italy', plundering and destroying at their ease.

Narses waited and kept watch. His strategic talents were not now to be employed against small and gallant armies like those of Totila and Teias, but to deal with this overwhelming horde of freebooters. Against the former, he had used a policy of rapid marches and imperative challenges to battle; against the latter, his strategy was to be of the 'Fabian' kind.

Perhaps he can be credited with the next move by the invaders; for on the confiñes of Samnium (near Sannio in Lazio), they divided their host into two separate armies. Not only that, but simply through folly or avarice the blundering barbaric brothers committed the ultimate strategical mistake of a division into two unequal parts.

Buccelin, leading the larger right wing, avoided Rome itself and marched down the western or Tyrannean coast of the peninsula, through Campania, Lucania and Calabria, all the way to the Straits of Messina at its toe. He probably despatched a message to King Theodebalt from Rhegium (Reggio di Calabria).[36] The smaller left wing under Leutharis went down the eastern, Adriatic, coast through Apulia, Abruzzo, Molise and Puglia, as far as Hydruntum (Otranto) on the heel.

All these provinces were systematically looted and enormous booty amassed as each brother went his own plundering way. When it came to despoiling however, there was a marked difference between the conduct of the Franks and that of the Alamanni. The Franks, as orthodox Christians, at least respected churches, but the heathen Alamanni had no scruples to restrain them from carrying off ecclesiastical plate, and destroying the sacred buildings.[37]

Pope Gregory The Great, in his Dialogues, relates the tale of Libertinus, Prior of the Abbey of Fundi (Fondi) in the province of Caserta, above Terracina and Formia. At the time that 'Buccellinus' entered Campania with an army of 'Frenchmen' [sic] it was commonly said that his Abbey had a great store of money. The intruders (more than likely, Alamanni) being very greedy for so good a booty, went into Libertinus' oratory, where the holy man lay prostrate at his prayers, to seek him out. To Gregory, it was 'a strange thing', that even though they stumbled upon him, they could not see him, and thus being deceived by their own blindness, went away as empty as they came.[38]

By the time summer was at its height, communication was re-opened

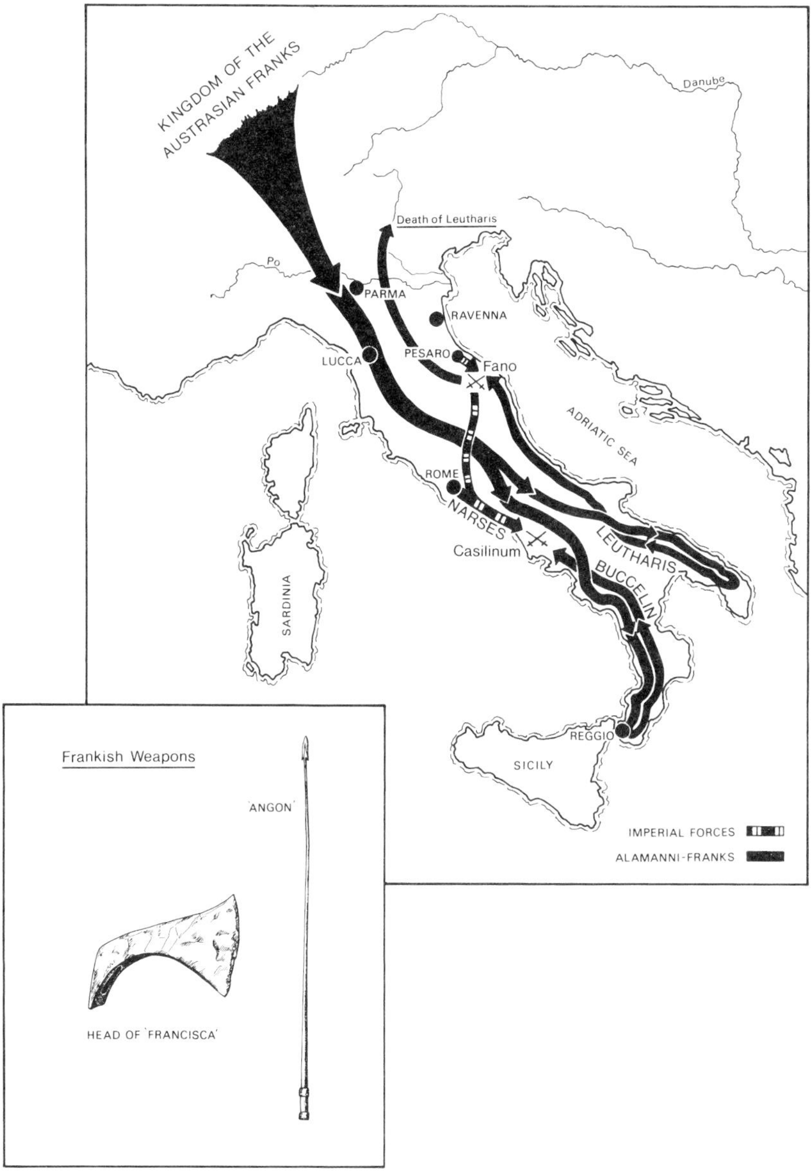

Fig. 7. The invasion of the Alamanni-Franks. The main map shows the battle-host sweeping down through Italy, before splitting into two to the east of Rome. The smaller part, under Leutharis, was eventually defeated near Fano by the imperial garrison from Pesaro. The larger part, under Buccelin, was annihilated by Narses at Casilinum. The detail shows the head of a 'francisca' and an 'angon'. The 'angon' would have had a short wooden shaft and the 'francisca' would have had a fairly long wooden handle.

between the two brothers, but the result was discord. Leutharis, it seems, had already had enough of plundering, and now only wished to return to the homeland with the souvenirs of his visit to Italy, i.e. prisoners and spoil. He exhorted Buccelin to follow his example and not risk the riches gathered so far on the doubtful event of a battle with Narses.

If Leutharis was motivated by avarice, Buccelin was activated by ambition, and consequently was the more enterprizing.[39] He was resolved to continue the campaign not only for the sake of spoil, but possibly to succeed to the kingship of the Ostrogoths. There are indications that an agreement had been struck between him and the Goths, some of whom may have joined him, that if he succeeded in ousting Narses from Italy, he would become their king. So Buccelin stayed on in Campania after the departure of Leutharis with his army, resolved to gamble all in battle with Narses, whom he had avoided up until now.

The Fate Of Leutharis

The fate of the less ambitious brother can be told briefly before relating the actions of Buccelin and Narses in Campania.

Leutharis was anxious to return home safely with his spoils without running any further risks. As his home may have been somewhere in the Black Forest, he had turned back marching northwards along the Adriatic coast as far as Fano. Here, he was ambushed by a foreguard of 3,000 men of the Imperial garrison from Pesaro, under Artabanes. The unsuspecting Alamanni leader suffered considerable losses among his followers; but, worse yet, all of his prisoners escaped, and the greater part of his booty was captured by the daring enemy.[40]

After this disaster, Leutharis left the coast, striking into the Apennines and succeeded in reaching the Po without further mishap, but very much broken in spirit. Beyond that barrier, he quartered his forces at a fortification of Theodoric's near Lake Garda between Verona and Tridentum (Trent). Here a plague broke out among his soldiers with Leutharis himself falling victim; in his death agony, Agathias has him 'rave and tear his flesh' as a fitting end to one who had plundered Christian churches. [41]

The Grapes Of Campania

Meanwhile, back down in Campania, the army of Buccelin was also suffering from disease, the climate of Italy ultimately serving justice on the invaders. Narses may have adopted a scorched earth policy against

Buccelin. By wasting the countryside and destroying its crops, he could have kept the barbarians from any means of sustenance, or at least from procuring wholesome food. There are various intemperate of the unwholesome sustenance that the intemperant barbaric warriors finally fell back on, but general agreement that it came from the plenteous supply of grapes in Campania.

It is possible that Buccelin was obliged to feed his army chiefly on ripe grapes or raisins, and that as a result his men suffered so severely from dysentery that he was forced into retreat. Then again, it is suggested that the barbarians indulged too freely in a raw wine of their own concoction, so that many of them fell victim to a fatal flux from the bowels.[42] No matter what form the grapes may have been taken in – fresh off the vine, dried as raisins or drunk as a raw wine – the army of stricken soldiers marched further up into Campania to meet Narses before it should become too greatly weakened.

This move, or 'retreat' by Buccelin may also have resulted from his desire to obtain a permanent base in the country where he could await the development of events. He found a suitable location for a strong fortified position on the banks of the river Vulturnus (Volturno) near Casilinum (the site of modern Capua).

Here, Buccelin founded a fortified camp, the river itself forming his front line of defence, with a wooden tower commanding the bridge of Casilinum. He also fortified the other side of the low, sandy banks of the Volturno with an enclosure of stakes, and wagons sunk down to their axles. His army may still have numbered around 30,000 men, even after being reduced by dysentery.

In addition, Buccelin held the expectation of reinforcements from the army of his brother, who had promised to send back his own warriors after he had safely deposited his share of the spoils. Either Leutharis had not as yet suffered his 'fate', or the news was slow in arriving from the north.

More bad news was to be in store from this direction for the barbarian chieftain who would be a king; for now Narses considered himself strong enough to engage the diminished host directly in the field. Marching down, he encamped on the northern side of the Volturno, almost in sight of the enemy. His entire army, however, could not have exceeded 18,000 men.

Nonetheless, it was Buccelin who was fortified 'as if for a siege' even though he still enjoyed a decided numerical advantage over his antagonist. Perhaps the ratio of the forces approximated that which had existed between Narses and Totila at Taginae, i.e. 5:3 (30,000:18,000).[43]

Once again, as at Taginae and Mons Lactarius, Narses showed his strategical superiority over barbarian leaders. His approach to the commencement of hostilities was to cut off the foraging parties that the enemy sent out for supplies of food. His movements not only intercepted the subsistence of the invaders, but deprived them of the advantage of the bridge at the river. Being unable to bear seeing them ravaging the nearby villages, Narses, with an indignant impulse (much as at Rimini) ordered Charanges, an Armenian, closest to the foe, to attack. His horsemen overtook the wagons of the looters, and slew their drivers. One of these wagons was filled with dry hay, and Charanges ordered it to be driven up close to the wooden tower at the bridge and set on fire. Its garrison was forced to flee to their camp, leaving the bridge in the hand of the Imperialists.[44]

As at Mons Lactarius, Narses drove and harassed his barbaric foe into beginning the battle by attacking first. Even the accidental was utilized by him to completely out-general his Alamanni antagonist; turning to account a quarrel with his chief barbarian allies, the Heruls.[45] It seems that Narses had ordered a Herulean officer put to death for killing a slave; the Heruls, deeply offended, left his camp vowing not to fight.[46] Two of them actually deserted to Buccelin, carrying the news of the mass defection, giving him further persuasion for an immediate attack. Buccelin's decision to attack was in spite of his German auxiliaries who were unwilling to fight because their augurs or soothsayers had declared that particular day to be 'unfavourable'.

Chapter XI

The Battle of Casilinum (Capua)

'One of the armies was destroyed by famine and pestilence, the other by Narses.'
Robinson Souttar[1]

Narses, in drawing up his line of battle, chose to ignore the Heruls. In his centre he placed his heavy infantry, true infantry men, not dismounted horsemen as at Taginae. These were picked troops, the 'Ante-signani', clad in long coats of mail that reached down to their feet and with stout helmets on their heads. In the rear of these spearmen were the light-armed infantry, the archers and slingers. This whole centre, however, was weak because of the absence of the 'angry Herulians' who should have been the core of its resistance.[2] These barbarian auxiliaries would have been a dismounted cavalry.

Highly trained cavalry, also completely clad in armour, and armed with bows and quivers, javelins and lances, constituted the larger portion of his army, and was placed on the wings. Narses himself commanded the right wing, formed of a strong corps of Hippo-toxotai; behind him was his major-domo, Zandalas, with all the slaves, apt in war, in his martial household.

On the left wing, there was a dense wood, and another body of Hippo-toxotai under the command of Valerian and Artabanes (evidently down from Pesaro after ambushing Leutharis). They had been directed to use the wood as a cover for a part of their force until the actual attack.[3] While the infantry in the centre had been ranged in a semi-circle, the cavalry, on both wings, would not be wheeled about or swung forward until the enemy had attacked and had penetrated into the centre of Narses' battle line.

Sindual, the leader of the Heruls, who was eager for fight and spoil, begged Narses to delay until he could bring his followers back to the battlefield. Narses refused, but did agree to reserve a space where they could fall in if they should arrive later on.[4]

The Arms of the Franks

Opposed to Narses was a barbaric host whose arms and tactics would be different from those of the Goths and other mounted tribesmen encountered so far. Although Buccelin might still have had about 30,000 effective infantry, he had no cavalry.

No matter the actual proportions of Alamanni to Franks in the army of invaders facing Narses, their arms and tactics are generally described as those of Frankish infantrymen. Agathias, who left a fairly complete description of the arms of the Franks, avows that they were 'very rude'. To begin with, their bodies were almost unprotected since they wore neither armour or greaves, their legs being protected only by bands of linen or leather. They were however, furnished with shields. Since the Franks had virtually no cavalry, their infantry at least were skilful in the use of the weapons that they wielded. The bow and the sling were not used by them, and their swords were worn on the left thigh, their main offensive weapons being throwing-axes and barbed spears, or hooked javelins.[5]

The single-bladed 'francisca' was the battle-axe of the Franks, which was a smaller cousin of the Danish weapon familiar in British history. It had a carefully weighted head and generally was for hurling and not for wielding; a typical tactic being a shower of these axes at the onset of a battle shattering shields and killing the foemen behind them.

The barbed spear known as the 'angon' was used either for thrusting, or as a hurling lance. It was of a moderate length with a long, narrow metal shaft attached to a short wooden shaft; its head had two barbs projecting backwards. As a battle tactic, this spear was cast at the enemy and became so firmly fixed in his flesh, by the two barbs, that it could not be withdrawn. If it only pierced his shield, it still could not be disengaged, for the iron shaft prevented him from removing it with his sword. At this crucial moment the angon caster would rush forward and place his foot upon the spear's shaft as it dragged along the ground, thus depriving his foe of any defence. He finished off his adversary by either cleaving his skull with an axe, or transfixing him with a second spear.[6]

These Frankish weapons can all be described as being of the 'close-range' type. This was to prove fatal in use against the array of Narses, and his tactical use of cavalry.

As for their battle formation, it was equally 'rude', being simply 'the wedge', or the ancient 'cuneus', used by the Germanic tribes as early as the time of Tacitus. This consisted of footmen formed into one deep, dense column with its head pointed directly towards the enemy. This close-ranked formation relied mainly on mass and momentum in its vehement charges against an opposing battle-line. Buccelin himself was most likely not acquainted with any other tactic, and adopted this basic arrangement for his central division, while the remainder of his host was marshalled in two wings.

Against these characteristic tactics Narses devised a shrewdly fitted trap. Gibbon even has him receiving them 'with a smile into the fatal snare'. [7] Not only the effectiveness of his own dispositions but the superiority of the armament of Narses' Imperial soldiers were to be conspicuous.

The Initial Assault

As usual, it was the barbarians who commenced battle by an impetuous charge. Narses' centre of bowmen and spearmen, on foot, serving as a defensive phalanx, was driven back and obliged to give way. He was not however, discouraged in the least during the early stages of this hurly-burly of battle. The formation in the centre must have been deeply enough massed to have been insured against disaster. Oman has the Heruls already back on the field, and with other Foederati, helping to slow up and then hold the attackers.[8]

While the enemy footmen were fighting hand-to-hand with his infantry, Narses wheeled his cavalry on both wings against their flanks. They promptly faced outwards ready to meet an expected charge, but his horsemen did not immediately charge the enemy faced to meet them. Narses knew that their formation was too solid to be broken by shock, and he held his cavalry out of range of the angons and franciscas (*c.*100 yards).

Instead, the horse-archers on both flanks were ordered to use their bows, emptying their quivers into the great weltering mass of half-naked barbarians. It became a prolonged missile assault, a rain of arrows on a mass formation that could not retaliate without disjointing itself. They harassed the flanks and rear of the unwieldy mass of confused barbarians who were a helpless target to their arrows for some hours.[9] At last, the stubborn foot-men undergoing this ordeal began to lose heart and started to break their tightly held formation. Checked in front, they sought relief by breaking their ranks, slipping off and edging away in the only direction open to them – the rear. Narses seized this opportunity by ordering a general charge.[10]

Narses Charges Home

This well-timed stroke by Narses shattered the broken column, cutting it to pieces; his cavalry rode through and through the enemy warriors.[11] Then the Heruls, in the excitement of the moment, forgetting all revengeful feelings towards Narses, charged the pointed head of the wedge.[12] This turned the already certain defeat of Buccelin's army into a savage annihilation. Fugitives were pursued, and those who had not perished on the actual field of battle did so in the waters of the Volturno, or later at the hands of the enraged natives.

By all accounts, it was an appalling massacre, Narses perpetrating at Capua what Belisarius, and Mundus, committed in Constantinople's Hippodrome. Agathias claims that only five men, out of the host that had faced Narses, escaped alive, and that his own losses for the day were only eighty. Gibbon found it incredible that only five barbarians survived and that such a victory 'could be purchased with the loss of fourscore Romans'.[13]

Evaluation of the Battle

Whether this battle is designated as Casilinum or Capua, it is generally regarded as one of the most annihilating ever fought, and one of the most terrible in history. It has been compared to those of Gaius Marius against the Teutons and Cimbri at Aquae Sextiae (Aix-En-Provence) in 102 BC, and at Campi Raudii (near Vercelli) in 101 BC.

It has been noted that Narses won this third great victory by a similar tactical plan to that which he had employed in his first against Totila.[14] In fact, similarities, as well as general principles, in their overall strategy have been seen in all three of his great battles; the Lactarian Mount as well as Taginae and Capua. The initial disposition of Narses' forces, a 'position defence', was of paramount importance in forcing those of the enemy, whether larger or smaller, into making an attack out of sheer desperation.

At Capua, the merit of Narses' formation was in its balanced combination of cavalry and infantry tactics; of missile and then shock effect. His most decisive victory was due above all to the tactical use of cavalry.[15] Once again, a barbarian leader's lack of acquaintance with strategy or any involved tactics, caused him to fall before the overall military skill of Narses.

While Hodgkin duly gave the chief credit for this splendid victory to Narses – 'that marvellous being' – he also ascribed credit to the barbarian chiefs who executed what he had planned. Singled out for distinguishing themselves were Aligern, the former Gothic enemy, and Sindual, the Herulian leader.[16] The prowess of Aligern may have helped to check the initial charge on the centre of the line in a long and fiercely contested fight.[17] Sindual, and his wayward tribesmen, could also have taken a hand in this, and then possibly mounted their horses to pursue a broken enemy.[18]

The implications of this battle were not lost on the Franks; the day of infantry was past; henceforth even they would rely more and more on cavalry. Oman saw 'Casilinum' as being already the beginning of the Middle Ages: 'With this last victory of the Roman army of the East in Italy we may close the transition period in the history of the art of war.'[19]

Narses himself most likely expected that his annihilating victory would only provoke the Frankish Kingdom into sending down yet a greater horde to avenge its warriors and regain Teutonic prestige. Fortunately for him however, Theodebalt, the sickly young king, died around this time (in 555), thus ending any further adventures beyond the Alps.

As a sort of post script to his vivid and clear description of the battle, Agathias also gave moral reflections on the victory, comparing it with Marathon, Salamis and Syracuse.[20]

The Aftermath of Capua

After the defeat and almost total destruction of Buccelin's host, the Imperial army returned to Rome flushed with victory. It would have been a direct march up from the old Capua along the Regina Viarum, or Via Appia, to the ancient Capital. Once there, the victors began to abandon themselves to the usual soldiers' delights and pleasures. They may have been a little more abandoned than usual as a large number of them were barbarians themselves. Once again, under these circumstances, the unusual qualities of Narses were to become evident.

As he realized the dangers of dissipation Narses addressed his troops in a 'manly oration' worthy of an ancient Roman censor.[21] Besides reminding them that they might soon have other perils to face (e.g. another and greater invasion by the Franks) he reproved their conduct as being unworthy of their 'Roman forefathers'.[22] This last reproof, strange to say, was sufficient to bring his motley muster of Heruls, Huns, Isaurians, Thracians, Warni, et al. back to their senses.

There was magic yet in the mighty name of Rome that an Armenian eunuch could utter it to such effect upon such representatives of the ancient Empire.[23] It was perhaps in keeping with this 'magic', and traditions of the once towering city, that Narses revived that ritual of conquest and victory – the Triumph.

Roman Triumph of Narses

There had been fewer and fewer triumphs to celebrate as once mighty all-conquering Rome ('Roma invicta') began to lose battles and wars, and was eventually conquered itself. Honorius visiting the City some 150 years previously (AD 404) had celebrated a triumph with the 'games', the first since Diocletian's a century before. These were to prove to be the last games in Roman history, with the possible exception of Totila's in the Circus Maximus in 550.[24]

Now, during the autumn of 554, Narses was to celebrate the last of the Roman Triumphs. Robert Payne, who devoted an entire book to the Roman Triumph, proposes that it was also 'perhaps the strangest', as no one in the actual procession was a Roman. Yet the dissolute military rabble of Narses, by virtue of their oath to an emperor in Constantinople, represented the power of the Empire. Payne maintains that there would be other conquerors with their triumphs, but that they were to be more in the nature of carnival processions.[25]

The city itself was still recognizably the scene for the ceremony in spite of the current state of its monuments. The triumphal arches remained, as well as the ancient temples and basilicas. Hadrian's mausoleum however, had already been fortified and only a few bronze statues remained standing in the Forum. The venerable Temple of Jupiter Capitolinus has been variously described as being despoiled of its ornaments; having its roof collapsed; and, being nothing more than a pile of ruins. Nonetheless, it was here that the 'classical' Triumph ended after going around the Palatine Hill.

In following the path of the Roman conquerors of old, Narses lacked only one thing that they had had in abundance – a great crowd of spectators.[26] From estimates of Rome's population at this time, he could only have heard the applause of a city of no more than 40,000 inhabitants.[27]

A small band of Roman nobles in purple-bordered togas greeted him at the Porta Appia; Narses then rode in a four-horse triumphal chariot over the Via Sacra.[28] Traditionally, he would have been dressed in purple and gold, in a tunica palmata and toga picta, and have had his cheeks painted red.[29]

His soldiers, carrying garlands, chanted his praises. There were great displays of the arms and treasures not only of the Franks and Alamanni, but of the Ostrogoths as well. Due to the annihilating nature of his victories, few, if any, prisoners could have marched in his procession.[30]

Proceeding to the Basilica of St Peter's, Narses was received on its steps by clergy in priestly pomp chanting hymns. Here, the pious eunuch prostrated himself in prayer at the grave of the Apostle.[31] The nature of his prayers, or the significance of his triumphal procession, have been given various interpretations. First, for the victories over the Germanic tribes that had overrun Italy; then, for the restoration of the Roman Empire under the rule of Justinian; and lastly, for the triumph of the Catholic Church over Arianism.[32]

No matter what his motives, Narses' ultimate destination through the more or less deserted streets of the ancient Capital was the old imperial palace of the Caesars. Here, he was to take ceremonial possession as the lawful representative of his highest majesty, Justinian.[33]

Ragnaris at Campsa

After his Triumph Narses had still to conduct one final siege before he could truly claim that Italy had been cleared of the Goths and barbarians. This was at Campsae (Campsa), a strong, well provisioned fortress that had been an important Roman military station, able to defy all direct assaults; so he had to resort to blockading it.[34]

A garrison of recalcitrant Goths, said to number 7,000, had taken refuge here under the leadership of Ragnaris. This was the same upstart who had behaved so treacherously down at Taranto in 552. After being defeated by Pacurius outside Taranto, he had fled to the hills up to Acherontia (Acerenza) northeast of Potenza.

Now, after the destruction of his erstwhile Frankish 'allies', he was in this Apennine stronghold, near the joint borders of Campania, Lucania and Puglia, which had been the centre of Gothic resistance in the south.[35] Campsa has been identified with Conza della Campania, in the province of Avellino, near Andretta.

Finally, at the beginning of spring 555, a parley was arranged, under the walls of the fortress, between Narses and Ragnaris. The Armenian eunuch, as a representative of courts and etiquette, acted with careful fidelity; but the bellicose, treacheous Hunnish leader behaved arrogantly.[36] As the meeting was breaking up, without any agreement being reached, Ragnaris turned and shot an arrow at the back of the departing Narses. But his aim was ill inspired, and the bodyguards of Narses mortally wounded him with a volley of their arrows.

Ragnaris died two days later, and the garrison began sincere negotiations for surrender; the only condition was that their lives be spared. This was granted by Narses, whose plighted word on all occasions was the wonder of a degenerate age. He did not permit any of the Goths to be put to death, but to guard the future peace of Italy sent this last remnant of the Ostrogothic nation to Constantinople.[37] He also did this so that their services might be utilized in the future defence of the Empire.[38]

Perhaps it was the fate of this garrison that led some historians to credit Narses with transporting Goths to Constantinople after the Battle of Mons Lactarius some two years earlier.

Nevertheless, with the capitulation of Campsa, Italy was to have a brief respite of peace, and Narses was to turn his talents in other directions.

Part III
Narses the 'Exarch'

Chapter XII

The Administration of Italy

'Narses, with an energy which belied his age, set
about reorganizing Italy.'
Robert Browning[1]

Having proven himself to be one of the greatest generals of his era, if not of all time, Narses now entered upon a new career, that of the unrestricted ruler, or administrator, of the Italy he had reconquered for the Eastern Empire.

Of the twelve years or so (554–67) that the Eunuch-Patrician held sway in the Peninsula, history has left scarcely any trustworthy details.[2] Enough is known of Justinian's administrative measures for the restored West (Africa and Italy) to give a good general idea of the extent of Narses' powers. The concept behind this 'Imperial Restoration' was to re-establish the literal counterpart of the old Roman Empire. The means was to be by reviving the ancient institutions. Steps along these lines had already been taken for Africa in April 534, and what proved to be slightly premature measures for Italy in the years 538 and 540. The Pragmatic Sanction of 554 was to complete these measures.[3]

Due to the constitution of the Vandals, the break in the old Roman rule was more complete in Africa than in Italy where, even under the Ostrogothic Kingdom, Roman civil administration had been left untouched. One major change however, which directly affected Narses and his rule over the ancient Italian praefecture, was the change of boundaries effected by the Vandal conquest. Not even Justinian himself could turn back the clock completely.

Corsica and Sardinia were already under the 'Viceroy' of Africa, who governed the former Vandal Kingdom. The old diocese of Africa was now considered to be independent of the rule of the praefectus praetorio per Italias.[4]

The Italian praefecture also lost Dalmatia, and the two Raetias; Noricum and Pannonia had been ceded to Narses' Lombard allies. Sicily was a special case, under its own Praetor; higher appeal being made to the Quaestor of the Sacred Palace back at Constantinople. Otherwise, the praefecture over which Narses ruled was still divided into thirteen provinces, although a new province, 'Alpes Cottiae', appears to have been cut out of Liguria.[5]

The main break with the old order of things was that the Empire was not to be ruled by two emperors as before, in the East and West, but by only one, who resided at Constantinople. Justinian was not going to set up an emperor, or 'Augustus' in the West again. Many of the offices which the Gothic kings had retained in the myth of their ruling Italy in the name of the Eastern Emperor disappeared or were amalgamated with the parallel central offices in Constantinople.[6] This could be seen as a blow to the old Roman senatorial aristocracy. Its members could no longer attain such high offices as comes sacrarum largitionum (minister in charge of gold mines and the mints), magister officiorum (master of the offices), rei privatae (head of imperial estates), or the quaestor (chief legal officer or magistrate) etc., except back in the East. The only 'illustrious' office available to them, in effect, would be the praefecture of the city of Rome itself, for even the praetorian prefecture of Italy was usually given to Easterners.

It is a moot point just how far the Roman Senate 'disappeared' during the course of the administration of Narses;[7] he has been referred to as a 'prototype of Napoleon'. Perhaps it lingered on as a local civic governing body. In any case, the one and only Imperial 'Roman' Senate was now in Constantinople.

If Justinian was the restored Emperor in the ancient province of Italy, Narses himself was to remain there as commander-in-chief, and a virtual 'viceroy'. He was not to have the title as such, officially only holding his military post, and being styled in official documents as praepositus sacri cubiculi et patricius (Grand Chamberlain and Patrician). This was, more or less, his old title back at the Sacred Court, which he was to retain possibly until the year 565.[8]

He was evidently not only supreme over the military but over the civil functionaries as well. At his side was a Prefect, who was the titular head of the civil service. This was initially the Antiochus, who may have given Narses occasion to check on his conduct during the early stages of the Frankish invasion. However, as Bury puts it, 'it is significant that the title of Antiochus was not that of Praetorian Prefect, but simply Prefect of Italy.'[9]

Fig. 8. The Ecclesiastical and Civil administrative divisions of Italy under Narses.

The Pragmatic Sanction

Justinian laid down the general lines for the reorganization of Imperial rule in Italy ostensibly at the request of the bishop of old Rome, Vigilius (exiled to Constantinople). This was in a collection of decrees; the Pragmatic Sanction (Pragmatica sanctio pro petitione Vigilii). These were addressed to Narses and Antiochus; they were dated 15 August, 554.

Among its 27 articles, the Pragmatic Sanction confirmed laws of Athalaric, and succeeding Gothic kings, but not those of Totila. Apparently, Justinian wished to effect with his stylus what Narses had done with his arms: cross out the very existence of the hated barbarian antagonist. Otherwise, his aim was to give back to Rome its ancient privileges.

Most important, the Pragmatic restored to the old Roman proprietors all the lands that they had held before Totila.[10] Narses' expulsion of the Gothic army, which had been quartered on the land, would have been the first step in this direction. But the Gothic warriors may have been on State lands (ager publicus) rather than on confiscated private estates.

The Pragmatic was to exclude civil cases from military jurisdiction, and put them under civil judges. These were to be chosen not only by the leading citizens in each region, but by the bishops as well.

This reorganization of Italy into a bureaucratic hierarchy of civil and military officers was a welcome change to the orthodox clergy; the more so because of the large powers it gave to their bishops in local administration. The granting of civil and administrative powers to bishops, and particularly to the chief bishop of Rome, was to have far-reaching consequences long after the time of Narses.

The immediate aim, as far as it concerned Narses, was to impose the theoretical separation of the civil and military powers. This may have been the function of Antiochus as Italy's 'Prefect'. In reality, Narses was the generalissimo who, reconquering the country with his army, had to defend and govern it with the same instrument. Opposing theories to the contrary, he wielded both powers, being in effect a military dictator.[11] His subordinate generals in the provinces, the Dukes (Duces), together with their underlings, the Tribunes, also combined military with civil functions. The prevailing conditions during most of Narses' administration seem to have called for martial law.

Another important aftermath to the administration of Narses, besides the future political power of the Church in Italy, was to be the continuity of the idea of Roman Law. Not only Italy, but the wider area of Europe, was to be integrated by its legal wisdom.[12]

Thus, Justinian's attempt to restore the status quo under the auspices of

Narses was initially fairly successful; the few changes that the Goths had introduced in the old system disappeared. The invasion of the far more barbaric Lombards after the end of Narses' reign was to bring the break-up of the Eastern Roman administration in Italy. For the next decade or so, however, Narses was to display the same vitality as the lingering Empire that he represented.

The 'Exarch'

The Pragmatic sanction had been addressed to Narses by his old official title back at the Court in Constantinople. Now, at this latest stage of his career, many historians no longer refer to him as a Grand Chamberlain, or a Treasurer, but generally use the term Exarch.

This word was never used by contemporary writers, therefore Narses was not in his own life time known as an Exarch in Italy. Both Procopius and Agathias referred to him as the general-in-chief of the Roman army. Pope Pelagius I addressed him as Patricius et Dux in Italia, and in letters sent to him, as Count. As a member of the highest class, he would have had the title of excellentissimus. Somewhat later, Pope Gregory I and Agnellus referred to him simply as Patricius (Patrician). The church chronicles that mention Narses, including the sixth century Liber Pontificalis, add Praefectus.

Hodgkin tackled this difficult subject of the origin of the Exarch's title, and traced its application to Narses back to Theophanes, 'The Confessor', in the ninth century (*c.*758–817). He had written a Chronographia of historical events from AD 284–813, but as he wrote over 200 years later, his is a none too trusty testimony. The Greek word exarchus in the time of Justinian denoted a high ranking military officer; a modern equivalent would be the rank of Field Marshal. Theophanes, therefore, may have applied the term in this sense to Narses when he called him 'Exarch of the Romans'.[13]

A further use of the original title was for any commander of a foreign expedition, e.g. Belisarius. On assuming his supreme command, Narses was already an 'exarch' in this sense. Both he and Belisarius were extraordinary military commanders acting without restriction, in the civil sector as well, subject only to any instructions given them by their Emperor.

Justinian may have deliberately deviated from Diocletian's principle of the separation between the civil and military authorities. This would concern, of course, only the supreme authority in a province, such as established in Africa and then in Italy. Thus, these high ranking military chiefs, superior to the praefectus of a province, were to develop into the office of the Exarch as understood late in the sixth century. Belisarius, and Narses, in this sense were predecessors.

In Italy, the word came to acquire almost the old value for the duties once entrusted to Theodoric and the Ostrogothic Kings governing the land in the name of, and representing, the Eastern Emperor. The Exarch, as a sort of 'vicar imperial', with the theoretical status of Theodoric was, after all, only a temporary governor, and could be removed at any time by the Emperor, as Narses was to discover to his sorrow at the end.

Unlike the Ostrogothic Kings, he did not have his own army. At best, like most generals of the time, he was surrounded by his private guards or comitatus who held a more distinguished position than soldiers of the regular army. His comitatus could be called gentlemen-at-arms. Narses, to all extents and purposes, was a real viceroy in Italy, and was to continue conducting military operations during his command there. In addition, Narses was a Patrician and still the holder of his high titles back at the Court in Constantinople. He most likely had a regular court of his own in Ravenna, with an 'officium', or governor's staff of assistants and advisers. Back in 534, Solomon the Eunuch, as the Praefect in Africa, had an official staff of 396 people.

It is a disputed point as to who was the first Byzantine Exarch. Among the candidates are Baduarius, Decius and Smaragdus; the latter usually accepted to be the first appointed with the title in 584. In that year, the Greek form of the title, instead of the Latin form Prefect, was first used. This change was made by the 'Armenian' Emperor, Maurice (582–602), and the newly coined title was to be used in Africa, as well as in Italy.

After the rule of Narses, it would no longer be a question of an Exarch of Italy, but more correctly the Exarchate of Ravenna. The Lombard invasion would leave the Empire holding only the cities and districts round Ravenna, Rome, Genoa, Perugia and Naples. The Exarchate of Ravenna was to be limited geographically to the territories within the area between the Adige and the Marecchia, and from the Adriatic over to the Apennines. The five marine cities of Rimini, Pesaro, Fano, Senigallia and Ancona, together with the territories of Numana and Osimo, joined together to form the Pentapolis – a form of maritime league.

Also, at this time, the Duces, theoretical subordinates of the Exarch (they received a stipend), having their territories separated from each other by great distances, became practically independent rulers. Thus, the Exarch at Ravenna was to rule over little more than a Duchy himself, raised over the others because he was still the supreme representative of the Empire.

Near the end of Imperial Byzantium the term Exarch was to be used not only for a Prefect, or provincial military governor, but for the bishop of a whole province, primates, or patriarchal delegates, and even the overseers of monasteries.[14]

The Duchies

The military defence system organized by Narses for Italy was ultimately to be an important factor in the future boundaries of that land. He was not being original, as such, in his military reorganization after the expulsion of the remnants of the Gothic army. The civil administration having remained 'Roman' in conception, only the military administration was left to be created anew. As military reform had already been implemented in the Eastern provinces of the Empire, the reconquered Western ones were to receive new guidelines.

Each province, Africa, Italy and Spain, formed a great command with a magister militum (commander-in-chief) at its head. Under them served duces (commanding officers) who governed the limites (military districts) along the entire length of the frontier. In Italy, there were four along the Alpine frontier where troops of a special nature were stationed, the limitanei, or 'borderers'. Much the same system had already been applied back East, in Asia Minor, but may have been modified by the background and local conditions existing in Italy.

The location of these border troops was probably influenced by the placement of garrisons under the Ostrogoths. An ominous difference from earlier times was that Noricum and Pannonia were now held by the Lombards. Some of the other barbarian troops who had entered Italy with Narses apparently were garrisoned and settled in the limites. These new military districts replaced the older 'ducatus' and certain generals who had accompanied Narses were now the commanders of these garrisons. Early on, these commanders were not ordinary duces, but high ranking generalissimos.

As for the geographical term, duchies, it came to be used in Italy, as in adjacent lands, for a district within a province.[15] After the first defeat of the Goths in 540, Justinian thought to restore the ancient Roman system that involved distinctions between the civil and military administrations. With the continuance of the war against Totila, he was induced to grant to Narses unlimited powers as commander-in-chief. Then, when Italy was divided into its various provinces, the duces, as subordinate generals, were placed in charge; an arrangement that persisted after the deaths of Justinian and Narses.

The headquarters of the Exarch, or the governor general, being in Ravenna, gave that city, with its territories, the name and status of the exarchate. It is known that Narses incorporated the city of Cremona (well to the northwest) into his exarchate.

After Narses captured Lucca, it was chosen as the seat of a duke (duce) Buono, who governed all of Tuscany. There was a duchy of Rome, as well as those of Naples, Benevento, Spoleto and Venetia, etc.

Chapter XIII

The Rebuilding Programme of Narses

'Narses was now faced by economic problems no less grave than the military problems had been.'
James E. Dunlap[1]

Among the grave economic problems faced by Narses were those resulting from years of devastating warfare; not only was he presented with problems of reorganization, but of reconstruction as well. The intrusions of the Franks into the arena of the East Romans and Goths had turned Italy into a three-cornered battlefield. The natives of that ruined land, from north to south, were faced with the immediate tasks of rebuilding its cities and towns, and renewing the cultivation of long abandoned fields.

Narses applied himself to the first of these tasks. Milan, which had been almost totally destroyed, was to rise again, as well as other cities damaged by the late hostilities. His compassion was aroused by the sight of the poverty all around him, and his well known generosity came to the relief of the needy.[2]

Naturally Narses' actual achievements would have been related to his administration of Justinian's policy towards the reconquered province. The Imperial restoration meant first of all the re-imposing of the laws of the Empire, including the collection of taxes under the system prevailing in the East. If any funds were allotted to public works, they may have existed only on paper; roads were said to have been left unrepaired; aqueducts fallen into ruins, and rivers left unbanked, allowing the lands to be flooded, etc. After a near generation of military campaigning, with its attendant destruction, agriculture was hindered by lack of implements. Additionally, there were the periodic disasters of famine and plague.

The City Of Rome

Milan had been destroyed and restored; but for Rome, the once mighty Capital not only of Italy, but of the Western World, it was to be the end as a major metropolis for a millennium. Not until the Renaissance, in the sixteenth century, was the city to ultimately revive.

There is a legend that during the Gothic War, Rome was almost completely deserted (for forty days) after Totila had abandoned it, and before Belisarius re-occupied it. Narses found it a vast and empty mass of tumbling ruins, little more than a village in a graveyard of monuments. The population was reduced to a few thousand dwelling in the lower part of the city, along the Tiber. The four sieges, along with the ruin of the aqueducts, had reduced the miserable inhabitants to drinking the river water much as before the time of the blind censor Appius Claudius over eight centuries previously. In 312 BC he had built the Aqua Appia as well as the Via Appia, both of which were named after him. The Tiber as the source of Rome's water was to continue until the time of Pope Nicholas V in the fifteenth century (1447–55). Funds may have been allotted to Narses for the repair of the aqueducts, and the upkeep of the Tiber's embankments, but they were most likely tied-up in bureaucratic red tape. The river was to have frequent, and dangerous, floods on into the twentieth century.[3]

Narses, as the 'Vice-Imperator', or at the very least, a military dictator, represented the Empire at Ravenna; but at first, he appears to have only half-resided there. Apparently, he lived in Rome and 'commuted' up to Ravenna on the official business of administration,[4] i.e. *c.*220 English miles (370km). After 560, he was to live in Rome until his death some seven to fourteen years later, with the exception of three or four years spent in exile in Naples (567–*c.*571).

He lived on the Palatine Hill, in one of the palaces of the Caesars or in the Flavian state apartments built by Domitian. These royal residences had been repaired during the Ostrogothic Kingdom by Theodoric and Athalaric, and were in use until the Byzantine period. The actual residence of Narses himself was to be the centre for the new Imperial administrative machinery in the west. It was to be the official residence of the later Byzantine Exarchs up at Ravenna when they visited Rome.[5]

Theoretically, the monuments of old Rome were the Imperial property of Justinian's 'New Rome', but apparently his policy was not to restore them, and the ancient Capital, to their former splendour. Although the Pragmatic Sanction had supposedly guaranteed the maintainance of public buildings by the state, Narses is not credited with the restoration of any of the classical buildings. Their ultimate fate, along with that of the other abandoned monuments, was to be used as quarries for the construction of the defences of medieval Rome.

One type of building activity, however, with which Narses was closely associated, was the construction of churches; he is said to have also been very zealous in their restoration. No doubt this was due to his piety, and

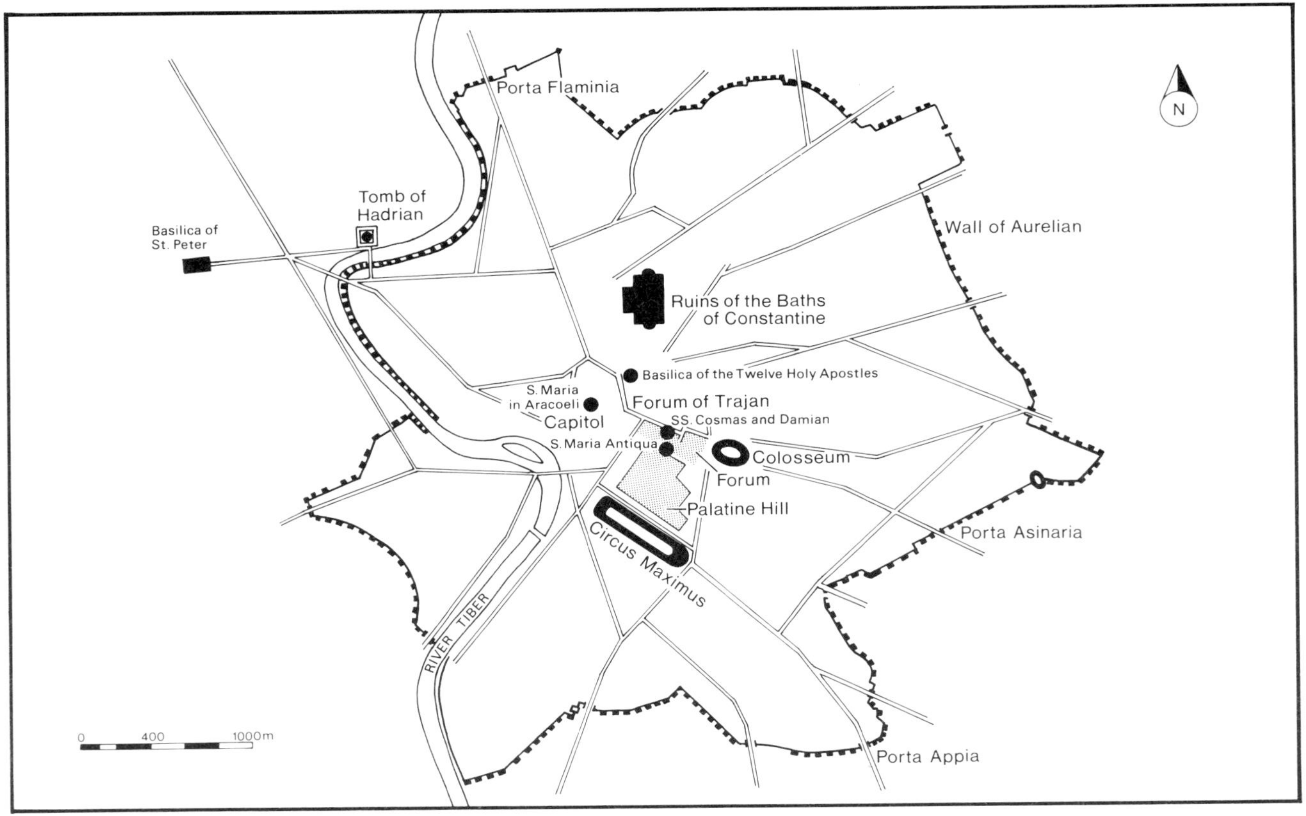

Fig. 9. Rome at the end of the Gothic Wars. Narses lived in a palace in the Palatine.

being an orthodox, fervent Catholic. Perhaps this should suffice to explain the charge that he neglected the old pagan temples, and all the other 'classical' buildings and monuments.

Even though a great general, he attributed his victories more to prayers to the Deity, and to following signs from the Virgin, than to mere military means. Therefore, he would doubtless have aided in the construction of a new basilica that was to be a monument to the liberation of Rome from the heretical Arian Ostrogoths.

Such an edifice was erected on the site of a church first built by Pope Julius I (337–52). It was dedicated to the apostles Philip and John, and is now known as the Basilica Santi Dodici Apostoli (Basilica of the Twelve Holy Apostles). The construction was begun by Pope Pelagius I (556–61) with the assistance of and under the auspices of Narses. However, Pelagius was to die before its completion.

The succeeding Pope, John III (561–74), claims to have contributed the larger share of the building which he finished and dedicated. John was certainly not averse to setting up metrical inscriptions to this effect: the apsidal one began:

> 'Here the priest before me has left his slight traces;
> Pope John has completed the work which he began.
> Standing the more erect in a season of cramping distress,
> The bishop scorns to be depressed by a failing world.'[6]

In all probability Narses continued his aid towards the completion of this church and this might, in part, explain why Pope John was later to befriend him at the time of his recall and exile.

There is however, some question as to the source of the materials used in the construction of the basilica. It has been considered probable that building components and decorative motifs, such as columns, marbles and mosaics, from the Baths of Constantine may have been used.[7] By the time of Pope Pelagius, the baths had either been destroyed by the Goths, or fallen into decay, ceasing to be of any service, due to the ruin of the aqueducts. Under such conditions, Narses need not have hesitated in adopting them for use as building materials.

Besides this, there is a fable, of a later date, that Narses gave permission for the removal and reuse of columns and marbles from the Forum of Trajan, the last of the Imperial Roman Forums. The basilica stands in the Piazza Santi Apostoli 51, close to the site of Trajan's Forum. This would have made the Forum a convenient quarry, especially as the basilica is 'downhill' from it. Eight antique spirally fluted columns of the original church are said to remain. Otherwise, no remains of the sixth century work can now be seen as the basilica was re-built in the fifteenth century and again in the eighteenth century.

Another place of Christian worship dating from the time of Narses is the Church of Santa Maria Antiqua in the Roman Forum. This was originally an Imperial building that was converted into a church.[8] Near a side oratory outside this church a Christian tomb inscription was discovered in its original position with the date 572. This is within a year or two of the death of Narses himself and shows that during his own period there was already Christian burial within the old pagan Forum.

There are two other sixth-century Roman churches that may have had some connections with Narses' period of administration. S.S.Cosma e Damiano is by the Roman Forum and was built in the ancient library of the Forum of the Peace or Vespasian. It is noted for the sixth-century mosaic in its apse. On the Capitol is the Church of Santa Maria in Aracoeli which was built upon the ruins of the temple of Juno Moneta. A Greek monastery was attached to it in the sixth century.

The Walls of Rome

Totila had gone so far as to start dismantling the fortification and walls of Rome, in addition to removing all its gates, when he swore to destroy the city in 546–47. Belisarius, on re-occupying the deserted metropolis, made hasty repairs in time to withstand another long siege by the Goths. The repairs that he made to Rome's Wall in April 547 consisted of brick, to save its outside facing, and rough, solid masonry. Blocks of tufo and peperino were the preferred materials as they were easy to handle and fit into place. Not long afterwards, to make this hasty work more permanent, the blocks were united with mortar and rough fragments of tiles.

Ian A. Richmond, who gave an account of *The City Wall Of Imperial Rome*, tracing 'Its Architectural Development From Aurelian To Narses', assigned this later work to either Bessas or Narses.[9] The wall of Aurelian (271–5) was originally about twelve miles long in extent. Bessas, when defending its walls against Totila in 546, was held to be negligent in the routine measures on which the safety of any besieged city depended. He had fled from Rome when Totila entered it on the night of 17 December.

As for its later fall to the Goths, and Narses' brief siege and final recapture of Rome, Richmond informs that there was no mention of any repairs in connection with either event. He does comment however, that since Narses rebuilt Rome's bridges, he probably also repaired its City Wall.[10]

Rome's future was to be no longer an 'Imperial Capital', but only the small metropolis of a Byzantine duchy. Richmond concluded that repairs on its

Wall dropped to their lowest level after the time of Narses, 'and become quite undistinguishable from one another for the historian's purpose.'[11]

The Bridge of Narses

Besides pulling down its walls and gates, Totila also destroyed bridges leading into Rome. One such was about two miles north of the city, where it crosses over the Aniene (Anio) on the Via Salaria. This consular road went from Rome, via Rieti, to the southern Adriatic coast; whereas the Via Flaminia went, via Terni, through Umbria to the northern Adriatic coast.

On this Pons Salarius, in one of the rare memorials of his time, was recorded the fact that Narses had rebuilt the bridge in the year 565. Besides two commemorative inscriptions, he had added a parapet with pilasters decorated with Greek crosses.

The first inscription informed that in the 39th year of the reign of the most pious and ever-triumphant Emperor Justinian the restoration was done. Assuming his official ascension to the throne was in 527, this work would have been done around 565. Otherwise, if the year 518 was the base date, then Narses would have done his rebuilding in 556 or 557.

Regardless of the actual year, the inscription described Narses as the late Praepositus of the Sacred Palace, ex-counsul and patrician. It testified that after victory over the Goths, overcoming their kings in open battle with marvellous speed, he liberated the city of Rome and all of Italy. This bridge on the Salarian Way, which had been destroyed by the tyrant Totila, down to the water level, he restored, cleaning the river's bed and building the bridge better than it was before.[12]

The second inscription was the inspiration of some poet of the period who recited:

> 'Lo! where the stream erst sundered the highway straight as an arrow
> Over the arched bridge leads the unbroken path;
> High o'er the angry stream we pass and the sound of the waters
> Murmuring under our feet fills the delighted ear
> Go then, Romans, in joy unhindered; ever resounding
> Let your applause ring forth, echoing Narses' name.
> Narses the stubborn hearts of the Goths did conquer, and Narses
> Set the unbridled streams under a yolk of stone.'[13]

These 'eulogistic distichs', were given by the German historian Ferdinard Gregorovius (1821–91) who commented on their 'pompous ostentation'. This was considering the work's insignificance, a small bridge over little more than a stream, as characteristic of the age. Gregorovius concluded 'even these solitary monuments to the memory of Narses have perished'.[14] He was referring to the fact that the bridge had been damaged and the inscriptions to Narses had been thrown into the river by Neapolitan troops retreating before the French, in 1798. On 25 October 1867, it was to be damaged again by Papal soldiers who blew it up during the panic caused by the capture of Monterotondo by Garibaldi.

After such vicissitudes only scant traces of its ancient construction remained in the smaller arches, up into the early decades of the twentieth century. Fortunately, engravings of the ancient bridge of Narses were made before the damage of 1798. Giovanni Battista Piranesi (1720–78), who specialized in such things, made one, entitled 'Veduta del Ponte Salario' from Two Views of Rome (1754). One of his teachers, Giuseppe Vasi, had also made an etching of the 'Torre e parte del Ponte sasso da Narsete', taken from a comparable angle.

There was even a literary memoir on his bridge published a scant year before the damage of 1798. Andrew Lumisden Esq. 'Member of The Royal And Antiquary Society Of Edinburgh', had printed in 1797 a book on the Antiquities of Rome, in which he remarked on this very bridge and its environs. He came upon the Ponte Salara [sic] about two and a half miles from the Porta Salara. He informs:

> 'By the inscription I find that it had been destroyed by Totila, and afterwards repaired by Narses, in the time of Justinian.'[15]

At the present time, no traces of the Bridge of Narses remain. A twentieth-century highway bridge brings one-way traffic into Rome from the North. Just to the East is a newer bridge carrying traffic out of the City.

Lumisden, in his 1797 opus, also referred to a Pons Nomentanus, (Ponte Nomentano); its name, by his day, had been corrupted to Ponte Lamentana. This bridge is also on the Aniene, as it meanders from the East to join the Tiber. Lumisden maintained that Belisarius fortified it against the Goths, and that later it was repaired by Narses.[16] Remaining intact since the time of Pope Nicholas V, and as one of Rome's most picturesque bridges, it was a favourite subject in the seventeenth and eighteenth centuries for painters and engravers. It retained its appearance well into the twentieth century.

There are other bridges over the river Aniene that may have had connections with Narses; one is the Ponte Mammolo, on the Via Tiburtina, of uncertain origins, but with a name that is not 'classical'. Gilbert Bagnani, writing in the second decade of this century, assumed: 'Like other bridges over the Anio it was probably cut by Totila and restored by Narses.'[17] It was to be destroyed again by the French in 1849.

On the Via Tiburtina (leading to Tivoli) was another bridge known since the twelfth century as the Ponte Lucan. Piranesi also made an engraving of the 'Ponte Lugano' (1763). It was reported by Bagnani that since the Aniene's bed had risen considerably over the years, only the tops of its arches were visible. Of the five original arches, one was completely buried in the river's bed.[18] Regarding the rest, Bagnani declared: 'One of the arches shows signs of having been cut by Totila and restored by Narses.'[19]

Narses And 'Venice'

While the actual city of Venice had not then been built, Narses became a benefactor to the peoples of the isles, lagoons and lidi that eventually emerged as the 'Queen of the Adriatic'. By his munificence, he was in effect rewarding these natives for the invaluable services they had rendered during his great march around the head of their future Sea.

At about this time, these 'Venetians' chose a tutelary saint, St Theodore. His identity is unknown, there being a military martyr, warrior saint, Abbot, Bishop and a monk of this name. There is a statue in his honour, standing over a crocodile, on top of a marble pillar outside the Doge's Palace.[20]

No matter his identity, Narses is said to have made a vow to build a church in his name. After the victory over Totila and the Goths in 552, he had it erected on the island of Rivus Altus (Rivo Alto). Supposedly, masters from Constantinople built the Church of St Theodore with spoils taken from the enemy. It was erected on a plot of ground known as the Bruollo, Brolio, or Broglio (i.e. garden), the site of the future Basilica of St Mark's; its location being below the chapel of St Isidore. As recently as 1956, some of its stones were found in the wall of the northern transept of St Mark's.[21] The first Doge of Venice, Pao Luccio Anafesto, was to be nominated at St Theodore around the year 697.

A second church was also built by Narses on a site opposite the first one during this time (in the middle of St Mark's Square). This was the Church of St Geminiano in honour of the martyrs Germinianus and St Menna; the first was a bishop of Modena, the latter a Phrygian martyr. This might have been the church that was altered by the Venetians – to improve the Piazza – who were placed under Papal interdict for their pains (1173). This particular structure was to be finally demolished by Napoleon.[22]

In the year 554, Narses also restored a church in Vicenza, northwest of Padova, with the spoils of the Goths. The Church of S.S.Felice and Fortunato was named for two natives of Vicenza beheaded at Aquileia during the reign of Diocletian in 296. Their bodies had been buried secretly at night, but the Vicintini reached an agreement with the citizens of Aquileia, receiving the head of S. Felice and the body of S. Fortunato. To the original church, built soon after 300, Narses added a sacristy, baptistery, or a chapel. Its plan was characteristic of his epoch, as were its mosaic decorations, known to have originally existed from old descriptions. Its apse, being polygonal on the outside, and semi-circular internally, is reminiscent of the churches at Ravenna.[23]

Ravenna

In the year 402 Ravenna had been selected as the capital in Italy, replacing Milan, after the final separation of the Roman Empire, by the first Emperor in the West, Honorius (395–423). This was done on the advice of his early guardian, the General Stilicho, for reasons of security and strategy. The young Emperor had been born there in the year 384.

Ravenna continued as a royal residence even after the fall of the Western Empire; first under Odoacer the Scirian (476), and then Theodoric the Ostrogoth (493) who held his Aula, or Court, in a royal palace with Romans as his officials. The other Gothic kings up to Vitigis also made it their Capital until Belisarius recovered the city for the Eastern Empire in May 540.

In 554, it became the official seat of the praefecture of Italy. It had been beautified all along, first by the Goths, and then under the joint reign of Justinian and Theodora. The famous San Vitale had been conceived by the Bishop Ecclesius in 525; construction started under Amalasuntha's regency, and was finished by 547. It was consecrated by Ravenna's first Archbishop, Maximian (of Pola), either on 19 April 547, or the following year, the year of Theodora's death. Maximian was also to consecrate San Appollinare In Classe on 9 May 549.

In the apse of St Vitale are the well-known mosaic portraits of Justinian and Theodora in the 'classical' Hellenistic-Roman tradition, and in the 'Byzantine' style. As suggested earlier, it is possible that one of the courtiers portrayed with Justinian might be Narses himself. On the façade of Theodoric's palatine Church of the Saviour, a mosaic representation of Justinian's bust had been put up during the later years of his reign (554–65). This church had been 'reconciled' to the Catholic faith, and dedicated to St Martin, Archbishop of Tours (316–87).

By an edict of Justinian, after 554 all Arian property was transferred to the Catholic Church. Other decorations had been completed (and possibly some Arian Gothic ones removed) when this church was consecrated by the Archbishop Agnellus between 556 and 565. Thus, it may owe some of its later ornamentation (mosaics) to the time of Narses.

The remains of Apollanaris, a Syrian, the first Bishop of Ravenna, and its tutelary saint (along with St Vitale), were not received until the middle of the ninth century. It was then rededicated to his name as the Basilica of St Appollinare Nuovo. Justinian's bust had been transferred to an interior chapel, but at the present time can be viewed just inside the entrance of the West door. The figure it portrays is grey-haired, and stouter than the one in San Vitale, which is obviously much younger in conception (Justinian was already sixty five years old in 547).

Narses is credited with taking an interest in the Ravennate churches, much as he did elsewhere. Of the works by the 'School of Ravenna', some of its later sixth-century churches were built or completed under his auspices.

It is known that the Church of San Vittore at Ravenna was in existence by the year 564.[24] The present day Basilica is on the original site.

The construction of the Church of San Pieto In Silvis, or the Parish Church of Bagna Cavallo (over by Lugo), shows evidence of being built around the same time as San Vittore at Ravenna. Another church, Santa Maria Di Pomposa, is ascribed to the years following the consecration of San Appollinare In Classe Basilica, and before the building of San Vittore.[25]

Other sixth-century churches were S. Agata Maggiore and S. Michele In Africisco of which a tower remains, just off the Piazza Costa, or Market Square.[26] There is also the Church of the Santo Spirito, facing the Arian Baptistry.

This late fifth-century Ostrogothic Baptistry was reconsecrated to the Catholic faith in 561 by the Archbishop Agnellus (557–66/69), with the authority of Narses, and transformed into the Oratory of Santa Maria in Cosmedin.

The Imperial benevolence that granted privileges to the churches of Ravenna, as the Capital, lessened the authority of the Popes at Rome at this time.

Campania

There are few references to any rebuilding programmes Narses may have undertaken in the South of Italy. Although he is mentioned by Church historians as retiring to Naples in about 567 for a period of perhaps three to four years, that city makes no claim to him.[27] During his active administration, he may have improved its ancient Greek harbour, to start it on the way to becoming a great commercial port. As he did at Rome, he further strengthened the walls, a large part of which had been razed to the ground by Totila back in 543.[28]

In a region where he fought two of his great battles, there are no local legends, or traditions, regarding Narses.

Further south in Campania, some 45 km beyond Salerno, on the Cilento coast below Paestrum, is the sea-side resort of Agropoli. Its name is Greek, but it has no connections with the ancient Magna Graecia. It was probably a foundation of the 'Greeks' of Justinian's time; Narses is said to have founded strongholds such as this.[29]

Chapter XIV

Narses and the Papacy

'Good order in the Church is the prop of the Empire.'
Justinian I[1]

Among the fews details known of Narses' actual administration are those of his relations with the Western Church in Rome, and in the North of Italy. Just what his final ecclesiastical policy may have been, remains, however, an open question.

Pope Vigilius (537–55)

By the year 555, the Roman clergy, through the offices of Narses, requested the Emperor in Constantinople to return their Bishop to them. Pope Vigilius had succeeded Pope Silverius (536–37) who had been arrested by Belisarius, deposed and exiled from Rome for 'treason' on 11 March 537, probably under orders from Theodora. He was either starved to death or murdered on the island of Palmaria (Palmarola) near Terracina. Theodora's protégé, the deacon Vigilius, was elected to his office on 29 March 537.

He, in turn, fell from favour when he refused to support Justinian in a dispute concerning ecclesiastical doctrine.

In 451 the Council of Chalcedon had decided against two rival doctrines in a critical debate about the true nature of Christ, thus establishing the basic doctrine that is still enshrined in the concept of the Trinity. The two defeated 'heresies' were the Monophysites and the Nestorians. The former believed that there was only one nature in Christ, thus reducing his human aspect to little more than a shell, while the latter stressed the humanity of Christ and concentrated on the historical life of Jesus. However, despite finding against both doctrines, the Council of Chalcedon accepted the writings of three Nestorians (Theodore of Mopsuestia, Theodoret of Cyrrus and Ibas of Edessa) as part of the Church's canon.

While it was agreed by the five Patriarchs of the Church, the decisions of

Chalcedon were not accepted by all the proponents of 'heretical' doctrines and strong, schismatic movements continued to develop.

At the start of his reign, Justinian strongly supported the orthodox point of view. However, in 543, perhaps as a gesture of conciliation towards the Monophysites, Justinian issued a condemnation of the three Nestorians in a document aimed against what have become known as The Three Chapters.[2] The Empress Theodora was, of course, an ardent supporter of the Monophysites, and this condemnation has been seen as her 'last triumph' before her death. Justinian was simply using his position as Emperor to impose his wishes on the church but, probably to his surprise, there was an outcry.

The four 'Eastern' Patriarchs only signed under duress, and Pope Vigilius refused. He was, therefore, arrested, and forcibly taken to Constantinople where, in 548, he was finally prevailed upon to issue a Judicatum supporting the Emperor. This caused uproar in the 'Western' church and the Pope was excommunicated by the North African Bishops. In Italy the protests were led by Macedonius, the Bishop of Aquileia and Vitalius, Bishop of Milan and, in August 551, Vigilius took refuge in the Church of St Peter in Hormisda. Soldiers entered, seized him by the beard and feet and in the ensuing struggle the altar fell over, crushing the Pope beneath it. Assembled on-lookers cried out in horror and the soldiers, or possibly demes-men, beat a retreat. Eventually, a delegation led by Belisarius himself escorted Vigilius back to Constantinople as a virtual prisoner.

He escaped from the Placidian Palace (the residence of the Roman nuncios) on the night of 23 December 551 and sought refuge in the Church of St Euphemia at Chalcedon.

Eventually, Justinian agreed to summon a Council to decide the matter and in 553 the Fifth General Council of the Church was held in St Sophia in Constantinople. Vigilius returned to the city, but the persecuted Pontiff, fearing violence, refused to preside over or even take part in its debates. Bury, in a preface, alleged that these Ecumenical Councils were like modern political conventions where the arts of lobbying were practised; bribery and intimidation even being employed to reinforce theological arguments.[3] No matter its actual methods, Justinian would not let Vigilius return to Rome until he accepted the decrees of this Council. The exiled Pope was given six months consideration.

The original source on the Life of Pope Vigilius I (Vita Vigilii), the *Liber Pontificalis*, gave a somewhat legendary version of his restoration to Rome. It avowed that the assembled clergy there asked Narses for his consent to request of Justinian that if the Pope, or any other exiled clergy were yet living, they be returned. When the Emperor received Narses' request, with that of the entire Roman clergy, he and his Senate rejoiced because 'God had given rest to the Romans'.[4]

Justinian supposedly yielded to these entreaties and allowed Vigilius and his fellow exiles, cardinals and clergy who had accompanied him, to return to Rome. The Pope in 'yielding' himself to the Emperor's wishes to leave Constantinople may have been influenced by the fact that Narses had recently subjugated the barbarians in Italy, and that his own proper place was to be back in Rome.

While it is likely that Narses assisted the Roman Church in its appeal on behalf of its Bishop and attendant clergy, it is also likely that Justinian's clemency resulted from other considerations. Their release probably hinged on their ultimate condemnation of the Three Chapters. Ironically, Pope Vigilius was destined never to see Rome again; he died when his ship reached Syracuse in Sicily, on 7 June 555.

Pope Pelagius I (556–61)

During the spring after Narses had gained possession of Campsa, Pelagius, a Roman, succeeded Vigilius as Pope (16 April 556). He had presumably been selected under pressure from Justinian's officials. Evidently he had served the cause of royal ecclesiastical policy well in the past. During the religious disorders at Alexandria in 536–37, Pelagius had been sent with Liberius, as a nuncio, to pronounce on the conduct of Paul, the Patriarch set up in opposition to Theodora's own monophysite candidate.

Now, as an Archdeacon, he had been Justinian's choice as the successor to the see of St Peter; especially as Pelagius was willing to publicly denounce the Three Chapters. But hostility and opposition arose among the Italian clergy as they believed that he was the cause of the suffering endured by Vigilius, and had even been involved in his death. The three chief centres of opposition were Rome, together with Aquileia and Milan in the North.

Pelagius, when he arrived in Rome, was received as a renegade, everyone keeping aloof from him; all classes of the Church, and the devout of Christian society, were united in rejecting him. Multitudes kept from communion with him, holding that he had had a part in the death of his predecessor, and therefore should be inflicted with such punishment. The new Pope even had difficulty in finding clergy to consecrate him. During this period it was Narses' protection that was the chief factor in placing Pelagius upon the apostolic throne.[5] It is generally agreed that the head of the civic administration in Italy, and the head of the Church, must have taken counsel together to devise a course of action to meet the situation.

The result was a rather striking religious ceremony participated in by the two, on 16 April 556, when Pelagius was finally consecrated by two Bishops, John of Perusium (Perugia) and Bonus of Ferrentum (Ferentino) assisted by a presbyter of Ostia named Andrea.[6]

First, a solemn litany was held at the Church of St Pancratius on the Janiculan Hill. Then, together with any other priests who were willing to accompany them, they marched in stately procession, chanting hymns, to the old original basilica of St Peter on the Vatican. Up its long nave, lined with columns taken from pagan temples, they proceeded to the apse. Pelagius mounted the ambo, or pulpit, with the gospels and held a cross above his head. He addressed the assembled congregation concerning the prejudice against him in the matter of the death of his predecessor, and defended himself against charges of heresy and betrayal of the Faith. He said that no one from a door-keeper to a bishop should accept advancement for worldly gain. He maintained that he had studied the works of God, led a good life, and not by bribes, but by honest means had risen to his present high office. It was pointed out that Vigilius had left him still in confinement back in the East, and that he too had been a fellow sufferer in the Three Chapters controversy.[7] His earnest words and manner apparently satisfied all those present.

The presence of Narses himself, acting as a sort of compurgator (oath-helper) of the accused pontiff, must have made his adjuration all the more impressive.[8]

The Letters of Pelagius to Narses

Not only was Pope Pelagius I a convincing speaker, he was also an inveterate letter-writer. During his Pontificat, which lasted almost five years (556–61), several interesting details of this period turn up in the ones that he addressed to 'Count Narses'.

The nature of their contents was given by Lewis Ellies Du Pin in the fifth volume of his History of Ecclesiastical Writers (London 1699). They deal chiefly with the schism in the Church in Italy, and the Pope's requests for assistance against the Bishops in the North. Following a letter to Pope Vigilius, Du Pin informs:

> 'The second is addressed to Count Narses [sic]. He prays him to assist Peter the Priest, and the Deacon Projectus, whom he had sent to Prosecute two Bishops of Italy, who disturb'd the Order of the Churches, and would appropiate to themselves all the Ecclesiastical Revenues.'[9]

Reference was then made to the administrative powers of Narses, and the use to which he should employ them.

> 'In the third he exhorts the same Count to employ the Authority which his Office gave him, for correcting and punishing the Bishops of Istria, Liguria and the Country of Venice [sic] who had separated from the other Churches for the Affair of the Three Chapters. . ..'[10]

The next letter contains the interesting fact that Narses, renowned for his orthodoxy and piety, was once excommunicated!

> 'In the fourth Letter he inveighs vehemently against the same Bishops for their boldness in excommunicating Narses. He exhorts him to employ his Authority for punishing Euphrasius, who was guilty of Murder, and an Incesturous Adultery. He counsels him to drive the Obstinate out of the Province, and to send the Authors of this Schism to the Emperor, and chiefly him who was in the See of Aquileia, who being, says he, a Schismatick, ought to have neither the Name nor Dignity of a Bishop.'[11]

After he was excommunicated by these 'Schismaticks' of Italy, Narses was actually congratulated by the Pope; Providence permitting it as a way of preserving him from their schism.[12] In yet another letter, Pelagius once again requested of Narses:

> 'to send the Bishops of Aquileia and Milan to the Emperor with a strong Guard because the first was incapable of being Bishop by his irregular Ordination, and the second ought to be punish'd for Ordaining after such a manner.'[13]

The promoters of all this disquiet were Paulinus of Aquileia, the head of the Eastern Bishops of Upper Italy (the seat of a patriarchate), and the Archbishop of Milan, the corresponding head of the Western ones. Roman clergymen were sent to bring these Northern Bishops back to communion with Rome, and Narses was requested to support them with the power of the secular arm. Pelagius also prevailed upon the King of the Franks, Childebert (one of the four sons of Clovis), to help end the schism by force. Evidently his endeavours to have Childebert (who died in 558) or Narses intervene in these affairs of the Church were in vain. There is no real evidence that Narses complied with his requests.

While Narses may have been anxious to please the Pope, he is generally credited with declining to do anything; or, if he did obey the recommendations of Pelagius, he did so only feebly. He may have been even more anxious not to offend his new subjects in Italy by enforcing orthodoxy on them by harsh measures. At this time, even Justinian's Imperial policy throughout his newly regained Roman Empire was one of unusual moderation. This could possibly be attributed to Narses' advice in the much needed interests of concord and peace.

In any event, Pelagius' efforts to use the authority of Narses to bring schismatic bishops into submission achieved no results and at his death they were stronger than ever. Some thirty years later, Pope Gregory I, the Great, had to deal with them, and, in fact, this schism in the Church in Italy lasted for more than a century.

Pope Pelagius I died on 2 March 561, and two days later was buried in the portico of St Peter's. The inscription on his tomb reads:

> 'Terrenum corpus claudant haec forte supulchra,
> Hic requiescit Pelagius Papa Qui sedit annos IV.
> Meses X Dies XVIII. Depositus IV Nonas Martii'

> 'May this sepulchre forever enclose his earthly remains;
> Here lies Pope Pelagius, who reigned 4 years 10 months
> and 18 days. Laid to rest on the 4th of the Nones of March.'[14]

During the life time of Pelagius, Narses can be credited with an ecclesiastical policy of not interferring in quarrels within the Church. With the successor, Pope John III (561–74) however, there may have been a change of policy. He must have been pursuing the Eastern theory of the Church being subordinate to the Empire, when he arrested several 'turbulent' bishops, and sent them to Constantinople for punishment.

Paul the Deacon, using a Roman annalistic source, mentioned Narses as also taking action against Vitalis, the Bishop of Altinum (Altino). Years before, Vitalis had fled to the Kingdom of the Franks, to Aguntum (Innichen) at the headwaters of the Drave, in The Tyrol. The Lombard historian expressed it this way:

> 'Narses the patrician whose care was watching everything. . . had him seized at length, and condemned Vitalis to exile in Sicily.'[15]

Marius of Aventicum, a historian of the old Kingdom of Burgundy, also referred to this event.

There are few, if any, references connecting Narses with Pope John III (who was consecrated on 17 July 561), until near the very end of both their lives and careers. In the year 571, this Pope befriended the aged ex-governor of Italy by journeying to Naples to bring him back to Rome. There was, in all probability, some connection with this event and John's own retirement to a secluded churchyard on the Via Appia.

Pope Gregory I, The Great

There remains one final, although indirect, connection of Narses with the Papacy during this period of history. This would be the time that one of the Church's great innovators spent his formative years in Rome. He was to be the future Pope Gregory I (590–604), also to be known as Saint Gregory the Great.

The generally accepted facts of his origins are that he was born in Rome around the year 540 when Vigilius was Pope and still in the City. Rome was once more in the possession of the Empire since Belisarius' entry in December 536. Gregory was to live through the period when the City was besieged by the Goths, betrayed to them, deserted, reoccupied, besieged again, betrayed yet again, and finally captured by Narses.

He belonged to the ancient nobility of Rome and was a descendant of two Popes, Felix III (483–92) and Agapetus I (535–36); both, incidently, were also saints. His father, the Senator Gordianus (Gordian), possessed vast estates, and had a palace on the Caelian Hill.[16]

None of this however, could have spared the young Gregory from the horrors of his day and age. During Totila's initial plan to destroy Rome by depopulating it, 300 youths of noble families were sent as hostages beyond the Po; there, they were put to death by Teias. Gregory may have been spared by his extreme youth, being only about seven years old. He is said to have had an exceptionally receptive mind and memory, and the sadness that pervaded his later writings has been attributed to the effect produced on him by such events in his early life. So much so that he clearly expected the world to come to its end during his own lifetime.[17]

Gregory could only have been around twelve years of age when Narses re-established the Imperial power in Rome with the final conquest in 552. He was to live out his youth in the family palace on the Caelian Hill during the time that Rome supposedly sank into the 'dark ages' of intellectual culture under the rule of Narses. The education and future career of Gregory should give the lie to such theorizing. Of course, he came from a noble, wealthy, and cultivated background, but the facilities for learning were yet intact, within reach of the Gordian Palace.

The Pragmatic Sanction, besides reviving the ancient custom of issuing free corn to Rome's citizens, also restored to lawyers, physicians and professors their salaries.[18] As a youth, Gregory attended the re-opened schools of grammar, rhetoric and dialectics; securing an education in all the learning that his age had to offer (but, by his own admission, he never learnt Greek). He undoubtedly received special training in law and for a civil career; therefore he could be called arte philosophus.

By the year 573, when Gregory was only in his early thirties, he attained the highest civil office still available to a citizen of Rome, that of Praefectus Urbi or Prefect of the City. Two years earlier (in 571) Narses may have returned to Rome with Pope John III to his own palace on the Palatine Hill where he is said to have died. The most liberal estimates of his age have him living to be ninety-five, which could have been in the year 573.

A year or two later, in 574 or 575, Gregory would resign his office and from secular life altogether. He also resigned his father's inheritance by founding six monasteries in Sicily and by turning the paternal home in Rome, the Clivus Scauri, into a monastery which he himself entered as a humble monk. (His mother, Sylvia, had become a nun after the death of Gordian.)

About three years later, he was ordained as a regionarius, or one of the seven deacons of the ecclesiastical regions of Rome by Pope Benedict I (575–79). Then, in the spring of 579, he was created the apocrysarius, or envoy, of Pope Pelagius II (579–90) to the Imperial Court at Constantinople. In all probability he was sent to seek aid against the Lombards who had invaded Italy eleven years earlier (568).

He was to remain at the Courts of the Emperors Tiberius II (578–82) and Maurice for the next six years. Evidently, in spite of his lack of Greek, he gained invaluable knowledge of the routine of administration on a grand scale at these Imperial Courts and households.

Returning to Rome in 585, Gregory was to head his own monastery of St Andrews (dedicated to the Apostle in 575) as its abbot for the following five years.

Pope Pelagius II (the son of an Ostrogoth) died during an epidemic, due to an overflow of the Tiber, early in the year 590. The Emperor Maurice sanctioned Gregory to be his successor as the Bishop of Rome.[19] After unsuccessfully evading this dignity, he, as the first monk, was consecrated as Pope on 3 September 590. Gregory, whose name means 'watchful', (fifty years earlier, he would have been Vigilius) lived until the year 604; his Feast Day is the date of his death, 12 March.

Chapter XV

Later Military Operations

'All Italy south of the Po was now restored to the Imperial authority. Of the subjugation of the Transpadane provinces where Goths and Franks were still in possession, we have no record.'
J.B. Bury[1]

The Franks not only threatened renewed warfare, but actually began a fresh campaign; kept from assuming dangerous proportions only by their internal dissentions, which kept them from crossing the Alps in force. It is recorded that they defeated a 'Roman' army in 555; these may have been Franks already settled in Italy; but the latter avenged this defeat by driving them back to their native land.

In 556, besides invading Thuringia, the Franks also made a successful inroad into Italy.[2] There is no specific mention of any military actions in the surviving sources from this date until the year 561; a lapse of five years.

Narses, most likely, had been engaged in the slow process of subjugating the regions beyond the Po. His task was to be complicated by the need to capture the important cities of Brixia (Brescia) and Verona from the Goth, Widin, aided by the Frank, Amingus.

Amingus And Widin

Around the year 561, there were raids, and a 'revolt' by the scattered Goths remaining in the province of Aquileia under the leadership of a Count Vidinus, or Widin. He may have held command in Verona, where the Goths had been prevented by the Franks from surrendering to Valerian in 552.[3] Alternatively, he may have taken Verona and Brescia by surprise at the beginning of the insurrection.

Widin was offered assistance by Amingus, which undoubtedly helped to prolong the campaign that Narses had to wage to put down the rebellion, and to capture the two important towns. There is some confusion in the accounts of this decade given by the old Church chronicals; the name of Amingus being coupled with that of Buccelin during the Frankish Invasion of 553–54. He was most likely a chieftain who first entered Italy with King Theodebert in the year 539. He may not have gone back after this 'raid', remaining south of the Alps for more than two decades. Nonetheless, Amingus, by aiding Widin, was to bring that old war-gelding, Narses, back into battle.

The first encounter may have occurred when Amingus with his forces opposed an Imperial army about to cross over the Adige. As some sort of treaty, or a truce, was then in effect between the Empire and the Franks, Narses sent envoys warning him to depart. Amingus reportedly replied that he would not retreat so long as his arm could wield and hurl a javelin.[4] His ultimate fate, along with that of Widin, was given by Paul the Deacon:

> 'Widin being captured, was banished to Constantinople, but Amingus, who had offered him assistance, perished by the sword of Narses.'[5]

As an example of the confusion regarding these events, the Lombard historian inserted this information in between his accounts of the fates of Buccelin and Leutharis in 554.

There is a further discrepancy as to the actual date when Narses recovered Verona and Brescia. Among the events listed for November 562, are Narses sending the keys of the two cities, as trophies of victory, to Constantinople; and the discovery there of yet another plot against Justinian, in which Belisarius himself was implicated.[6] This relatively late date for their capture was also given by John Malalas and Theophanes.[7] The even later date of 20 June 563, was mentioned by Agnellus of Ravenna in his *Liber Pontificalis*.

Whether it was in 562, or even 563, Narses did complete his task of reconquering the ancient homeland province of Italy for Justinian's restored Roman Empire. No attempt was made to reconquer Gaul, or the regions beyond the Alps. And, none too soon, for the Emperor's reign over his extended domain came to an end with his death in November 565.

The Revolt of Sindual

Also in 565, Narses was called upon to crush another revolt. This was under the leadership of Sindual (Sinduald), the Herulian chief, who had distinguished himself fighting for Narses at the Battle of Capua in 554. By bringing his disaffected tribesmen back onto the field the already certain defeat of Buccelin's army was turned into savage annihilation.

Now, a year or so after the conclusion of the campaign against Amingus

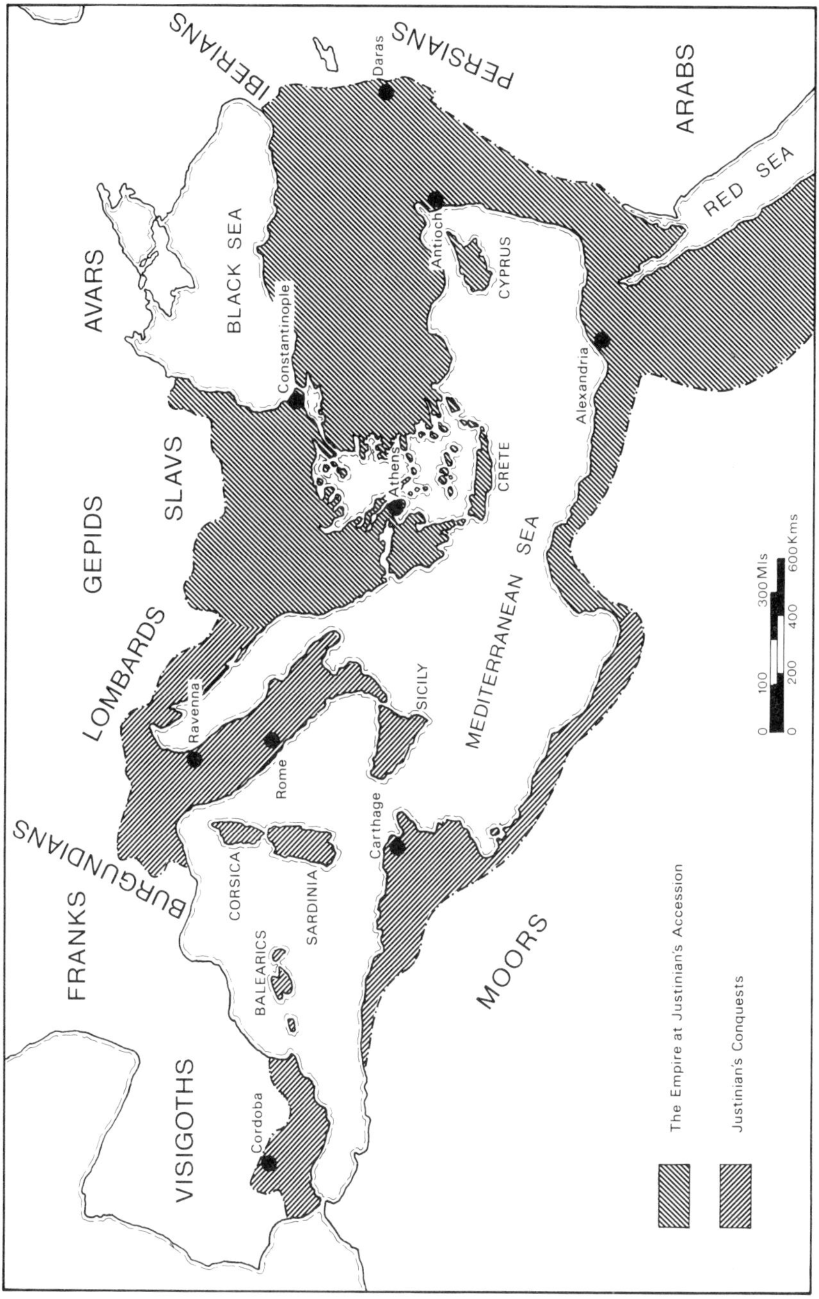

Fig. 10. The Empire of Justinian I.

and Widin, the Heruls were disaffected enough to actually revolt. There is some doubt whether these wandering mercenaries, longtime allies of Narses, really constituted a full tribe, much less a nation, by this date. They, and Sindual, are now mentioned in conjunction with the Brenti, perhaps the same as the Breones or Briones, from the Alps of Noricum, or the Tyrol, near the Brenner Pass. Sinduald himself was said by Paul the Deacon, and Otto Bishop of Freising, to have entered Italy with Odoacer, and was the sole survivor of his Counts. There must be some more chronological confusion here, as in the case of Amingus. For Odoacer (434–93) was the barbarian general who deposed the last Roman Emperor in the West, Romulus Augustulus, nearly ninety years previously (AD 476). This would mean that Sinduald would have had to be around the same age as Liberius, who had served both barbarian rulers; in other words, about a decade older than Narses himself, who by now was anywhere from eighty-five to eighty-seven years old. Notwithstanding his actual age, Sinduald had until now been a faithful supporter of Narses, receiving many benefits in return. There are two extant letters from Pope Pelagius I addressed to 'Sindula' as 'magister militum'.

It could have been a wish on the part of the surviving Heruls to recreate their ancient glories and freedom or the further ambition of the high-ranking Sinduald, that elevated him to a sort of sovereignty over the Brenti-Heruli. There are no details of this rebellion, and the struggle with 'king' Sinduald, but Narses' reaction to such ingratitude was given by Paul the Deacon: [Narses] 'defeated him in war, captured him and hung him from a lofty beam.'[8]

As for the fragmented nation of the Heruli, their defeat by Narses gave them a second fatal blow from which they would never recover. Earlier in the sixth century (507–12) the Lombards, at that time subjects of the Heruli on the plains of Hungary, had defeated them in battle and entirely destroyed their kingdom. A part of the Heruls had attached themselves to the Gepidae, another Gothic tribe; the remainder may have migrated back to Scandinavia, through the forests of eastern Germany.[9] As barbarian mercenaries for hire, Narses was highly successful in recruiting them for the service of the Empire. Now, he was to give the death blow to the remnants of this tribe; they gradually died out, disappearing entirely as a 'nation'.

Gundovald The Pretender

Earlier in his career, in 545, Narses had unmasked the pretender, Chilbudius. Now, a decade or two later, he had occasion to protect a different kind of pretender. This was Gundovald, an illegitimate son of Chlotar (Lothair) who had, as the sole survivor of the four sons of Clovis, inherited the Merovingian dominions. Lothair was also the uncle and great uncle respectively of Theodebert and Theodebalt. Upon Lothair's death, in 561, said to be in remorse over the murder of a rebellious son, Chramnus, the kingdom was divided by four other 'legitimate' sons. These were Charibert (d.567), Chilperic, Guntram and Sigebert, who became the Kings of Paris, Soissons, Orleans with Burgundy, and Metz. Sigebert also became the husband of Brunhilda, a daughter of the King of the Visigoths in Spain, Athanagild, the 'ally' of Liberius. Not to be out-done, Chilperic, a half-brother (and possibly not legitimate) married her elder sister Galswintha.

Gundovald, even though a bastard son, perhaps expected a share in the inheritance of the Frankish Kingdom. He had been detained by his father, while still alive, and afterwards by his half-brothers, in Agrippina (Cologne). As a means of rendering him incapable of assuming regal power, his long hair was cut short. He escaped from the banks of the Rhein and, letting his hair grow long again, made his way down to Italy and its ruler Narses. Gregory of Tours cited Gundovald as saying:

> 'No man is ignorant that my father Lothar [sic] ever detested me, or that my hair was cut short first by him, and later by my brothers. This was why I joined Narses, prefect of Italy, in which country I took a wife and begat two sons.'[10]

Evidently, he stayed on with his family in Italy during the rest of Narses' administration there. Later, after the death of his wife, he was to be accorded a welcome by the Emperors Justin II and Tiberius in Constantinople. Therefore, Narses granting asylum to this Frankish pretender may well have been deliberate 'Byzantine' policy.

'The Long-Haired Kings'

This cutting short of Gundovald's long hair, compelling him to join Narses in distant Italy, was definitely barbaric German policy. The wearing of long, particularly blond, hair as a badge of sovereignty by barbarians of rank, first became known to the Romans during the time of Marius and the invasion of the Cimbri and Teutons. Magical properties, as well as social status, could have been symbolized by this custom.

The Merovingian dynasty may have perpetrated this hair-style as a mark of antique regal distinction or significance. The Visigothic kings in Spain also retained this mode as an outward mark of royal authority.[11] Their assumption of the title of 'Flavius', (from the Latin flavus, meaning golden-yellow) was indicative of this august and highly esteemed distinction.[12]

Conversely, if a king was to be degraded, a chief dishonoured, or as in the case of Gundovald, a rival rendered incapable of opposition, he was not put to death; he merely had his long hair cropped short. No matter how popular he may have been, no degree of righteousness in his cause could rouse any support for one who had been cropped. When his hair did grow back again, he might become formidable once more; but the 'scissors' were always near at hand.[13] Gundovald mentioned his own hair being first cut by his father, and then again by the other sons; after his escape, he did not enter into the presence of Narses, as a royal pretender, until his hair was long again.

Eventually, he was brought back from Constantinople by Frankish nobles to be set up in opposition to Guntram, the King of Orleans and Burgundy, and his adopted nephew Childebert II (575–95). It was the latter's formidable mother, Brunhilda, whose name was invoked in suppressing this revolt.

The pretender Gundovald was besieged, betrayed, and forced to surrender at the town of Saint-Bertrand-de-Comminges in a Pyrenees valley in 585.[14] His long hair was not enough protection to prevent Boso, a Frankish count, from dashing out his brains with a large stone. Then his hair and beard were pulled out by a mob.

Chapter XVI

Financial Administration

> 'Narses, the commander renowned for generous and pious acts, was gradually transformed into Narses, the superintendent of enforced levies of money, and his very name before long was a mark of universal fear and hatred.'
>
> Eleanor Shipley Duckett[1]

One of the sore points of Justinian's restoration of the Empire in the West, and consequently of Narses' administration of the Praefecture of Italy, was the introduction of the oppressive system of taxation prevailing in the East. The Western provinces, were expected to support the complicated administrations imposed on them, and to pay for the costly armies necessary to defend them. In addition, they were even obliged to contribute to the general maintenance of the Imperial Court in Constantinople.

The barely conquered Italy that Narses governed for his distant autocratic master was weaker than Africa, which had also known war and reconquest. If it had been accomplished with the same speed as that of Africa a whole generation of campaigning and destruction would have been avoided. As it was, Italy had been reduced to utter misery by the Gothic War. The invasions of the Franks, and moreover the ferocity of the Imperial barbarian merceneries, had further contributed to its ruin and depopulation. The aristocracy and middle-classes were both diminished at this time; commerce and industry disappeared in many of the towns; there were large uncultivated and deserted tracts in the country. Fugitives, dispersed by the warring armies, gradually congregated in the towns, thus helping Milan and some other cities to recover part of their populations, but leaving the countryside deserted. Agriculture was probably reduced to a mere subsistence level, engaged in by the inhabitants of the towns.

Narses, as Justinian's 'alter ego' may have wished to prove that the Italy he had reconquered was not only self-supporting, but could even remit tax revenues back to the Capital on the Bosporus. The work of relief and restoration done by him was laudable, but as it required the extraction of large taxes from the more fortunate of the native Italians, it engendered much ill-will. It came to be felt that the Eastern Imperial 'finger was thicker than the loins' of the Ostrogoths from whom Italy had been delivered.

The attempt to establish a highly centralized and bureaucratic government at Ravenna called for more taxes from even the common people than the Gothic Kings had extracted. The very ignorance and limited wants of these barbarian rulers had made for less demand on the ruined productive system of the peninsula. Consequently, in the eyes of its natives, the re-imposed laws of the Empire, and the costliness of their upkeep, came to seem more 'foreign' than the alien and heretical Ostrogoths had been. This was compounded by the fact that Narses had to import his administrative officials, especially in the higher categories, from the East.

Notorious among these were the 'logothetae' (the very name is Greek) or tax-auditors of the Imperial Treasury. They applied the burdensome Eastern system of taxation without making any allowances for the prevailing distress of the ruined country. They were to enrich themselves at the expense of taxpayers by demanding arrears dating back to the Ostrogothic Kingdom; they even falsified the registers to increase their returns. Thus, an elaborate system of fiscal oppression was established, and apparently under the direct auspices of Narses himself.

The career of one especially notorious logothete is often referred to for this aspect of Narses' administration, although he apparently flourished during Justinian's initial reorganization, following Belisarius' capture of Ravenna in 540. This was Alexander Psalidios, 'the Snips'; so-called for his ability to clip, or trim, the edges of gold coins. His fine art of tax-gathering enabled him to accumulate a fortune from his office. As he was legally entitled to one-twelfth of everything collected, there was no limit, except human endurance, to what he imposed.[2]

Even the soldiers of the Imperial armies were cheated in their pay and bonuses and fined for any and every breach of discipline – logothetes were also paymasters of the army.

There is some evidence that Justinian himself heard appeals from the Western provinces on their misery. He is even said to have actually taken measures to restore prosperity to his new subjects by tax-relief from the well-known greed of his officials. His exertions, in Africa at least, did result in a real prosperity. Similar measures taken in Italy, e.g. public works to repair the ravages of war, were in vain in regard to achieving any real revival.[3]

The ultimate wisdom of Justinian's attempts to re-establish the Roman Empire that had skirted the shores of the Mediterranean, and his wish to restore its ancient prosperity, is really impossible to determine. The 'reconquest' barely survived his own life-time; the Lombards, Persians, Visigoths, and lastly the Arabs, annulling his expanded Empire.

C.R.L. Fletcher in his work attempting '*To Trace the Fortunes of the Children of the Roman Empire*' [in Western Europe] made some interesting comments on Justinian's tax-gathering. First, that the cost of warfare in his day and age did not fall directly on the tax-payers. Fletcher felt that the expense of Justinian's wars in the West, i.e. Africa and Italy, even though lasting some twenty years, could have been greatly over-estimated. The armies were generally small, and ill-paid; Belisarius' second campaign in Italy being a case in point. Many of the troops engaged were barbarian auxiliaries who had joined for the prospect of spoils and plunder from the enemy. Narses himself has been accused of using this bait in his recruiting missions, and later operations.

Linked to this aspect of booty and loot helping to pay the soldiers' way, Fletcher cited the existence of hoarded treasures. He is convinced that the Imperial government must have had its share of the 'enormous' hoarded treasure taken from the Vandals and Ostrogoths. The part played by such deposits in unsettled, once rich, societies was very great; Totila's hoards in the palace at Pavia, and the fortress of Cumae, readily come to mind. Even Narses himself was to later give rise to a legend of buried treasure; an amassed fortune of gold and silver that he is supposed to have taken out of Italy (see Appendix 4).

Fletcher, after setting forth the needs of taxation for good and orderly government, came to this conclusion:

> 'Before I condemned Justinian as an exorbitant tax-gatherer, I should want to know the incidence per head of the peoples he ruled, of the amount he levied, and this we have no means whatever of ascertaining.'[4]

Plague In Italy (565)

Narses was to have other problems to contend with besides trying to rebuild Italy after years of devastating warfare, and the depredations of barbarian raids. The economic problem of collecting the revenue to finance this work had led to his transformation from the deliverer of Italy to being considered its oppressor. In addition there were disasters which, though often aided and abetted by man himself, generally come under the heading of 'due to natural causes'. Chief among these were the double scourge of plague and famine over which armies, or even tax-collectors, have no control. Paul the Deacon, after mentioning the revolt of Sindual in 565, had continued: 'In the times of this man a very great pestilence broke out, particularly in the province of Liguria.'[5]

Evidently, this was a periodic recurrence of the same bubonic plague which had originated in Egypt back in 542. For over fifty years, it was to break out in recurring epidemics throughout the known world. Italy had also been visited by it in 543; now, twenty-two years later, it was to be stricken again. This could possibly have been a result of the recent movements of the barbarian forces in northern Italy under Amingus, Widin, and Sindual.

Paul proceeded to list some of its symptoms: first, a swelling, the size of a nut or date, would appear in the glands, followed by a fever, then death on the third day. If, however, anyone should survive the third day, there was a chance of recovery.

As for the reactions to this epidemic, there was a mass flight away from the plague; dwellings were deserted, flocks left untended, sons left their parents unburied, parents abandoned children with raging fevers. In descriptions of death and desolation that contain the elements of a pastoral elegy, Paul stated:

> 'You might see the world, brought back to its ancient silence: no voice in the field; no whistling of shepherds; . . . The crops out-living the time of the harvest, awaited the reaper untouched; the vineyard with its fallen leaves and its shining grapes remained undisturbed while winter came on; . . . pastoral places had been turned into a sepulchre for men, and human habitations had become places of refuge for wild beasts.'[6]

Unfortunately for Narses, and his administration, these evils occurred only within Italy itself, up to the boundaries of the Alps.

The Death Of Justinian I

The year 565, as a whole, was an eventful one for the Emperor Justinian's 'viceroy'. There was not only plague in his Praefecture, the revolt by the Heruls, the destruction of the Sibyl's cave at Cumae, the memorials of the restored bridge on the Via Salaria, the seizure of Vitalis, Bishop of Altino and exiling him to Sicily; but also the deaths of Belisarius, and then Justinian himself. Especially fateful for the future of Narses was the succession to the throne of Justin II together with his consort, Sophia.

The Emperor Justinian I died on 14 November (Theophanes states 11 November) at the age of eight-three years and six months. Belisarius had died the previous March, at the relatively young age of sixty. Theodora had been dead for seventeen years, and Tribonian for twenty-two. Thus, of the principle characters connected with the Imperial Court, there only remained Antonina, an eighty-one year old widow possibly retired to a convent, and Narses.

The death of his Imperial master was to shake his favourite's position as the over-lord of Italy. Apparently, he had been given a free hand to do as he chose, and his age of eighty-seven or so would have prevented him from changing his methods, and adapting to a new order of things.

A deputation of disaffected well-placed Roman nobles made loud-voiced complaints to the new emperor in Constantinople about the intransigent, extorting old governor. They insinuated that they would rather serve heathen barbarians than be ruled and oppressed by the eunuch Narses. They credited their most devout emperor with being ignorant of the true state of affairs. Justin, and his wife, Sophia, may have already suspected that Narses was less liberal in sending a share of the taxation back to them than he had been to Justinian.

Italy was the part of the Empire that was suffering the most at the time of Justinian's death. It was shattered and exhausted by the lengthy war, and the calamities, natural or otherwise, that had ensued. There are indications that even the soldiers of Narses were deserting the country, depriving it of means of defence against renewed barbarian invasion.

Narses personally suffered under the new regime, being reduced to far more than mere physical impotence; just when the frontiers should have been strengthened in the North. The Ostrogothic Kingdom had extended as far as Noricum and Pannonia; now Italy was almost unprotected on the very border where the barbarian tribes had always found passage into the country. Narses was unsupported, and his Praefecture unprepared; he could expect no assistance from the disaffected Italians themselves; or from any other quarter for that matter. He thus found himself rewarded with the hatred of his subjects, and the ingratitude of the new Court back in Constantinople.

Then, in the year 567, Narses was recalled from his office and duties, with a successor, Longinus, being sent out to Italy immediately to take his place. This fall of Justinian's favourite was perfectly in keeping with the role of favourites at the Eastern Court; especially considering the dread which Narses' power in Italy must have awakened in the new rulers there.[7]

The Accession of Justin II

Since Theodora had never given Justinian any offspring, there was no direct heir to the succession. She was, however, to have one last posthumous triumph; her long-laid plan to keep the throne in the family after all. She is credited with arranging the marriage between Justinian's nephew, Justin, the son of his sister, Vigilantia, and her niece, Sophia, the daughter of her older sister Comita, and Sittas. (See Genealogical Table, p.67)

During his lifetime, Justinian had not associated any colleague with himself, as his own uncle, Justin I had done, by making him Caesar. The intended succession was only indicated by his nephew's appointment to the post of curopalatesor cura palatii (controller of palace bureaucracy). Otherwise, the elder son of Germanus, Justin, could have been considered as a possibility. Even on his death-bed, Justinian gave no sign, but the Senate was already agreed on his successor. All through the long night of 13–14 November, Justin and Sophia could only sit and wait.

Then finally, before dawn, the news arrived that the Emperor was dead, and a new ruler was expected for the Roman Empire. After the formalities of tears and refusals were satisfied, Justin was finally persuaded to accept the senators' offer of the throne. He went to the palace, guarded by the future emperor Tiberius; there, he was acclaimed by the Army and the Church. Later that morning, he went to the Hippodrome, where he was acclaimed by the populace.

Justin II returned to the palace at midday, where the last honours were paid to Justinian, and his embalmed body was then carried to the Church of the Twelve Apostles. The new Empress, Sophia, laid a purple cloth over the bier on which were embroidered, in gold, scenes of the achievements of his reign.

There were rejoicing and festivities in the Capital at the accession of the new emperor, and apparently genuine relief throughout the Empire that the old one was finally dead. Flavius Cresconius Corippus, a Latin epic poet, sang 'The world renews its youth'.[8]

It was not to be long however, before the weakness of the Realm, and its new ruler, became obvious to the rest of the then known world. Unfortunately, Justin II had delusions of grandeur when it came to the might and power of his inherited Empire, and even as to his own personal dignity as its emperor. By the year 569, it had become apparent that he was 'ailing', and even subject to occasional bouts of mental weakness. In fact, already in 567, the year of the recall of Narses, Justin may have been suffering from the effects of fits of irrational and unreasonable anger. In the words of Paul the Deacon, after hearing the accusations of the Romans against their eunuch-ruler: 'Then the emperor was so greatly moved with anger against Narses that he straightway sent the prefect Longinus into Italy to take Narses' place.'[9]

The following year, 568, a series of disasters marked his reign, beginning with the invasion of Italy by the Lombards. During the years 569–71, there was a Moorish rebellion in Africa, and in 571–72, the Visigoths recovered much of the Empire's conquests in Spain, including Cordova. Also in 571, Justin tried to take under his protection the Armenians in Persarmenia who had revolted against Persia, and asked the Empire for aid. This, and his refusal to pay the annual subsidy stipulated in a treaty of 562, provoked a war with Chosroes in 572. The next year, after one of his generals invaded Syria, capturing Antioch and sacking Apamea, Chosroes took Daras on 15 November 573. Thus eight years, almost to the very day, after Justinian's death, his restored Roman Empire was all but shattered.

Justin himself was devastated by the shock of the loss of Daras, the rampart of the Eastern Empire, and never recovered. It was by now quite clear that the Empire's affairs could not be managed by a hopelessly violent and weak-minded madman. A story goes that the once exalted emperor was reduced to being pulled about the palace floors in a little cart; and, like a naughty child, was frightened from violence by the mention of the name of an Arab border sheikh.

By the year 574 the Empress Sophia, who was a virago governing Justin absolutely, was carrying on the government in concert with Tiberius, the comes excubitorum, or commander of the palace guards. She went so far as to have Tiberius adopted as the son of the Emperor, and on 7 December 574, in a formal impressive ceremony, he was created Caesar, or Augustus. As such, he created Maurice the comes excubitorum.

Justin, recovering his reason temporarily in 578, crowned his adopted son as the Emperor Tiberius II on 26 September. Eight days later, on 4 October 578, Justin II died; Sophia wanted to marry Tiberius Constantinus but he already had a secret and lawful wife named Anastasia.

The Lombards

The last of Italy's barbarian tribal invaders, in the third year of Justin's reign, were also the most savage. This small tribe was branded by the Roman historian, Velleius Paterculus (*c.*19 BC–after AD 30) as: 'gens etiam Germana feritate ferocior' or, 'the German people fiercer than ferocity itself'.[10]

They were to be even more detested by the native Italians than the Ostrogoths had been, remaining 'nefantissimi' (Italian for cursed, execrable, filthy, heinous, lewd, loathesome, obscene, etc.) from beginning to end (568–774).

The present Italian version of their name is the Longobardi – in English, they are known as the Langobards or Lombards. They were to give their name to the north central region of Italy (its most populous) of which Milan is the centre – Lombardia (Lombardy).

Traditionally of Scandinavian origins, they came from the home-land of the Gothic races (Ostrogoths, Visigoths and Gepidae), the large island of Gotland (Gothland or Gottland) in the Baltic Sea, off the east coast of Sweden. Their migrations through Central Europe had followed the general pattern of the other Teutonic tribes; their legends were similar and interchangeable with the main body of Germanic experience.

Historically, they first emerged from the banks of the lower Elbe at Bardengau, on the left bank, near Lüneburg. They were neighbours of the Saxons, whose customs were similar to their own. They came to dwell in the regions above the northern banks of the Danube; during the three centuries after the reign of Marcus Aurelius (AD 161–80). In conjunction with the Marcomanni, they had been repulsed by the Romans from an initial incursion into Pannonia in 165. In the life-time of Narses, under their 'king', or war-leader, Godeoch, they took possession of the territories known as Rugianland, or Rugiland. These had been occupied by the Rugians, a tribe originally from Norway, who were destroyed by Odoacer in a two-year campaign (487–88).

The Lombards being cattle-breeders (they used conquered peasants to till the land), moved on to pasture in the low plains of Alföla, or 'Feld', in Hungary. It is known that they themselves were subject for a time to the Heruls, although this may have meant nothing more than the payment of tribute. Sometime during the period between the years 507 and 512 the Lombards, under King Tato, defeated the Heruls in a battle somewhere in south-western Hungary.

In 547, Justinian gave Noricum and Pannonia to the Lombards, to be used as a counterpose to the Gepidae. Not only did he bestow Noricum (Belgrade) and the strongholds of Pannonia, but 'a very great amount of money' as well.[11] (King Wacho had refused aid to the Ostrogoths in 539, citing friendship with Justinian.)

In the year of Narses' recall, 567, the Lombards defeated the Gepids, destroying their Kingdom. King Alboin, slaying King Kunimund by his own hand, took his daughter Rosamund prisoner and made her his queen. Later, at a banquet, in Verona, he was to force her to drink from, a 'scala' (cup or goblet) made out of her father's skull, bidding her to 'drink merrily with her father'.

By the Spring of the year following their destruction of the Gepids, and despite their alliance with the empire, the Lombards were ready for their incursion into a weakened Italy.

In April 568, King Alboin led a host, traditionally numbered at 200,000, consisting of subjugated tribes and allies (including 20,000 Saxons) out from Pannonia, and then over the Julian Alps, into the region of Friuli. The first important place captured was Forum Julii (Cividale), the centre of a chain of small fortresses on the south side of the Alps.

By 4 September 569, Milan had surrendered without opposition, but Pavia, just to the south, was to resist for three years. Cremona, over to the east, withstood the invaders for thirty-three years, until 603, when she was destroyed along with her neighbour Volturnia.[12]

While the Lombards never entirely conquered the Italian peninsula, as the Ostrogoths had done, they were to break up the whole of the Imperial administrative system within a decade. Longinus, the successor of Narses, may have already abolished the provincial dukes, setting up a prefect in each city with the ducal title.

The Lombard chieftains who conquered such duchies as Benevento and Spoleto styled themselves dukes trying to preserve something of the Imperial administration. But such political uniformity was impossible under the changed conditions and the title of duce, or duke, became little more than a designation of social honour.

Not only did the Lombard invasion prove to be fatal to the Justinianic system, as restored in Italy, but it was also to be the final, and most controversial event in the long life and career of Narses the Eunuch. Rumours and tales arose that were eventually to assume the status of a Saga.

Chapter XVII

The Saga of Narses

'Narses the Patrician, after he had under Justinianus Augustus, overcome Totila, King of the Goths in Italy, being terrified by the threats of Sophia Augusta, the wife of Justin, invited the Langobardi from Pannonia, and introduced them into Italy.'

Isidore of Seville[1]

This celebrated legend had its origins in the events that led to the downfall of Narses in 567. Then, there had been the malice and accusations of the Romans, and the reaction of the new, and ultimately mad, Emperor Justin II, to their pleas for release from the 'slavery' that the aged eunuch governor had reduced them to.

When Narses came to hear of all this, and of his recall to Constantinople, he is reported to have become so alarmed and frightened that he did not dare return to the capital. Instead, he departed from Rome, withdrawing southwards to Naples in Campania. The conqueror of the Franks, Goths, and assorted barbarian warrior nations, was reputedly terrified by the threats of the Empress Sophia.

She had added insult to injury by sending an offensive message to the effect that if Narses returned to the Palace, she should have him rule over the women's chamber, instead of nations, portioning out the daily allotment of wool for spinning there. This biting taunt was accompanied by a golden distaff.

Offended and aroused to indignation, Narses reputedly replied that he would spin a thread of which neither she nor the Emperor Justin would be able to find the end.[2] Then followed the far-famed vengeance of the eunuch on the Empress; he sent messengers to his old allies the Lombards under King Alboin, up in Pannonia, inviting them to abandon their barren reign and come down to possess Italy with its riches of every sort. He also sent samples of the many fruits and other produce with which that land was well supplied.

The Lombards received the invitation and the gifts joyfully, as they already had the desire to return to the land they had left reluctantly fifteen years earlier (552). Throughout Italy itself, terrible omens of the bloodshed and disaster to come were continually seen at night; fiery 'swords', or streamers (blood-red comets?).

Eventually, Pope John III went down to Naples. There he began soothing the aged, dejected ex-governor, entreating him to return to Rome. Narses asked of the most Holy Father, what evils had he done to the Romans? He offered to go as a supplicant to the feet of the ones who had sent the Pope, and all of Italy would know how he had toiled with all his strength for that land. The Pope replied by stating that he, himself, would go to them. The end result was that instead of possibly going to Constantinople, the two, eunuch and Pope, returned to Rome together.

The year generally given for their return is 571; if correct, there would have been a lapse of some four years since his exile, and the Lombards would have been well on their way to the conquest of northern Italy. Narses went back to live in the Palace of the Caesars on the Palatine Hill. The situation in Rome during the period of his disgrace and eventual return is unknown. However, Pope John III retired to an abode in the churchyard of Saints Tiburtius and Valerian, a small church standing over the catacombs of Pretextatus on the Via Appia, about two miles below the city. His retirement to such a secluded spot may have had some connection with the confusion and the uproar of this time; he even consecrated bishops while living there, up until his death on 13 July 574.

There is much chronological confusion regarding the actual year of Narses' own death. Historians have placed his demise anywhere from the year 566 to 573, and even 574.[3] However, if one assumes the generally accepted date of 478 for his birth, and accepts the assertion of Andrea Agnellus of Ravenna, a ninth century chronicler (*c.*830), that Narses died in his ninety-fifth year, then the year of his death must have been 573.

Assuming Narses to have still been living in the year 567, there yet remain the sources, and the evidence, of the Saga to be considered, and accepted or rejected.

Sources of The Saga

The origins of this celebrated and legendary story of Italy's betrayal by Narses are to be found years after the Lombard invasion in 568.

Thomas Hodgkin traced the tale forwards and backwards through the centuries, seeking the evidence for Narses' crime. According to him, the story seems to have been unknown to 'strictly contemporary authors';[4]

Agathias (who wrote between 566–94), Marius of Aventicum (*c.*530–94), or Gregory of Tours (*c.*538–94). *The Liber Pontificalis*, which was more or less contemporary, did mention the notorious invitation. In the section on the life of Pope John III are the details of the delegations of Romans to Justin, the departure of Narses from Rome to Campania, and his writing to the tribe of Lombards to come and possess Italy. It also narrated the intercession of the Pope, the return to Rome, and John's retiring to his abode in the churchyard on the Appian Way.

About half a century after the Lombard incursion, appeared the citation of the invitation and introduction of that tribe into Italy in the Chronicle (to the year 615) of Isidore of Seville. He was not a historian as such, but an early encyclopaedist; his Chronicles are full of facts and fictions. He died on 4 April 636. After the *Liber Pontificalis*, Isidore is considered the strongest support for the story of the 'invitation'.

The story also occurred in the *Origo Gentis Langobardorum* (The Origin of the Nation of Lombards) which was an extract from a lost history of Secundus of Trent. He is mentioned several times in the letters of Pope Gregory I; of his career it is known that in January, 596, he was a deacon to the Archbishop Marinianus of Ravenna, and that by 603, he was an abbot. The work in question was a *History of the Acts of the Lombards* which had been brought down to the year 612. The Origo itself is dated around 650, and simply stated that Alboin led the Lombards into Italy after being 'invited by Narses (chief) of the secretaries'. [sic]

The so-called Fredegarius, who wrote towards the middle of the seventh century, (*c.*642–58) supplied one of the saga-like details. In his Epitome he said that the empress sent a golden instrument used by women, together with the insulting instructions for its use. Fredegarius also gave Narses' response to this gift of Sophia.

Then, towards the close of the eighth century, i.e. over 200 years later, Paul the Deacon, drawing on the *Liber Pontificalis* and possibly Fredegarius, filled in the more minute details in his *History of the Langobards* (last chapter of the first book, and first seven chapters of the second book). He began his narrative of the Saga with an initial statement on the destruction of the Gothic nation, and the conquest of others, possibly Sindual and the Heruli. Then, Paul has Narses acquiring great wealth, and incurring the envy of the Romans, in spite of his labours for them against the common foes. Their insinuations made to Justin and Sophia were followed by the emperor's anger, and his being replaced by Longinus. When he knew of his fate, Narses feared to return to Constantinople, especially because of Sophia's message threatening to make him portion out the wool in her women's chamber.[5]

Paul changed Fredegarius' answer, made by Narses, to a more personal note by having him say he would begin 'to weave her [Sophia] such a web as she could not lay down as long as she lived'.[6] Next, racked by fear and hate, Narses withdrew to Naples, from where he sent messengers to the nation of the Lombards with the invitation to, and the samples of, the riches of Italy. Paul concluded by relating the terrible signs, i.e. 'fiery swords', that were seen in the Italian night skies, as omens of the future blood-shed.[7] His history enjoyed immense popularity, surviving in many manuscripts, largely because of these and a variety of other engaging legends. The Historia Langobardorum was written after the year 787; Paul the Deacon died, possibly on 13 April, in the year 799. Thereafter, the Lombard invasion has been told, and retold, by various historians, and assorted authors, all drawing chiefly from the pages of one who wrote over two hundred years after the event.

As one example, Niccolo Machiavelli (1469–1527) included it uncritically in his Florentine History (1525). An English translation, dated 1595, by Thomas Bedinfeld, captured some of the Renaissance seasoning to the original narrative. Recalling that the government of Italy was taken from Narsete (Narses) after he had got it by his 'verture and blood'; it added that Sophia also injured, reviled and threatened to call him home to 'spinne with women'. Narses was so greatly moved by this 'to chollor and offence that he persuaded Alboino King of the Lombardi. . .to come into Italy, and conquere it.'[8]

Besides his chronological distance from the events of Narses' time, Paul the Deacon cannot be considered a particularly trustworthy source; Foulke prefaced him as 'a kind of humbler Herodotus of mediaeval times'.[9] He also added this warning to early twentieth century readers: 'He has not that critical judgment which the requirements of modern history demand.'[10]

Much like the famous phrase used by her aunt and predecessor the Empress Theodora, during the crisis of Nika, the message of Sophia to Narses could have had a 'classical' literary source. Either she, Fredegarius, or even Paul, could have been versed enough to have been familiar with the verse of the 'last poet of classical Rome', Claudian, or Claudius Claudianus (*c.*370–404?). He was a Greek-speaking native of Egypt, who wrote Latin poems, and even though a probable pagan, was the poet courtier of Christian emperors (e.g. Honorius). The work that specifically comes to mind is his Invectives against Eutropius.

Eutropius was an ex-slave eunuch, possibly of Armenian origins, who, as the praepositus sacri cubiculi was in power during the reign of the Eastern Emperor Arcadius about 170 years earlier (395–99). He was made a Consul in 399 which came to be known as 'The Year of the Eunuch'. His career excited the ire and literary wrath of Claudian enough to be penned with the following lines:

'Old, sexless lump! what, – try the sword to wield?
Or Pallas seek amid the bloody field?
For other studies, with Minerva rest:
The loom, not lance, for thy employ is best.
Learn threads to weave; or wenches keep to work,
Who, full of sloth, from labour wish to lurk;
Or snowy wool, around the shuttle, wind,
That, for a mistress' fingers is designed.'[11]

In commenting on the eunuch silentiary presiding over his council, Claudian referred to him as an odious dame overseeing girls at the loom.[12] Along the same general lines, but with the metaphor twisted the other way:

> 'If eunuchs o'er the state and laws preside, let men the twining thread on distaffs guide.'[13]

Regarding all the sources, Hodgkin remarked that though the dealings of Narses were too well vouched for to be dismissed as entirely fabulous, they still could not be placed as undoubted historical facts.[14] Tracing the tale backwards, he found that the nearer one got to the date of the events, the less the narrators knew of all the freely imputed secret motives, and dramatically described dialogues of great personages.[15] Thus the celebrated Saga of Narses could be considered to be more scenario than 'storia' (history).

Status of the Saga

Through the centuries the Saga has found varying degrees of acceptance, or rejection, according to the critic's point of view. The possibly contemporary Anastasius in the Liber Pontificalis, presented the initial popular belief that Narses was disloyal to Italy and his sovereigns. This opus was copied by both 'the Venerable Bede' (673–735) and Aimoin of Halberstadt (d.853) to prove this popular belief.

Cardinal Cesare Baronius (1538–1607), denied the treason of the 'favourite of the Virgin'; but the weakness of the defence by this protector was supposedly shown by many severe critics.

On into the eighteenth century, Charles Le Beau (1723–51), and Gibbon himself (1737–94), were of the opinion that there was little ground for disbelieving the charge against Narses. In the early nineteenth century, Lord Mahon, Philip Henry, Fifth Earl Stanhope (1805–75), as a biographer of Belisarius (1829), readily accepted the Saga. He diminished the fame and all the glories of a long life by having Narses blot them out with treason; calling in the enemy to avenge his personal wrongs.[16]

Near the end of the century, however, the acceptance of the Saga became tinged with doubt, or it was almost rejected altogether. Hodgkin warned about distinguishing between popular suspicion, and the judicial evidence on such a 'crime'.[17] There had been parallel historical cases of high treason involving Stilicho, and the Roman general Bonifacius.

The Vandal general and guardian was arrested on orders from the Emperor Honorius, and executed by beheading at Ravenna on 28 August 408. As the Governor of Africa, Boniface was recalled in the year 427; during the ensuing civil war, the 'Procopian' story is that he invited the Vandals in Spain, under King Gaiseric, over to Africa (in the spring of 429).[18]

Hodgkin came to the conclusion that there was 'hardly sufficient evidence' to convict the eunuch of taking such vengeance on the Empress.[19]

Gregorovius had grave doubts about the statements of the Latin chroniclers that the Lombards had been summoned into Italy by Narses. Nevertheless, even he had Narses dying at tragic variance with himself, and with his past. While it might still be impossible to free him of all suspicion, serious historians have begun to question the evidence of the Saga itself when it came to actually convicting Narses of treason. In other words, this legendary tale itself has been put on trial.

Its Evidence

A.A. Vasiliev considered the accusations and allegations to be unfounded as he stated that Narses died before he had time to commit treason. Gregorovius did not think it probable that after his dismissal he could have lived quietly in retirement, with all his reputed treasures, for six years (i.e. until 573) and therefore placed his death in 567.[20]

Hodgkin found it 'strange. . .though not impossible', that before sending so treacherous a message he went south, all the way to Naples. This, in effect, was increasing the distance and toil for his messengers, and at the same time decreasing his own chances of being saved by the invaders.[21] (This was in reference to the 'evidence' presented by the *Liber Pontificalis*.)

Dunlap, evidently following the lead of Hodgkin, commented that if Narses had wanted to betray Italy, to avoid detection and punishment he would have awaited the arrival of the Lombards in the north. There he would have had their protection as soon as possible; but the *Liber Pontificalis*, and Paul the Deacon, had him deliberately going to Naples before sending his embassy to Pannonia. To Dunlap, the introduction of this element of improbability brought the whole story into doubt.[22]

Other historians, remarking on the distance of Naples from the point of the invasion, observed that the Saga's legendary character was too obvious. Besides, many of the Lombards had already been in Italy, fighting under Narses, and needed no gifts of fruits to be informed as to the country's fertility.

Pasquale Villari stated an obvious objection, that if these supposed gifts had been sent all the way from Campania up to Pannonia 'one may easily imagine in what condition they arrived'. He felt that the Lombards had been moved to cross the Alps by stronger motives than any one man's capricious spite.[23]

Yet the invasion did not start before the early spring of 568. Therefore, the otherwise perishable gifts of fruit could have been dispatched during the late autumn, or even the winter months of 567–68. Interestingly enough, some 500 years later, Norman adventurers would send fruits from Salerno to their brethren all the way back in Normandy in order to show that 'Sicily' was a paradise.[24]

Besides their knowledge of its agricultural wealth, the Lombards may have also been well aware of the weakness of Italy and not only Italy, but the Empire of Justin II as a whole. Furthermore, the Lombards need only to have heard of Narses' recall, knowing him to be the only general capable of resisting them, to take advantage of the confusion attending his retirement to seize the opportunity of returning to Italy.

William Plate, drawing on the Saga, went so far as to frame the hypothesis that Narses issued his invitation, not with any treasonable intent, but only as a strategem to recover his former position of power. As such, it ran as follows: Narses' disposition was not only one of unlimited ambition, but was coupled with an 'irritable and resentful temper which is peculiar to women and eunuchs.' [sic] The bitter taunt of the woman, Sophia, could not but provoke the ill-temper of the eunuch. Thus, Narses invited the Lombards, not with the intention that they conquer Italy, but to force Justin to place him in command of the army again, as he was the only one who could check these barbarians. It is not quite clear whether he would have offered his services to the new emperor, or merely waited, hoping to be begged to repel the invaders. For Plate, his death alone prevented his using the Lombards as mere pawns in his scheme to triumph over his enemies, and gain ample revenge for the insults he had endured.[25]

Somewhat similar speculations based on the evidence of the Saga had been made by Gibbon. In his opinion, the Lombards might have failed in their invasion if they had had Narses as the antagonist. And the Lombard veterans who fought under him in the Gothic victory would have reluctantly encountered an enemy they both dreaded and esteemed. Gibbon also felt that Narses' death, even at an extremely old age, was unseasonable and premature.[26] Acceptance of the Saga seems to be implied by the statement 'since his genius alone could have repaired the last and fatal error of his life'.[27]

Such armchair speculations seem to be based on the logic that if Narses had faced his former allies in battle, with his knowledge of the barbarian mind, he would have continued his mastery over them. The psychology of the tribal warriors was all the same, having remained unaltered since the time of Tacitus; with their lack of discipline, or tactical ability, they relied almost solely on their time-worn onsets against the foe.

Narses, as a genius of the deadly science of war, would have continued his successful meld of the strategic offensive with the tactical defensive, as at Taginae and Capua. Assuming that he had not entirely neglected the defences of Italy, as often charged, his Imperial troops would also have had a superiority in armament. Finally, even to Gibbon, the Lombards barely qualified as barbarians; he referred to them at the time of their dismissal by Narses (in 552) as 'valiant savages'.[28]

One final test of plausability to the 'evidence' or suppositions, of the Saga is made by Dunlap. He questions if it was actually known that some temporary ill-feeling had existed between the empress and the eunuch.[29]

There could not have been any permanent hostility between the two, since Sophia was present at Narses' burial.[30] The Liber Pontificalis, and Paul the Deacon, stated that after dying in Rome, his body was sent back to Constantinople.

The contemporary John of Ephesus (507–86) in his Ecclesiastic History (571–85), avowed that Narses was buried in a splendid monastery, built for himself, in Bithynia, in the presence of the Emperor and the Empress.

Perhaps this is a final piece of evidence that not even Justin, not to mention Sophia, had cause to resent his 'Treachery.'

> 'So vanishes from history the mysterious figure of the great Eunuch-general.'[31]

Appendix 1

Some Dimensions for the Hippodrome in Constantinople

The overall length of the track at the Hippodrome, 320 yards, has been calculated by the distances between these monuments.

From the northeast end to the Obelisk	300 paces
From the Obelisk to the Column of Delphi	47 paces
From the Column of Delphi to the Brazen Column	47 paces
From the Brazen Column to the southwest end	245 paces
	639 paces or cubits

A cubit was a measurement from the elbow to the tips of the fingers – *c.*18 inches. Thus two paces, or cubits, were equal to a yard, and 639 paces would equal *c.*320 yards.

The overall width of the track was 158 paces or *c.*79 yards.

The actual length of the whole structure, including seating tiers, has been calculated at between 550 and 600 yards.

Appendix 2

The Ostrogothic Kings in Italy (493–553)

Theodoric the Great	493–526
Athalaric	526–534
Theodahad (Theodatus)	534–536
Witigis (Vitigis)	536–540
Ildibad	540–541
Eraric	541
Baduila (Totila)	541–552
Teias	552–553(?)

Appendix 3

The Eastern Roman Military System

The armies of Rome had conquered her Empire through stern discipline and drill. The victories of the East Roman Empire were won by studied strategy and generalship. In other words, by a system that was Greek rather than Latin; here alone in Europe were the principles of strategy and tactics actually studied.

Its army, although small in numbers, was highly trained and excellently equipped. The estimated total strength under Justinian was only some 150,000 men, although the extent of the frontiers it was expected to defend may have called for an army of *c.*645,000. The largest force sent out on a single campaign was rarely more than 35,000. The army that Narses was to lead against Totila could have been such a force. Naval power was never well developed, any more than it had been by Republican or Imperial Rome.

Yet in the final analysis, the secret of the military and political strength of the Eastern Empire lay largely in its continued economic prosperity.

Its Mercenary Character

Even before the time of Justinian the old legionary system had ceased to exist. The disappearance of the ancient city-state and its citizens extinguished the type of man who made a good legionary soldier. It is an obscure and difficult subject to determine the various stages after the legion that evolved into the mercenary armies of Justinian. The comitatus of Narses himself were mercenaries of the wilder barbarians from the borderlands of the Empire, owing loyalty only to him. These private military guards, or retainers, had a curiously complex origin.

Both in East Roman, and on into Byzantine times, the army was to be characterized by an increasing prevalence of barbarian elements, particularly Germans and Illyrians. From the fourth century on, they had been rising to officer rank. The first phase of military significance that can be termed Greek, or 'Byzantine', was when the army was divided into two commands.

The first was a static force, settled part-time in each region; the basic unit was the 'numerus': 200–400 men under a tribune. This was a smaller unit than in the legions, suitable for times when garrisons were needed in many places. A town would have had one or two numeri. The second command was a mobile field force, mercenary in character. It was of two types: a light cavalry (foederati) and a heavy cavalry (cataphracti).

Cavalry had long been gaining steadily in importance, having been adapted to the Sassanid warfare. The best soldiers came from Illyria, Thrace and Isauria. Barbarian mercenaries included Antae, Arabs from Syria, Moors from Africa, the Huns, Heruls and Lombards. These served as cavalry scouts, being less reliable than the regular cavalry. There were also the private guards, regiments modelled on the comitatus of the Northern Kings.

The Bucelarii

The foederati, or barbarian auxiliaries, as the personal followers of their own chiefs, left behind a bad system of recruiting that had spread to the whole army. It was the individual generals, as 'condottiere' and not the Imperial government who not only collected, but also supported the soldiers. There were now no regiments, or legions, with their own names; each corps was called after its commander. Collectively they were known as the bucelarii. This word may be derived from 'buccella', a biscuit, or a better sort of a baked bread than that served to the common foot soldiers. Then again, it may have referred to the little 'bits' drawn from the commanders.

Justinian made this system worse by not entrusting any of his generals, before Narses, with much money or power. The result was discontent, and even mutinies. In a certain sense this has been seen as a decline of the Empire, the pay and equipment of its soldiers being left to their commanding officers. Generally the commissariat was badly arranged with the pay in arrears, and even the treasury officials ('logothetae') under various pretexts, sought to cheat the troops. Narses, as an adviser to Justinian, recognized this dangerous side.

In effect, everything depended on the commander-in-chief of a campaign; victories were due to the military genius of a great general e.g. Belisarius or Narses. The Empire was fortunate in having great and glorious commanders such as these two, capable of defending it with brain as well as sword. Until Belisarius appeared, and brought in a new military system, emperors had relied almost exclusively on negotiation and diplomacy in conducting foreign affairs.

The Comitatus

The Greek tyrants had armed bodyguards; a Roman oligarch of the late Republic was surrounded by a household of gladiators, and there were 'clients' surrounding Roman patricians. Under Diocletian's re-organization, the comitatus became the retinue of the Emperor himself when the commander-in-chief of the field army during a major campaign. This system was copied from the Roman Empire by the Northern barbarian kings.

Belisarius copied it back in a new form. He raised his comitatus into a corps of considerable size, from 1,500 men after Daras, to having as many as 7,000. Narses was to have only 400. These personal retainers were recruited from all sources, but barbarians such as Goths, Heruls and Huns came to prevail as a general rule. As long-term professional soldiers, they took an oath of allegiance to their employer.

This was to be a dangerous feature of the system which was, in a sense, illegal. Licences, however, were issued in approved cases to permit their enrollment. Ultimately not only generals, but military officers of subordinate rank, Praetorian Prefects and other civil officials, even wealthy private persons, came to possess them. From Egyptian papyri it is known that large land owners in Egypt employed them.

One of the indirect implications of the system was that they became almost too great a force for a subject of the Empire to possess and control, constituting a royal household in itself. Although the law required an oath of allegiance to the emperor, this was too frail a guarantee. Its members were not Imperial soldiers, but a private staff engaged and paid by their employer, taking orders from no one else. Finally they were in most cases not even subjects of the Empire; many barbarians were hired or recruited, military excellence being the sole qualification.

The comitatus differed from the foederati in that its members had a standard equipment of full body armour and weapons. This consisted of close-fitting steel helmets and shirts of mail, greaves to the knees, round shields worn on the left shoulder (worked with a strap, not a handle), long lances or spears, broad swords, daggers and, at the saddle-bow, a stronger bow than any then in use. All of this represented Belisarius's inspired invention, or at least evolution, of the Cataphracti – an armoured rider mounted on an armoured horse.

The Cataphracti

Belisarius did not attempt to revive the old legionary foot-soldier, who had been armed in cuirass mail coat, helmet and greaves and equipped with lance, sword, bow and arrow. Instead he took the typical first-class fighting man of his own time, the armoured cavalry man who was equipped with spear and sword, plus the bow and quiver. In their equipment the cataphracti were close to that of the Persians, and even closer to the medieval knight.

A standard training was given in the use of these weapons and also in how to be a tactical improviser. These specially picked and trained troops became the core, as the legion had once been, around which to assemble all the other elements of the East Roman military sevices.

There had been an evolution over the centuries for Belisarius to have the elements on hand for his 'invention'. Ironically, he is said to have lost the licence to maintain his own comitatus after his recall from Italy in 549. In a sense the cataphracti had been known since the time of Hadrian (AD 117–38) as one unit of armoured lancers called the 'clibanarii' ('cuirassiers'). This was a word used of those, possibly of Persian origins, recruited in the Eastern dependencies.

In fact, the Parthians had had heavy armoured cavalry divided into 'clibanarii', armed with heavy lances, and the 'cataphractii', who were archers. They were mounted on the armoured 'great' Nesaean horses from the Zagros mountains (the wide Plain of Nysa in Media).

From the second century onwards, cavalry began to replace the infantry. Weapons were to change from swords and javelins to the bow and lance; there was the use of body armour, and the introduction of composite and flexible army corps. In the third century only the smallest part of the Roman army was infantry, which was heavily equipped, more noted for its solidity than mobility.

The cavalry units, both mounted archers and armoured lancers, were introduced into the Greco-Roman world by the Parthians, and the Sarmatic tribes coming into contact with it. As early as 55 BC the Parthians had defeated Crassus at Carrhae. Archers of Moorish or Syrian recruitment were common in the auxiliary arms.

In the age of Belisarius and Narses the cataphracti were generally unbeatable on the field of battle, but in other ways were unsatisfactory. They were expensive, cruel, overbearing, even mutinous and were owned by their commanding general.

The cataphracti therefore came to represent a 'chef d'oeuver' of Greek military technique, but not a further stage in its native development. They were, after all, an adaptation from the Persian enemy.

The Horse in Battle

As for the prime mover of these mobile cavalry arms, the use of horses in warfare can be divided into three periods or stages:

1. As used by charioteers, i.e. they were driven rather than ridden: first before two-horse cars, then four horses and scythed chariots.
2. Ridden bareback by a mounted warrior, who had to cling to the steed by the pressure of his knees. Primarily, he was a mobile bowman and a hurler of javelins; if he tried using a sword, and missed his target, he would wind up on the ground. A spear had to be wielded at the end of the arm, the blow delivered with the strength of his shoulders and biceps.
3. The rider was equipped with saddle and stirrups, which replaced human energy with the power of the animal, increasing the warrior's ability to damage the enemy. This was, it is thought, a Chinese invention; the rudimentary idea had appeared in India in the late second century BC. Hindu cavalrymen were using them in the first century BC. These 'stirrups' fitted about the big toe of a bare-footed rider. By *c.*AD 300 the Chinese had adapted it to take a whole booted foot. Its introduction to the West was most likely by way of the tribes north of the Black Sea. It immediately made possible the tactic of mounted shock combat.

There is no literary evidence that the Greeks, Romans or Franks used the horseshoe. If they did, there should at least be the archaeological evidence.

Besides the technological break-through of the stirrup, there were two other developments that increased the effectiveness of the mounted warrior. First of all was the saddle, replacing horse-blankets and riding cushions. In the West its earliest use was by the second century AD, usually appearing on heavier horses. The frame, or 'tree' saddle evolved later.

The second was nothing less than the development of a new type of mount, the heavy horse, the ancestor of the medieval destrier. The common derivation of 'dextrarius' is thought to come from the assumption that the right hand held the reins to lead the horse. The use of the cataphracti themselves was made possible by such a breed of great horse; such a beast was able to carry a heavily armed rider, and could even be armoured itself. The Romans, together with the Moors, Gauls, Germans, and the later invaders of the West, had only light cavalry.

This heavy cavalry mount is said to have been developed in the rich grasslands of Mesopotamia, and its use learnt from the Parthians. Large areas of lush meadow were comparatively rare in the Eastern Empire; there were large Imperial estates in the upper Halys around Caesarea (in Cappadocia) where horses had been bred in earlier times for the Great King of Persia. Justinian had even attempted legislation to keep such possible stud farms for his own cavalry from private encroachment.

The importation of such a 'super' steed was to revolutionize European warfare, eventually leading to the development of the feudal army. However, this is a subject that remains obscure through a comparative lack of investigation; the use of cavalry in these early Christian centuries demands more careful study than it has received.

It is known that the Hunnish and Persian horse-archer, and then the Gothic lancer, combined the value of mobile fire-power with that of mobile shock-power. In conclusion, the knightly array of the Carolingians could be said to have been derived from the cataphracti, 'invented' by Belisarius, and used with deadly effect by Narses.

The Hippo-toxotai

One further cavalry arm to which both Belisarius and Narses could ascribe their astonishing successes was the mounted bow-men, or the hippo-toxotai. The main body of Narses' army was to consist of such cavalry 'cuirassiers' armed with the bow and arrow, his horse archers charged an often demoralized foe shooting arrows with a deadly aim, much as the cuirassiers of Louis XIV charged, shooting pistols. Or, to bring the simile on up into the late nineteenth century, they were the 'Mounted Rifles' of the Empire.

Appendix 4

The Treasure of Narses

> 'Narses indeed returned from Campania to Rome and th ere not long afterwards departed from this life, and his body, placed in a leaded casket, was carried with all his riches to Constantinople.'[1]

Even after his death, Narses continued to give rise to legends; now, to one of the oldest and most fabulous of all – that of buried treasure.

Already in the Saga there had been various references to his great wealth. To the impoverished Italians, the Imperial system of taxation had seemed oppressive, and apparently there arose a widespread feeling that Narses had enriched himself by such relentless extortions. Thus the popular tales of his avarice and accumulated wealth; such ideas may have prompted the complaints of the Romans to Justin.

The short chronicle of Agnellus which reported that Narses lived in the Palatine Palace at Rome up until his death, also added that he had removed its statues. 'Narsis' is also said to have apparently removed the statues from the Capitoline temple in 571.'[2] These were presumably part of the treasures he is said to have dragged off as plunder from all over Italy. Shortly after his death legends began to spout about the amassed treasure of Narses.

Dunlap traced the initial belief that he was extremely wealthy back to the heavy taxes he had levied upon the whole province for the rehabilitation of its desolated regions. His construction and renovation of churches, together with the public works from these revenues, and his very generosity itself to the destitute, only added conviction to this belief.

It was conceeded by Dunlap that the Eunuch-Exarch possessed a considerable amount of the 'world's goods', but he maintained that it would have been strange if a governor of a province the size of Italy during Justinians's time had not. As the bulk of this wealth was derived from Italian sources, it needed but little imagination on the part of the credulous natives to develop Narses' possessions into a fabulous treasure.[3]

The original version of the legend that this treasure became a buried one is by the contemporary Gregory of Tours (538–94) in the Fifth Book of his ten-book *Historia Francorum* (The History of the Franks). Some two centuries later, much as he had done with the Saga, Paul the Deacon retold the tale of the hidden treasure of Narses; but following Gregory closely as to details and even language. Between the two, the story was related as follows:

Narses, as the 'duke' or 'patrician' of Italy, owned a great house in a 'certain city' (otherwise unspecified). He went there with his great treasures, and secretly digging out a very large cistern within the house, deposited 'many thousand centenaria' of gold and silver. Then, much as a pirate captain, he put to death on the spot all those who knew of its location.

The buried private fortune of Narses was entrusted to a solitary old man, from whom an oath of secrecy was exacted. This wealth was still hidden beneath the ground at the death of Narses, in 568, according to Gregory's English translator, O.M. Dalton.

This old guardian, seeing the unceasing charities of the emperor, went to the 'Caesar' Tiberius [sic]. This could imply a lapse of time of from six to ten years, depending on whether Tiberius was addressed as 'Caesar', or Emperor, as early as the year 574, or not until 578. No matter the actual year, the old man offered to reveal his great secret to the ruler, but only after holding out for a promise of reward. Tiberius' interest aroused, he was told to continue as he would surely gain if his story showed any promise of profit.

It was then explained by the old guardian that he held the concealed treasure of Narses, but being near the end of his days, he could no longer keep it hidden. Delighted with this revelation, Tiberius had his servants follow the old one to the place of concealment.[4]

When the cistern was opened and entered into, so much gold and silver was found inside, that it took many long days to empty it out by carrying away the contents.[5]

Gregory of Tours has been highly praised as a historian, being referred to as almost the sole one of the Merovingian period, just as the Ravenna educated Fortunatus was its poet. His apparent naivete was said to be deceiving as it was a matter of deliberate art. Therefore, to M Christian Pfister, a professor at the Sorbonne, Gregory had a real gift for story-telling, and was justly called 'the barbarian Herodotus'.[6]

Be that as it may, between him and Paul the Deacon, 'the humbler Herodotus', questions are raised regarding the final Estate of Narses. For example, was the 'certain city' where he had his house, with the secret cistern, in Italy, or in a suburb of Constantinople? (Under Roman law, a treasure trove was the property of the owner of the land on which it was found.) Did Narses hide away all of his riches before his death, or were some of them returned with his body? Finally, just how long after his death did the old guardian wait until revealing the existence of the treasure of Narses to Tiberius?

A possible clue as to the location of the 'great house', with its cistern full of gold and silver, may be contained in a reference made by A.G. Paspates to 'the house of Narses'. He told how, over two centuries after Narses' death, the Emperor Theophilus (829–42) had imprisoned a Persian named Theophobos, and when the Persians made inquiries, had the prisoner executed.

Then, Theophilus himself died miserably of dysentery, and his body was borne to the Church of the Holy Apostles. Meanwhile, the body of Theophobos had apparently been recovered by his countrymen, and was secretly conveyed through the Bucoleon Harbour, within the palace complex, over to the neighborhood of the house of Narses. It was deposited in a place that was to be called the Theophobeia.

Paspates noted that his own source, Byzantios, placed a monastery of the Theophobeia on the Asiatic shore of the Bosphorus in a village then called Kuzghuntzúk.[7] This is at present known as Kuzguncuk, a northern sector of Usküdar (Scutari) across from Constantinople (Istanbul). Thus there is at least this much evidence as to the neighborhood of the so-called house of Narses.

Of course, there is no certainty that this 'house of Narses' was anything more than another stretch of the popular imagination developing more legends, and again there is no indication as to just which Narses was meant. There is always the chance of confusion with the Narses who had assisted at the coronation of Justin II and was the general of Tiberius and Maurice. In addition, the name, as initially stated , was not an uncommon one, at least not in the eastern world.

Dunlap, for one, took issue with the whole 'picturesque tale', and its disregard for all considerations of time and place. He characterized the narrative as being typical of wonder-tales and stated that even to Gregory himself, it was plainly nothing more. Besides going into detail as to the origins of the belief in a 'fabulous treasure' of Narses, Dunlap also defended him against the charge of being avaricious. To begin with, there was no suggestion of avarice in his earlier life and career. In fact, more than once, his generosity towards his soldiers (e.g. the barbarian mercenaries) and the more unfortunate of his Italian subjects had been mentioned. From this, Dunlap came to the conclusion that, by all accounts, it was power rather than wealth that had been the aim of Narses' ambition.[8]

Notes and References

References are abbreviated or referred to by author only after the first full citation. Abbreviations used for frequently cited works:

Bury, *Hist. Later Rom. Empire*	(From the Deaths of Theodosius I – Justinian)
C.M.H.	*Cambridge Medieval History*
S.H. [Secret History]	*The Anecdota*
TLCL	*The Loeb Classical Library.*

Part I. The Origins and Early Career of Narses the Eunuch

Chapter I. The Background of Narses

1. Procopius, *History Of The Wars I.* xv.31. TLCL Vol.I p.139
2. Pauly and Wossowa, *Real-Encyclopädie der Classischen Altertumswissenschaft*
3. Procopius, I.xii 21. p.101 (cf. Iliad xxiv.348; Odyssey x.279)
4. Procopius, I.xv.32 Vol.I p.139
5. Procopius, S.H. xxiv. 16 TLCL Vol.VI p.285
6. Runciman, *Byzantine Civilisation.* p.181
7. Lang, *Armenia Cradle of Civilization.* p.172
8. Runciman, p.181
9. Bury, *Hist. Later Rom. Empire.* Vol.II (footnote 1, p.346)
10. Runciman, p.181
11. R.H.C. Davis, *A History Of Medieval Europe From Constantine to Saint Louis.* p.66
12. H.W. Haussig, places Tauresium near Bederina (Uskub), *A History of Byzantine Civilization.* p.115
13. Procopius, S.H. vi. 27–8 Vol.VI p.77
14. Ibid., S.H. vi. 11 Vol.VI p.71 Robert Browning cautions not to 'take too seriously' this 'tale' of Procopius. *Justinian & Theodora.* p.38 (1971)
15. Ibid., vi. 16 Vol.VI p.73
16. C.M.H. Vol.II Chapter I. p.2
17. Bury, *Hist. Later Rom. Empire.* Vol.II p.32
18. Procopius, S.H. xvii. 5–6 Vol.VI p.199 (see also Buildings I. ix.3. TLCL Vol.VII pp. 75 & 77)
19. Gibbon, *The History of the Decline and Fall of the Roman Empire.* Ch. XL
20. Haussig labels Justinian, 'half monk, half pagan Emperor'; considering him 'Similar in many respects to Philip II of Spain'. A Hist. of Byz. Civilization. p.115

21. Stein, *Histoire Du Bas-Empire*. Tome Second. De le disparition de l'Empire d'Occident a la mort de Justinien (476–565) p.356
22. Pernice, Article in *Enciclopedia Italiana*. Vol.XXIV p.275 (1934)
23. Thomas Hodgkin, Article on Narses in *Encyclopaedia Brittanica*. 11th edition Vol.XIX. p.241 (1911).
24. Hodgkin, *Italy and her Invaders*. Vol.IV p.273
25. *Smith's Dictionary of Greek & Roman Biography & Mythology*. Vol.II p.1139
26. Finley, *A History of Greece*. Vol.I p.211.
27. Graves, *Count Belisarius* (Penguin) pp.126–7 (For Goronwy-Eugenius, see pp.43–5)
28. Vandercook, *Empress Of The Dusk*. p.174
29. Gibbon, Ch. XLIII
30. Kraus, *Theodora The Circus Empress*. p.111
31. Agathias, cited by F.M. Crawford, *The Rulers Of The South*. Vol.II pp.35–36
32. Gibbon, Ch.XLIII
33. Dunlap p.285 (The other 'Prominent Grand Chamberlains' were Eusebius, Eutherius and Eutropius.)
34. Diehl, C.M.H. Vol.II pp.11–12
35. Oman, *The Dark Ages*. p.103
36. *Smith's Dictionary*. Vol.II p.1141
37. Bradshaw, *The Bearkeeper's Daughter*. p.33
38. Baker, *Justinian*. pp.178–79
39. This suggestion was made by Richard Bryant, Academic Director of Alan Sutton's, during the editing of this book. He pointed out that other possible identifications have included Julianus Argentarius and the Pretorian Prefect of Italy, and that Dr Andreeseu Tredgold felt that the identification with Narses was unlikely, as he was not actually in Italy at the time the mosaic was produced. (pers. com.).
40. Evagrius, *Ecclesiastical History*. Book IV Ch.XXIV pp.214–15 (1844)
41. Paul the Deacon, Book II Ch.III p.56 (Foulke)
42. Dunlap, p.190
43. Ibid., p.190
44. Ibid., p.189–90
45. A.H.M. Jones, *The Later Roman Empire 284–602*. Vol.II pp.568–69
46. Ibid., Vol.III Note 13 p.163
47. J.S. Reid, C.M.H. Vol.I Ch.II p.29
48. J.B. Bury, *The Imperial Administrative System in the Ninth Century*. p.25
49. Dunlap, p.245
50. Ibid., p.284
51. Wallace-Hadrill, *The Barbarian West* 400–1000. p.41

Chapter II. The New Rome and the Rise of the Greens and Blues

1. H.M. Gwatkin, *The Cambridge Medieval History*. Vol.I, Ch.1 p.18
2. It has to be added that, as the city was semi-rural between the Walls of

Constantine and Theodosius, an estimate of no more than 225,000 has been made. J.G. Russell even suggests that under Justinian the population of the city proper was only 160,000. Norman J.G. Pounds, *An Historical Geography of Europe 450 BC–AD 1330*. pp.194–95 (and Note 43 p.446)

3. Gibbon, Ch.XL
4. Suetonius states that Domitian (89–96) tried adding two more colours – Purple and Gold
5. Virgil (70–19 B.C.) had used a similar simile for the unleasing of warfare: 'even as when from the barriers the chariots stream forth. . . .' Georgics Book I 512ff
6. Gibbon, (footnote 3) Ch.XL
7. Ostrogorsky, *History of the Byzantine State*. p.67 (footnote 1: 'This is the view of [G.] Manojilovic, [Le] Peuple de Constantinople) Ibid.
8. Gibbon Ch.XL
9. Procopius, S.H. vii. 8–14 TLCL Vol.VI. pp.79 & 81
10. Gibbon, Chap. XL.

Chapter III. 'Nika'

1. Procopius, *Hist. Of The Wars*. I xxiv.10. Vol.I p.223 and footnote 1)
2. Gibbon, Ch.XL
3. Bury, *Hist. Later Rom. Empire*. Vol.II. p.74 (added an Appendix 'A Scene In The Hippodrome', pp.71–74)
4. Gibbon, Ch.XL (see footnote on Theophanes)
5. The 'Roman' Ides fell on the 15 March, May, July and October; on the 13th of the rest of the months
6. Fletcher Pratt, *The Battles That Changed History*. pp.65–67.
7. Bury, *Hist. Later Rom. Empire*. Vol.II. footnote 2 p.41
8. Procopius, I.xxiv.18. Vol.I. p.225
9. The eunuch body-guard under Narses would be loyal to Justinian
10. Procopius, Buildings I.ii.14. Vol.VII p.37
11. Procopius, I.xxiv.19. Vol.I p.227
12. Ibid., I.xxiv.24. Vol.I p.227
13. H.St.L.B.Moss, *The Birth Of The Middle Ages*. 395–814. p.84
14. Procopius, I.xxiv.33–38 Vol.I pp.231 & 233.
15. Hodgkin, Vol.IV. p.570
16. Browning, *Justinian And Theodora*. p.72 (1987 edn.)
17. Procopius (more than 30,000 dead) was not only contemporary, but being on the staff of Belisarius, was most likely on, or near, the scene; as was John Lydus (491–565) (50,000 dead). Zachariah of Mitylene (80,000 dead) was also a contemporary, dying after 536. Otherwise, Theophanes 'The Confessor' (35,000 dead) wrote between 811–15 and Johannes Zonarus (40,000 dead), at the end of the eleventh and the early twelfth century
18. Ostrogorsky, *History of the Byzantine State*. p.73
19. Jack Lindsay, *Byzantium into Europe*. pp.121–22

20. Procopius, IV.ix.15. Vol.II. p.283. (This was not an actual 'triumph', but only a triumphal celebration of his inauguration as consul.) Ibid., footnote 2 p.283

Chapter IV. The First Command of Narses

1. Gibbon, Ch. XLI
2. Procopius, VI.xiii. 16 TLCL Vol.III. pp.401 & 403
3. Procopius, VI.xvi. 4 Vol.IV pp.3 & 5
4. Ibid., VI.xvi. 5 Vol.IV p.5
5. Ibid., VI.xvi. 6–13 Vol.IV pp.5 & 7
6. Ibid., VI.xvii.24 Vol.IV p.19
7. Ibid., VI.xviii.3 Vol.IV p.19
8. Robert Browning observes: 'Henceforward subordinate commanders could play off Narses and Belisarius against one another.' *Justinian and Theodora*. p.111 (1987 edn.)
9. Procopius, VI.xix.13 Vol.IV p.31
10. Ibid., VI.xix.21 Vol.IV pp.33 & 35
11. Ibid., VI.xviii.28 Vol.IV p.27
12. Ibid., VI.xxi.39 Vol.IV p.55
13. Ibid., VI.xxii.4–5 Vol.IV p.57

Chapter V. After the Recall

1. Dunlap, *The Office of the Grand Chamberlain*. p.287
2. Procopius, I.xxv.26. TLCL Vol.I p.247
3. Ibid., I.xxv.30. Vol.I p.249
4. Ibid., I.xxv.42–43 Vol.I pp.251 & 53
5. Ibid., II.xxx.54 Vol.I p.555 & 57
6. Ibid., II.xxiii.20 Vol.I p.473
7. Ibid., II.xxiii.20 Vol.I p.473
8. Procopius, S.H.IV.1. TLCL Vol.VI p.43
9. Ultimately this pandemic moved across to the British Isles to be known in England as the Plague of Cadwalader's Time. Philip Ziegler, *The Black Death*. p.25
10. Procopius, VII.xiii.23. Vol.IV. p.261 cf II.xix.15. Vol.I p.423
11. Procopius, VII.xiv.9–11. Vol.IV. p.265
12. Ibid., VII.xiv.18–20 Vol.IV pp.267 & 69
13. Ibid., VII.xiv.32–34 Vol.IV pp.273 & 75
14. Ibid., VII.xiv.36 Vol.IV p.275
15. Cited by Diehl, C.M.H. Vol.II Ch.II p.50
16. Hodgkin, Vol.IV. p.581
17. Gibbon commented on its further history: 'which has filled more volumes than it deserves lines' Ch.XLVII
18. Procopius, VII.xxxi.12. Vol.IV p.417

19. Sergius having married a granddaughter of Antonina. Bury, *Hist. Later Rom. Empire*. Vol.II footnote 3 p.56
20. Procopius, IV.xxviii.43. Vol.II. p.457
21. Procopius, VII.xxxi.13–15. Vol.IV. p.419
22. Ibid., VII.xxxii. 3–4 Vol.IV. p.421
23. Ibid., VII.xxxii. 34–35 Vol.IV p.431
24. Ibid., VII.xxxii. 42–43 Vol.IV p.433
25. Procopius, S.H.IV. 7–12 Vol.VI p.45
26. Procopius, VII.xxxii. 46 Vol.IV p.435

Part II. The Victories of Narses

Chapter VI. The Supreme Command of Narses

1. Gibbon, Ch.XLIII
2. Procopius explains: 'It was impossible for me, through fear of the Empress, to reveal the truth of what took place.' S.H.xvi.3 TLCL Vol.VI p.189
3. Ibid., S.H.xvi.1–5 Vol.VI pp.189 & 191 (and footnote 1 p.191)
4. Procopius, I.xix.35–37. Vol.I. pp.187 & 89
5. Gibbon actually refers to – 'the arms of the eunuch Narses' – that 'wasted the third capital of the Roman world.' Ch.XLVII
6. Procopius, VII.xxxix.7. Vol.V p.31
7. Ibid., VII.xl.14–17 Vol.V pp.43 & 45 (Melita was most likely Malta)
8. Ibid., VII.xl.9 Vol.V p.41
9. G.P. Baker, Justinian. p.300
10. Procopius, VIII.xxi.8 Vol.V p.273
11. Ibid., VIII.xxi.10–16 Vol.V pp.273 & 75
12. W.G. Holmes, *The Age of Justinian and Theodora*. Vol.II note, p.648
13. H.D. Sedgwick, *A Short History of Italy (476–1900)*. p.22
14. Procopius, VIII. xxvi. 17 Vol.V p.333
15. Hodgkin, Vol.IV p.625
16. Dunlap, p.288
17. White, *The Eighteen Christian Centuries*. p.127
18. John G. Sheppard, *The Fall of Rome*. p.307
19. Procopius, VIII.xxvi. 8–9 Vol.V p.329
20. B.H. Liddell Hart, *The Strategy of Indirect Approach*. p.64
21. Procopius, VII.xl.35. Vol.V p.49
22. Lewis, *Naval Power and Trade in the Mediterranean*. p.25
23. Ibid.
24. Procopius, VIII.xxiii.30–31. Vol.V p.297
25. Ibid., VIII.xxiii.32 Vol.V p.297
26. Lewis, p.25.

Chapter VII. The Italian Expeditionary Force

1. G.P. Baker, *Justinian*. p.298
2. Procopius, VIII. xxvi.12 TLCL Vol.V p.331
3. Ibid., VIII. xxvi.13 Vol.V p.331
4. Ibid., VIII. xxvi.5 Vol.V p.327
5. Brig-Gen. G.F. Young, *East And West Through Fifteen Centuries*. Vol.II Note 1 p.299
6. Procopius, VIII. xxvi.24 Vol.V p.337
7. Ibid., VIII. xxvi.25 Vol.V p.337
8. Ibid., VIII. xxviii.1 Vol.V p.349
9. Ibid., VIII. xxviii.2 Vol.V p.347
10. Ibid., VIII. xxviii.2–4 Vol.V p.347
11. Ibid., VIII. xxviii.4 Vol.V pp.347 & 49
12. Procopius, Index Vol.V p.431
13. Procopius, Buildings and General Index. Vol.VII p.480
14. Procopius, VIII.xxviii. 10 Vol.V p.349 & 51
15. Edward Hutton, *Cities Of Romagne, The Marches*. p.274
16. Augustus J.C. Hare, *Cities of Northern And Central Italy*. Vol.II p.432
17. Procopius, VI.xi 4–20 Vol.III pp.379–385. These 'gates' were at the southern (upper) end with a 'small gate' at the northern end, footnotes 1–3. p.383
18. Procopius, VIII.xxix.5 Vol.V p.353. H.B. Dewing added that Procopius – 'is far from the truth' – the 'Busta Gallica' [Gallic Pyres] of Livy V.xlviii were actually in Rome, footnote 1 p.353
19. Ibid. Dewing again qualifies Procopius by stating that Taginae is 'more properly' Tadinum and in modern times Gualdo Tadino, footnote 1 p.353
20. Hodgkin, Vol.IV pp.710–13
21. Ibid., Vol.IV p.672
22. Procopius, VIII.xxviii 13 Vol.V p.351
23. Bury, *Hist. Later Rom. Empire*. Vol.II pp.288–89
24. Ibid., Vol.II p.289
25. Procopius (VIII.xxix.5) may have been referring to the siege of Rome by the Gauls almost a century earlier still (390 B.C.)
26. Bury, *Hist. Later Rom. Empire*. Vol.II. pp.289–90
27. Hodgkin, Vol.IV p.692
28. Ibid., Vol.IV pp.726–28. Hodgkin also deals with the problem (or adds to the confusion) in his *Theodoric The Goth* (p.364) and by a 'Note F on the Site Of The Battle Of 552'. Vol.IV pp.643–45
29. Bury, *Hist. Later Rom. Empire*. Vol.II. p.290
30. Ibid.,Vol.II p.290
31. Procopius, VIII.xxix.3 Vol.V p.353
32. Brig-Gen.Young, Vol.II. p.301
33. See note 19. As names for the battle, 'Taginae', or even 'Gualdo Tadino' are geographically inaccurate.

34. Brig.Gen.Young, Vol.II. p.301
35. C.W.C. Oman, *A History Of The Art Of War*. p.33
36. Brig.Gen.Young, Vol.II p.301 (and note)
37. Bury, *Hist. Later Rom. Empire*. Vol.II. p.291 (Appendix, pp.288–91)

Chapter VIII. The Battle Of Taginae

1. John W. Barker, *Justinian & The Later Roman Empire*. p.164
2. P.N. Ure, *Justinian And His Age*. p.56
3. Procopius, VIII.xxix. 8 TLCL Vol.V. p.355
4. Ibid., VIII xxix.10 Vol.V p.355
5. Major-Gen. J.F.C. Fuller, *A Military History of the Western World*. Vol.I note 1 p.324
6. G.P. Baker, *Justinian*. p.308
7. Oman, *The Art Of War In The Middle Ages*. p.33
8. Ibid., pp.33–34
9. Gibbon, Ch. XLIII
10. Oman, *The Art Of War In The Middle Ages*. p.34
11. Procopius, VIII.xxxi. 3–4 Vol.V pp.369 & 71
12. Liddell Hart, *Strategy*. p.59
13. Hodgkin, Vol.IV pp.635–36
14. Liddell Hart, *Strategy*. p.70
15. Bury, *History Later Rom. Empire*. Vol.II p.268
16. Procopius, VIII.xxxii. 7 Vol.V p.377
17. Oman, *A History Of The Art Of War*. p.33
18. Procopius, VIII.xxxii.7 Vol.V p.379
19. Ibid., VIII.xxix.16–21 Vol.V pp.357 & 59
20. A. Jones, *The Art Of War In The Western World*. p.98
21. Procopius, VIII.xxix. 22–28 Vol.V pp.359 & 61
22. Ibid., VIII. xxxi. 8–9 Vol.V p.371
23. Ibid., VIII.xxxi. 14–16 Vol.V p.373
24. Ibid., VIII.xxxi. 18–20 Vol.V p.373 & 75
25. Hodgkin, *Theodoric the Goth*. p.366
26. Hodgkin, *Italy and her Invaders*. Vol.IV p.637
27. Procopius, VIII.xxxi. 21 Vol.V p.375
28. Ibid., VIII.xxxii. 4 Vol.V p.377
29. Bury, *Hist. Later Rom. Empire*. Vol.II p.266 (Yet according to Procopius, the 'entire army' was under orders to use no other weapon except the spear VIII.xxxii.7 Vol.V p.377)
30. G.F. Young, *East & West Through Fifteen Centuries*. Vol.II pp.301–2
31. Bury, *Hist. Later Rom. Empire*. Vol.II. p.266
32. Ibid., Vol.II footnote[1] p.266
33. Procopius, VIII.xxxii. 8 Vol.V p.379
34. Oman, *The Byzantine Empire*. p.95
35. Oman, *The Art Of War In The Middle Ages*. p.35

36. Hodgkin, *Theodoric the Goth.* p.320
37. Liddell Hart, *The Strategy Of Indirect Approach.* pp. 65–66
38. Bury, *Hist. Later Rom. Empire.* Vol.II p.267
39. Procopius, VIII.xxxii. 20–21. Vol.V p.383 Belisarius had earlier stated that it would be necessary 'to treat them as enemies'. Ibid., VII.xi. 7–10 Vol.IV p.239
40. Procopius, VIII.xxxii. 33–35 Vol.V pp.387 & 89
41. Procopius, VIII. xxxii. 22–28 Vol.V pp.383 & 85
42. Bury, *Hist. Later Rom. Empire.* Vol.II footnote[1] p.291
43. Ibid., Vol.II p.268
44. Procopius points out that Totila even saw to it that the famished Roman garrison was gradually nursed back to health. VII.viii.1–5 Vol.IV pp.213 & 15
45. Bury, *Hist. Later Rom. Empire.* Vol.II p.269
46. Hodgkin, Vol.IV pp.641–42
47. Henry Bradley, *The Story Of The Goths.* p.308
48. Oman, *The Dark Ages* 476–918. p.105
49. Bury, *Hist. Later Rom. Empire.* Vol.II p.269
50. Ibid., Vol.II p.267
51. Oman, *History Of The Art Of War.* p.35
52. J.F.C. Fuller, *A Military History of the Western World.* Vol.I p.458
53. Hodgkin, *Theodoric the Goth.* p.320 & 365
54. Procopius, VIII.xxxii. 11–12 Vol.V pp.379 & 81
55. Rodgers, *Naval Warfare Under Oars 4th to 16th Centuries.* p.22
56. Procopius, VIII. xxxiii.1. Vol.V p.389
57. Bury, *Hist. Later Rom. Empire.* Vol.II p.270. (See also Gibbon, Ch.XLIII and Procopius, VIII.xxxiii.2. Vol.V p.389)
58. Ibid., VIII.xxxiii 2 Vol.V pp.389 & 91
59. Paul the Deacon. *History Of The Langobards.* Book II Ch.I (Foulke) p.34
60. Gibbon, Ch.XLIII

Chapter IX. The Destruction of the Ostrogothic Nation

1. Ault, *Europe In The Middle Ages*, p.117
2. Procopius, VIII.xxxiii.6 Vol.V p.391
3. Hodgkin, Vol.IV p.647
4. Procopius, VIII.xxxiii.7 Vol.V p.391
5. Ibid., VIII.xxxiii.3–5 Vol.V p.391
6. Ibid., VIII.xxxiii.9–10 Vol.V p.391 & 93 Two 'Roman' deserters, Meligedius and Ulifus, were in command at Perugia; the former had to kill the latter before he could surrender the city. VIII.xxxiii.10–12 Vol.V p.393
7. Ibid., VIII.xxxiii.14 Vol.V p.395
8. Ibid., VIII.xxxiii.18–19 Vol.V p.395
9. Ibid., VIII.xxxiii.21–22 Vol.V p.397
10. Ibid., VIII.ix.1–3 Vol.V p.131
11. Emil Ludwig, *The Mediterranean.* pp.250–51
12. Procopius, VIII.xxxiii.26–27 Vol.V p.399

13. Gwatkin, C.M.H. Volume 1. p.1.
14. J.W. Thompson, *Economic & Social History Of The Middle Ages*. p.122
15. Procopius, VIII.xxxiv.10 Vol.V. p.401 Ragnaris had originally given up six Goths as hostages during his earlier negotiations. VIII.xxxiv 9 Vol.V p.401
16. Ibid., VIII.xxxiv.13–15 Vol.V p.403
17. Ibid., VII.vi.3 Vol.IV p.199
18. Ibid., V.xiv.2 Vol.III p.143
19. Ibid., VIII.xxxiv.19 Vol.V p.405
20. Ibid.
21. Procopius, S.H.v.5–7. Vol.VI p.57 Yet in the *History Of The Wars*, Belisarius is said to have threatened to call Herodian to account for his 'previous record' VII.xii.16 Vol.IV p.253
22. Procopius, VIII.xxxiv.16. Vol.V p.403. Besides taking Nepa (Nepi) a fortress in Tuscany, Narses' forces also captured the previously invested Portus. Petra Pertusa may have been another place on the Via Flaminia, but closer to Rome. See Bury, *Hist. Later Rom. Empire.* Vol.II footnote 2 p.272
23. Bury, *Hist. Later Rom. Empire.* Vol II footnote 1 p.272. [O.Korbs, Untersuchungen zur ostgotischen Geschichte I. 1913])
24. Procopius, VIII.xxxv.11 Vol.V p.411
25. Bury, *Hist. Later Rom. Empire.* Vol.II footnote 3 p.272
26. H.F. Clinton, *An Epitome of the Civil and Literary Chronology of Rome and Constantinople.* p.253
27. Procopius, VIII.xxxv.14. Vol.V. p.411
28. Gibbon, Ch.XLIII (in antiquity, milk was from ewes or goats)
29. Procopius, VIII.xxxv.19 Vol.V p.413
30. At least this is the conjecture of Hans Delbrück. (1848–1929) See Bury, *Hist. Later Rom. Empire.* Vol.II footnote 2 p.273
31. Hodgkin, Vol.IV p.655
32. Bury, *Hist. Later Rom. Empire.* Vol.II p.273
33. Procopius, VIII.xxxv.20 Vol.V p.413
34. Ibid., VIII.xxxv.22–26 Vol.V pp.413 & 415
35. Procopius simply states: 'Now the battle began early in the morning.' VIII.xxxv.22 Vol.V p.413
36. Ibid., VIII.xxxv.26–31 Vol.V p.415 & 417
37. Bury, *Hist. Later Rom. Empire.* Vol.II footnote 1 p.274
38. Procopius put forth: 'the two armies separated and passed the night on the battle field in their equipment.' VIII.xxxv.31 Vol.V p.417
39. Procopius, himself, avows: 'large numbers were being slain on both sides.' VIII.xxxv.32 Vol.V p.417
40. Ibid., VIII.xxxv.33–35 Vol.V p.417 & 419
41. Prince Hubertus Zu Loewenstein, *The Germans In History*. p.53
42. Alexander M. Rackus, *Guthones* (The Goths) etc. p.104
43. John G. Sheppard, *The Fall of Rome*. pp.307–308
44. C.R.L. Fletcher, *The Making Of Western Europe*. Vol.I p.131
45. Procopius, VIII.xxxv. 37–38 Vol.V p.419

46. Bury, *Hist. Later Rom. Empire.* Vol.II footnote 2 p.181
47. J.W. Thompson, *Economic & Social History Of The Middle* Ages (300–1300). p.122
48. Crawford, *The Rulers Of The South. Sicily, Calabria, Malta.* Vol.II p.35
49. Bury, *Hist. Later Rom. Empire.* Vol.II p.275
50. In ancient warfare 'winter' was from November through February. The season of active compaigning resumed in March (Martius) the first month of the pre-Julian Roman year, sacred to the god of war Mars.
51. Procopius, VIII.xxxv.38 Vol.V p.419
52. Ibid., VIII.xxxv.33 Vol.V pp.417 & 19 Actually, this was a 'reasonable settlement' brought by their notables for Narses to take under consideration. Ibid., p.417
53. Gibbon, Ch.XLIII
54. Ibid.
55. Ibid.
56. Bury, *Hist. Later Rom. Empire.* Vol.II p.275
57. Ibid., Vol.II pp.275–6
58. H.A.L. Fisher, *A History Of Europe from the Earliest Times to 1713.* p.131
59. Ibid., pp.131–32
60. Hodgkin, Vol.IV p.657
61. Hook, *The Hero in History.* p.165
62. Edward Hutton, *Ravenna A Study.* pp.103–4
63. Pratt, *The Battles That Changed History.* p.72
64. Hook, p.165

Chapter X. The Invasion of the Alamanni-Franks

1. *The Book of the Popes (Liber Pontificalis)* to the Pontificale of Gregory I. (Trans. L.R. Loomis) p.164
2. Christian Pfister, C.M.H. Vol.II Ch.IV p.119
3. Ibid.
4. Procopius, VIII.xxiv.6 Vol.V p.305 (Otherwise, Gregory of Tours has him dying after 'a long illness')
5. Fr. Funck-Brentano, *The National History Of France.* Vol.I p.257
6. J.C.L. De Sismondi, *The French under the Merovingians.* pp.94–95
7. Procopius, VI xi.38–39 Vol.III p.395
8. P.N. Ure, *Justinian And His Age.* p.58
9. Ibid.
10. P. Villari, *The Barbarian Invasions of Italy.* Vol.II pp.263–64
11. Victor Duruy, *The History of The Middle Ages.* (Note by George Burton Adams) p.33
12. Bury, *Hist. Later Rom. Empire.* Vol.II p.275
13. Agathias, cited in Hodgkin, Vol.V p.16
14. Gibbon, Ch.XLIII
15. Ibid.

16. Hodgkin, Vol.V p.25 See Virgil, TLCL Vol.I p.512 There was a Stoic maxim: 'The brave man may rise superior to fortune, however adverse.' Ibid., footnote 4 pp.512–13 (Yet, a footnote in Gibbon comments that these and the following line 'would become ridiculous if [the Trojan] Aeneas were actually in a Greek city' Ch.XLIII.
17. Bury, *Hist. Later Rom. Empire.* Vol.II p.276
18. Gibbon, Ch.XLIII
19. Bury, *Hist. Later Rom. Empire.* Vol.II p.276
20. Ibid.
21. Ibid., p.277
22. Hodgkin, Vol.V pp.29–30
23. Bury declares that they 'decended into Italy in the spring of A.D.553.' *Hist. Later Rom. Empire.* Vol.II p.275 Gibbon, on the other hand, has it that 75,000 'Germans' 'descended in the autumn from the Rhaetian Alps into the plain of Milan.' Ch.XLIII
24. Roberto Berti, *Storia dei Goti.* p.252
25. Hodgkin, Vol.V p.30
26. Ibid., Vol.V pp.30–32
27. Ibid.
28. Ibid., Vol.V footnote p.32
29. R. Berti, p.252
30. James E. Dunlap, pp.289–90. (See also Gibbon, Ch.XLIII).
31. P. Villari, Vol.II p.264
32. G.F. Young, Vol.II p.311
33. Funck-Brentano, Vol.I p.256
34. Villari, Vol.II p.264
35. Hodgkin, Vol.V p.32–33. Gibbon avows that all these drills and exercises were 'By the command and after the example of Narses,. . .' Ch.XLIII
36. Bury, *Hist. Later Rom. Empire.* Vol.II footnote 1 p.278
37. Ibid., Vol.II pp.277–78
38. *The Dialogues of Gregory the Great.* The First Book. Ch.2
39. See Gibbon, Ch.XLIII
40. Hodgkin, Vol.V p.34
41. Ibid.
42. W.G. Holmes, Vol.II p.664
43. R. Berti, p.253
44. Hodgkin, Vol.V pp.39–40
45. P.N. Ure p.59
46. Gibbon remarks: 'The justice or passion of Narses was awakened' but that he appeared as a 'Cruel master' imposing an 'arbitrary execution' that was unjust and imprudent to the indignant Heruls. Ch.XLIII.

Chapter XI. The Battle of Casilinum (Capua)

1. R. Souttar, *A Short History of Mediaeval Peoples.* p.373

2. Hodgkin, Vol.V p.42
3. Ibid., pp.42–43
4. Bury, *Hist. Later Rom. Empire.* Vol.II p.279
5. Agathias, Historiae. II 5
6. Ibid.
7. Gibbon, Ch.XLIII. He earlier commented: 'Perhaps the talents of the Roman general were most conspicuous in the calm operations which preceed the tumult of a battle.' Ibid.
8. Oman, *The Art Of War In the Middle Ages.* p.18
9. Bury, *Hist. Later Rom. Empire.* Vol.II p.280. As the 'Franks' faced both ways, they could only see the enemy in front of them and not those who were 'raining arrows upon their backs'. Ibid.
10. Liddell Hart, *The Strategy Of Indirect Approach.* p.66
11. George T. Denison, *A History of Cavalry.* p.102
12. Oman, *A History Of The Art Of War.* pp.36–37
13. Gibbon, Ch. XLIII. Buccelin himself paid the same price as Totila and Teias in giving battle to Narses-death. However, unlike the Ostrogothic kings, there is apparently no version of how it came about.
14. Bury, *Hist. Later Rom. Empire.* Vol.II p.280
15. Denison, p.102
16. Hodgkin, Vol.V pp.44–5
17. Villari, Vol.II p.265
18. Lynn Montross, *War Through The Ages.* p.110
19. Oman, *The Art Of War In The Middle Ages A.D.378–1515.* p.18 and p.37
20. Hodgkin, Vol.V p.45
21. Gibbon, Ch.XLIII
22. Agathias, Hist.II. 11–12 (cited by Dunlap p.291)
23. Hodgkin, Vol.V p.46
24. S.B.Platner-Thomas Ashby, *A Topographical Dictionary of Ancient Rome.* p.119
25. Robert Payne, *The Roman Triumph.* p.209
26. Ibid., pp.209–10
27. Grant Showerman, *Eternal Rome.* p.352
28. Payne, p.210 (this chariot was the currus triumphalis)
29. Gibbon, Ch. XLIII
30. The ancient triumphs had been granted to Roman generals who had defeated a foreign enemy, slain at least 5,000 of his men, and brought their armies back to Rome
31. Gregorovius, *History of The City Of Rome.* Vol.I p.482
32. Ibid.
33. Dunbar von Kalckreuth, *Three Thousand Years Of Rome.* p.139
34. Agathias, Hist.II 13–14
35. Diehl, C.M.H. Vol.II Ch.I p.18
36. Hodgkin, Vol.V p.47
37. Ibid., Vol.V p.48
38. W.G.Holmes, Vol.II p.665

Part III. Narses the 'Exarch'

Chapter XII. The Administration of Italy

1. Robert Browning, *Justinian And Theodora*. p.234 (1971)
2. Hodgkin, Vol.V p.65
3. Diehl, C.M.H. Vol.II Ch.I p.20
4. L.H. Hartmann, Ibid., Vol.II Ch.VIII (A) p.222
5. Bury, *Hist. Later Rom. Empire*. Vol.II footnote 1 p.283 [from Diehl] (or, even possibly from Alpes Maritine in Gaul)
6. Hartmann, C.M.H. Vol.II Ch.VIII (A) pp.222–23
7. Lynn Thorndike, *The History Of Medieval Europe*. p.88
8. H.W. Haussig comments: 'It was no coincidence that Narses, commander-in-chief of the imperial army in Italy, wielding the most extensive powers, had held the office of praepositus sacri cubiculi'. p.54
9. Bury, *Hist. Later Rom. Empire*. Vol.II p.282
10. Their former slaves, that had been freed by Totila, were restored to them as well (plus any offspring who had been born in the meantime).
11. Villari, Vol.II p.267
12. Sir Henry Slesser, *The Middle Ages In The West*. p.23. See also, H.W.C.Davis, Medieval Europe. Second Edition p.29
13. Hodgkin, Vol.VI p.531
14. Carl Stephenson, *Medieval History, Europe from the Second to the Sixteenth Century*. Rev. Edition p.113–15
15. Edward Hutton, *The Cities Of Lombardy*. p.223

Chapter XIII. The Rebuilding Programme of Narses

1. Dunlap, p.293
2. Ibid.
3. Gilbert Bagnani, *Rome And The Papacy*. pp.107–8
4. H.B. Cotterill, *Medieval Italy*. pp.154–55
5. F.S. Burnell, Rome. p.20
6. Gregorovius, Vol.I p.494
7. Ibid.
8. Michael Grant informs that it was a guard house of Domitian's palace. *The Roman Forum*. p.180
9. Ian A Richmond, *The City Wall Of Imperial Rome*. p.90
10. Ibid., p.43
11. Ibid., p.267
12. Gregorovius, Vol.I p.498 See also Bury, *Hist. Later Rom. Empire*. Vol.II footnote 5 p.283 for the Latin inscription.
13. Gregorovius, Vol.I p.498
14. Ibid., Vol.I p.499

15. Andrew Lumisden, *Remarks on the Antiquities of Rome and Its Environs:* p.45
16. Ibid., p.50
17. G.Bagnani, *The Roman Campagna and its Treasures.* p.206
18. Ibid., p.212
19. Ibid.
20. Jan Morris lists the military martyr as St Theodore of Heraclea; the warrior-saint, Theodore Tiro; the Abbot, Theodore the Sanctified; the Bishop, St Theodore of Sykeon and the monk as St Theodore the Studite. She concludes that he could have been a former commander-in-chief, 'canonized for his belligerence.' As for the crocodile, it could even be a dragon. *A Venetian Bestiary.* p.44
21. Janet P. Trevelyan, *A Short History of the Italian People.* p.89
22. Doge Sabastiano Ziani (1172–78) actually 'pulled down' the first church dedicated by Narses. Peter Lauritzen, Venice. *A Thousand Years of Culture and Civilization.* p.40
23. Arthur K. Porter, *Lombard Architecture.* Vol.III pp.554–55
24. G.T. Rivoira, *Lombardic Architecture.* Vol.I p.90
25. Ibid., pp.90–92
26. The later's mosaics were sold to the King of Prussia in 1847. Bury, *Hist. Later Rom. Empire.* Vol.II footnote 4 p.285
27. Narses may have actually lived in a villa outside the city
28. Naples was not re-taken by the Empire until 553
29. Edward Hutton, *Naples And Southern Italy.* p.142

Chapter XIV. Narses and the Papacy

1. Cited by Charles Diehl, C.M.H. Vol.II Ch.II p.43
2. Herbert Waddams, *The Church and man's Struggle for Unity.* pp.55–6 and pp.83–5
3. Bury, *Hist. Later Rom. Empire.* Vol.I Preface p.viii
4. *The Book Of The Popes (Liber Pontificalis)* I [L.P. LX1] L.R.Loomis. p.159
5. Robert Browning relates that Pelagius could only enter Rome 'Under the protection of Narses' troops.' *Justinian And Theodora.* p.234 (1971)
6. Andre Lagarde, *The Latin Church in the Middle Ages.* pp.265–66
7. *Book Of The Popes (Vita Pelagii)* [L.P. LXII] Loomis. pp.161–62
8. Hodgkin, Vol.V pp.53–54
9. L.E.Du Pin, *A New History of Ecclesiastical Writers.* Vol.5 (1699) p.58
10. Ibid., p.59
11. Ibid.
12. M. L'Abbe Fleury, *Ecclesiastical History.* Vol.IV Book XXXIII p.206
13. Du Pin, Vol.5 p.59
14. Ferdinand Gregorovius, *The Tombs Of The Popes.* (R.W. Seton-Watson, transl.) pp.15–16 (note 1)
15. Paul the Deacon, *History of the Langobards.* Book II Ch.IV (W.D. Foulke, transl.) note 1 p.58

16. Mons Caelius was the most south-easterly of Rome's seven hills.
17. G.R. Huddleston, *The Catholic Encyclopedia*. Vol.VI (1913) p.780
18. A.H.M. Jones, *The Later Roman Empire. 284–602* Vol.I (1964) p.291
19. Legend alleges that Gregory saw an angel sheathing its sword, signifying that the plague was over, on the summit of Hadrian's mausoleum; thus, the Castel Sant' Angelo.

Chapter XV. Later Military Operations

1. Bury, *Hist. Later Rom. Empire*. Vol.II p.281
2. H.F. Clinton, *Fasti Romani*. Vol.I Tables p.236
3. Procopius, VIII.xxxiii. 5 TLCL Vol.V p.391
4. Bury, *Hist. Later Rom. Empire*. Vol.II footnote 3 pp.281–82
5. Paul the Deacon, *History of the Langobards*. Book II Ch.II (Foulke) p.55.
6. Clinton, *Fasti Romani*. Vol.I p.239
7. Bury, *Hist. Later Rom. Empire*. Vol.II p.281 (and footnote 3)
8. Paul the Deacon, Book II Ch.II pp.55–56
9. F.G.M. Beck, (in part) Article on 'Lombards' or Langobardi. *Encyclopaedia Brittanica*. 11th Edition Vol.XVI pp.932–33
10. Gregory of Tours, *The History Of The Franks*. VII 36 Vol.II Text. p.314
11. J.M. Wallace-Hadrill, *The Long-Haired Kings*. pp.156–57
12. S.P. Scott (editor's Preface) *Forum Judicum*. p.xxi
13. James White, *The Eighteen Christian Centuries*. p.152
14. Christian Pfister, C.M.H. Vol.II Ch.IV p.122

Chapter XVI. Financial Administration

1. E.S. Duckett, *The Gateway To The Middle Ages*. p.51
2. Robert Browning, refers to Alexander as the 'chillingly efficient financial officer' of Maximinus, appointed the supreme commander in Italy during Belisarius' disgrace (543–4). *Justinian And Theodora*. pp.184–85 (1971)
3. C. Diehl, C.M.H. Vol.II Ch.I pp.23–4
4. C.R.L. Fletcher, *The Making Of Modern Europe*. p.137–38
5. Paul the Deacon, *History of the Langobards*. Book II Ch.IV (Foulke) p.56
6. Ibid., pp.57–58
7. Henry Hart Milman, (Dean of St. Paul's) went so far as to maintain that the Emperor Justin [II] was jealous enough to fear his greatness. *History of Latin Christianity*. Vol.II p.97
8. Corippus cited by Norman H. Baynes, C.M.H. Vol.II Ch.IX p.264
9. Paul the Deacon, Book II Ch.V p.59
10. Velleius Paterculus, *Compendium of Roman History*. (Frederick W. Shipley transl.) II cvi.2 TLCL p.271 (closer to the original Latin – 'a race surpassing even the [other] Germans in savagery')
11. Procopius, VII.xxxiii–10 Vol.IV p.441
12. Edward Hutton, Cities Of Lombardy. p.223

Chapter XVII. The Saga of Narses

1. Isidore of Seville, cited by Hodgkin, Vol. V p.63
2. Hodgkin, Vol.V footnote 2 p.62
3. A.A. Vasiliev (*History of the Byzantine Empire 324–1453*. p.172) stated that the aged ruler of Italy died shortly after retiring, because of old age, after the accession of Justin II, thus possibly in 566, and probably no later than 567. If so, this would rule out as unfounded the 'invitaion' in the popular tradition of the Saga. Eduard von de Muralt (*Essai de Chronographie de 395 a 1057* p.226) had Narses, 'avec Jean III', returning to Rome on 31 October 568, thereby giving him time to have called the Lombards into Italy. (Even so, this would not rule out an earlier date for his death than 571.) Ferdinand Gregorovius apparently did not accept 571 as the date of the return from Naples, as he found the assertion of Agnellus to clearly be an exaggeration. Moreover, he has Narses, soon after his return, dying in his palace, sunk in grief and dejection. Gregorovius fixed the date of death in 567. (*History of the City of Rome in the Middle Ages*. Vol.1 p.502) Henry Fynes Clinton did not think it 'probable' that Narses lived until 573. (*Fasti Romani* p.833) He listed among the events of that year, Cassiodorius being in his eighty-third year, and the murder of King Alboin by his Queen, Rosamund, who had conspired with his foster brother, Helmechis. Clinton dated Narses as dying a little before 'Joannes III', probably after 568 (from Paul the Deacon) but before 573. Architectural historians, citing Agnellus, have the eunuch ex-governor living in the Palatine Palace as late as the year 570. Thomas Hodgkin reckoned that Narses died about 573, or perhaps even a year or two earlier. James E. Dunlap concluded that his death took place in Rome, either in 573, or even 574; reasoning from Pope John's death in the later year. A footnote in chapter XLV of Edward Gibbon's monumental History flatly declared that he could not share with Agnellus the belief that Narses reached the age of ninety-five; further exclaiming 'Is it probable that all his exploits were performed at fourscore?' The reference here must be to the great victories that led to the conquest and defence of Italy during the years 552 to 554. In that case however, the relevant date would be the year of Narses' birth, 478 to 480, not the questionable point of his death.
4. Hodgkin, Article in the *Encyclopaedia Brittanica*. (11th edition) Vol.XIX pp.241–42 (see also footnote 2 p.242)
5. Paul the Deacon, *History Of The Langobards*. BookII Chap.V (Foulke) pp.58–59.
6. Ibid., p.59
7. Ibid., p.61
8. Niccolo Machiavelli, *The Florentine History*. p.31 (1905)
9. Paul the Deacon. Foulke, Preface, p.iii
10. Ibid., p.iii–iv (1907)
11. Claudian, *The Works of*. Vol.II. Invectives Against Eutropius. (A.Hawkins, transl.) Book I lines 409–16 p.14

12. Ibid., Book II lines 545–52 pp.50–1
13. Ibid., Book I lines 773–74 p.26
14. Hodgkin, *Encyclopaedia Britannica.* (11th Ed.) Vol.XIX footnote 2, p.242
15. Hodgkin, Vol.V p.63
16. Lord Mahon, *The Life of Belisarius.* p.252
17. Hodgkin, Vol.V p.64
18. Procopius, III. iii. 14–28 TLCL Vol.II pp.29 & 31. Justine Davis Randers-Pehrson reviewing the case of Narses remarked in referring to Stilicho and Boniface on people's need for 'scapegoats'. She continued: 'If we look ahead we find the Venerable Bede having similar things to say about Vortigern, on whose shoulders he lays the blame for the Saxon invasion of Britain.' *Barbarians And Romans.* p.217
19. Hodgkin, Vol.V p.64
20. Gregorovius, Vol.I pp.501–2
21. Hodgkin, Vol.V pp.62–3
22. Dunlap, p.295
23. Villari, *The Barbarian Invasions of Italy.* Vol.II p.273
24. Gregorovius, Vol.I pp.502–4
25. Plate, Article on Narses in *Smith's Dictionary of Greek And Roman Biography And Mythology.* Vol.II. p.1141
26. Gibbon, footnote Ch.XLV
27. Ibid.
28. Ibid., Ch.XLIII
29. Dunlap, pp.295–6
30. Ibid., p.299
31. Thomas Hodgkin, *Italy and her Invaders.* Vol.V Ch.II ('The Rule of Narses') p.67.

Appendix 4. The Treasure of Narses

1. Paul the Deacon, *History of the Langobards.* Book II Ch.XI (Foulke) p.68
2. This has been qualified by extracting that Narses appears to have removed 'many of them'. S.P. Platner (and Thomas Ashby) *A Topographical Dictionary Of Ancient Rome.* p.301
3. Dunlap, *The Office Of The Grand Chamberlain.* pp.297–8
4. Gregory of Tours, *The History Of The Franks.* V 13–19
5. Paul the Deacon, Book III Ch.XII (Foulke) p.109
6. M. Christian Pfister, C.M.H. Vol.II Ch.V pp.156–7
7. A.G. Paspates, *The Great Palace Of Constantinople.* p.176
8. Dunlap, p.298

Bibliography

Printed Works consulted in compiling Narses: Hammer of the Goths

BASIC SOURCES AND RECORDS

The Book Of The Popes (Liber Pontificalis) To The Pontificale Of Gregory I. Translated with an Introduction By Louise Ropes Loomis, New York: Columbia University Press, 1916.

Cassiodorius. *An Introduction to Divine and Human Readings.* Transl. with an Introduction and Notes by Leslie Webber-Jones. N.Y.: Columbia. Univ. Press 1946.

The Letters of Cassiodorius, Being a condensed translation of The Variae Epistolae. (With an Introduction by Thomas Hodgkin.) London: Henry Frowde, 1886.

Claudian. *The Works of Claudian*, trans. into English Verse by A. Hawkins, Esq. Vol.II. Invectives Against Eutropius. London. 1817.

Diodorus Siculus (Of Sicily). *Library of History.* Vols. VI & X. The Loeb Classical Library with an English transl. by C.H. Oldfather & Russel M. Geer. London: William Heinemann. Cambridge, Mass: Harvard Univ. Press 1954.

Du Pin, Lewis Ellies. *A New History of Ecclesiastical Writers.* (etc) Volume the Fifth, containing the Authors that Flourished in the Sixth Century. London: 1699.

Eusebius. *The Ecclesiastical History.* Vol. II. The Loeb Classical Library. Transl. J.E.L. Dulton. London: Wm. Heinemann, 1932

Evagrius, Scholasticus. *Ecclesiastical History.* A History of the Church in Six Books From A.D. 431 to A.D. 594. London: Samuel Bagster and Sons, 1844

Forum Judicum. (The Visigothic Code). Translated & edited from the original Latin by S.P. Scott. Boston, Mass: Boston Book Co., 1910.

Gregory of Tours. *The History of the Franks.* Vol.I Introduction. Vol.2 Text. Transl. with an Introduction By O.M. Dallon. Oxford: Clarendon Press, 1927.

Gregory, The Great. *The Dialogues of Gregory the Great,* Transl. into Our English Tongue By P.W. – Printed at Paris 1608. Re-edited – Edmund G. Gardner, London: Philip Lee Warner, 1911.

Isocrates. *Archidamus.* Vol. I The Loeb Classical Library. Transl. by George Norlin. London: Wm. Heinemann 1928.

Jordanes. *The Gothic History* (an English version with an Introduction and a Commentary By Charles Christopher Mierow). Princeton, N.J: Princeton Univ. Press. London: Humphrey Milford. Oxford Univ. Press, 1915.

Malalas, John. *Chronicle of John Malalas,* Books VIII–XVIII. (Transl. from the Church Slavonic by Mattew Spinks & Glanville Downey) Chicago, Ill.: The Univ of Chicago Press, 1940.

Otto, Bishop of Freising. *The Two Cities.* A Chronicle of Universal History to the Year 1146 A.D. Transl. Charles C. Mierow. N.Y.: Columbia Univ. Press, 1928.

Paul the Deacon. *History of the Langobards.* Transl. William Dudley Foulke. Philadelphia: Univ. of Pennsylvania, 1974.

Polybius. *The Histories.* Vol.V. The Loeb Classical Library. Transl. W.R. Paton. London: Wm. Heinemann, 1927.

Procopius. *History of the Wars.* In V Volumes. The Loeb Classical Library. Transl. H.B. Dewing. London: Wm. Heinemann, New York: Macmillan – G.P. Putnam's Sons, 1914–28.

Procopius. *The Anecdota or Secret History* – Vol. VI. TLCL. Transl. Dewing) London: Wm. Heinemann. Cambridge, Mass.: Harvard Univ. Press, 1935.

Procopius. *Buildings.* General Index to Procopius – Vol.VII TLCL. H.B. Dewing with the collaboration of Glanville Downey. London Wm. Heinemann. Cambridge, Mass.: Harvard Univ. Press. 1940.

Putnam's Dark And Middle Ages Reader. *Selections from the 5th to 15th Centuries.* (Harry E Wedeck). New York: Putnam's, 1964.

Velleius Paterculus. *Compendium of Roman History*. Also Res Gestae Divi Augusti. Transl. by Frederick W. Shipley. The Loeb Classical Library, London: Wm. Heinemann. Cambridge, Mass.: Harvard Univ. Press 1924/55

Zachariah Of Mitylene (Zacharias rhethor). *The Syriac Chronicle*. Transl. F.J. Hamilton & E.W. Brooks. London: Methuen, 1899.

ARCHITECTURE

Bagnani, Gilbert. *The Roman Campagna and its Treasures*. New York: Charles Scribner's Sons, 1930.

Gyllius, Peter. *The Antiquities of Constantinople* etc. Transl. John Ball). London: 1792.

Lanciani, Rodolfo. *The Destruction of Ancient Rome*. A Sketch Of The History of the Monuments, London, N.Y.: Macmillan, 1899.

Lumisden, Andrew. *Remarks on the Antiquities Of Rome and its Environs: Being A Classical and Topographical Survey of the Ruins of that Celebrated City*. London: W. Bulmer and Co., 1797.

MacDonald, William L. *The Architecture of the Roman Empire*. New Haven, Conn: Yale Univ. Press, 1965.

Marucchi, Horace. *The Roman Forum and the Palatine. According to the Latest Discoveries*. Paris, Rome, 1906.

Middleton, J. Henry. *The Remains of Ancient Rome*. Vols. I & II, London and Edinburgh, 1892.

Paspates, A.G. *The Great Palace of Constantinople* (Trans. from the Greek by William Metcalfe). London 1893.

Piranesi. *Etchings and Drawings* selected with an Introduction by Roseline Bacou. London: Thames & Hudson, 1975. (Paris 1974)

Porter, Arthur Kingsley. *Lombard Architecture*. Vol.III. Monuments. New Haven: Yale Univ. Press. London: Oxford Univ. Press, 1917.

Richmond, Ian A. *The City Wall of Imperial Rome, an Account of its Architectural Development from Aurelian to Narses*. Oxford: Clarendon Press, 1930.

Rivoire, G.T. *Lombardic Architecture*, Vol.I. Its Origin, Development and Derivatives. (Transl. G.McN. Rushforth) London: Wm. Heinemann, 1910.

Scherer, Margaret R. *Marvels of Ancient Rome*. (Published by the Phaidon Press for The Metropolitan Museum of Art). New York & London, 1956.

Swift, Emerson Howland. *Hagia Sophia*. New York: Morningside Heights, Columbia Univ. Press, 1940

Van Millingen, Alexander. *Byzantine Churches in Constantinople.* London: Macmillan, 1912.

Van Millingen, A. *Byzantine Constantinople, the Walls of the City and Adjoining Historical Sites.* London: John Murray, 1899.

Wilton, Ely John. *The Mind and Art of Giovanni Battista Piranesi.* London: Thames & Hudson, 1978.

Young, George. *Constantinople.* London: Methuen, 1926.

BIOGRAPHIES

Bridge, Anthony *Theodora, Portrait in a Byzantine Landscape.* London: 1978

Dodge, Theodore Ayrault. *Gustavus Adolphus.* Cambridge Mass: The Riverside Press, 1895.

Hodgkin, Thomas. *Theodoric the Goth.* London (Heros of the Nations series) 1891.

Mahon, Lord. *The Life of Belisarius.* London: John Murray, 1829

Vasiliev, A.A. *Justin The First. An Introduction to the Epoch of Justinian the Great.* Cambridge, Mass: Harvard Univ. Press, 1950. Church and Ecclesiastical Histories

CHURCH AND ECCLESIASTICAL HISTORIES

Bagnani, Gilbert. *Rome and the Papacy.* An Essay On The Relations Between Church And State. London: Methuen, 1929.

Burns, C. Delisle. *The First Europe. A Study of the Establishment of Medieval Christendom A.D. 400–800.* London: George Allen & Unwin, 1947.

Cheetham, Nicolas. *Keepers of the Keys. The Pope in History.* London & Sydney: Macdonald, 1982.

Daniel-Rops, H. *The Church in the Dark Ages.* (Transl. from the French by Audrey Butler). London, 1959.

Fleury, M. L'Abbe. *Ecclesiastical History*, Vol.IV. Containing the sixth and seventh Centuries. London, 1830.

Hefele, Joseph. *A History of the Councils Of The Church.* Vol. IV. A.D. 451 to A.D. 680. (Transl. from the German by William R. Clark). Edinburgh: 1895.

Lagarde, Andre.	*The Latin Church in the Middle Ages.* (Transl. Archibald Alexander). New York: Charles Scribner's Sons, 1915.
MacCulloch, J.A.	*Medieval Faith and Fable.* Boston, Mass., 1932.
McKilliam, A.E.	*A Chronicle of the Popes.* From St Peter to Pius X. London, 1912.
Milman, Henry Hart.	*History of Latin Christianity.* Vol.II. Third Edition. London: John Murray, 1864.
Mourret, The Rev. Fernand	*A History Of The Catholic Church.* (Transl. Rev. Newton Thompson). Vol.III. Period Of The Early Middle Ages. St. Louis, Mo., & London, 1936.
Robinson, John M.	*A Short History of Christianity.* London, 1902.
Waddams, Herbert	*The Church and Man's Struggle for Unity* London: Blandford Press 1968
White, The Rev. James.	*The Eighteen Christian Centuries.* From the second Edinburgh Edition. New York: D. Appleton, 1890.
Wilkes, G.A.F.	*The Popes: an Historical Summary;* Comprising A Period of 1784 Years: From Linus to Pius IX. London 1851.

DICTIONARIES AND ENCYCLOPAEDIAS, ETC.

The Catholic Encyclopedia.	Volume VI (Hudleston, Gilbert Roger). N.Y.: The Gilmary Society, 1913.
Encyclopaedia Brittanica.	Vols. VII, XVI & XIX. 11th Edition, 1911.
Encyclopedia Italiana.	Volume XXIV. Roma, MCMXXXIV–XIII
Everyman's Atlas of Ancient and Classical Geography.	London: J.M. Dent. New York: E.P. Dutton, 1907. (Revised 1952)
The Oxford Classical Dictionary.	Edited by N.G.L. Hammond and H.H. Scullard. Second Edition. Oxford: Clarendon Press, 1970.
The Oxford Dictionary of the Christian Church.	Edited by F.L. Cross. Second Edition. by Cross and E.A. Livingston. London: Oxford Univ. Press, 1974.
Pauly-Wissowa.	*The Pauly-Wissowa Real-Encyclopädie Der Classischen Altertumswissenschaft*, Stuttgart, 1894ff.
The Penguin Companion to Literature.	Classical and Byzantine. Edited by D.R. Dudley (and Oriental and African, edited by D.M. Lang) Allen Lane. The Penguin Press. Revised Edition 1971.
Platner, Samuel Ball.	*A Topographical Dictionary of Ancient Rome.* Completed and revised by Thomas Ashby. London: Oxford Univ. Press. London: Humphrey Milford, 1929.

Smith, William (Editor). (William Plate – a long article on Narses.) *A Dictionary of Greek and Roman Biography and Mythology*, Vol.II. London 1849.

FICTION (NOVELS AND DRAMA)

Bradshaw, Gillian. *The Bearkeeper's Daughter.* London: Methuen, 1988.

Franzero, Carlo Maria. *The Life and Times of Theodora.* London: Alvin Redman, 1961.

Graves, Robert. *Count Belisarius.* London: Cassell. New York: Seizen Press, 1938. Penguin Books, (1954) 8th Reprint, 1988.

Kraus, René. *Theodora. The Circus Empress.* Garden City, N.Y.: Doubleday, Doran, 1938.

Lamb, Harold. *Constantinople. Birth of an Empire.* New York: Knobf, 1957. London: Robert Hale, 1958.

Lamb, Harold. *Theodora and the Emperor. The Drama of Justinian.* Garden City, New York: Doubleday, 1952. London: Robert Hale, 1954.

Presland, John. (pseud. Mrs Gladys Skelton.) *Belisarius, General of the East (A Tragedy).* 4 Act Historical Drama. London: Chatto & Windus, 1913.

Vandercook, John W. *Empress of the Dusk. A Life of Theodora of Byzantium.* New York: Reynal & Hitchcock, 1940.

Wellman, Paul I. *The Female.* Garden City, N.Y.: Doubleday, 1953.

GENERAL WORKS

Abbott, John Stevens Cabot. *Italy the Monarchies of Continental Europe.* New York. 1860.

Andrieux, Maurice. *Rome.* (Transl. Charles Lam Markmann). New York: Funk & Wagnalls, 1968. (French Edition, 1960)

Ault, Warren O. *Europe in the Middle Ages*, New York: D.C. Heath, 1937.

Baker, G.P. *Justinian.* New York: Dodd Mead & Co., 1931.

Barker, Ernest. *Social and Political Thought In Byzantium from Justinian I to the Last Palaeologus.* Oxford: Clarendon Press, 1957.

Barker, John W. *Justinian and the Later Roman Empire.* London: The Univ. of Wisconsin Press, 1966.

Baynes, Norman H. — *The Byzantine Empire* (The Home University Library of Modern Knowledge). London, New York, Toronto: Oxford Univ. Press, 1962.

Baynes, N.H. and Moss. H. St.L. B. — *Byzantium An Introduction to East Roman Civilization.* Oxford: Clarendon Press 1961.

Bemont, Charles and Monod, G. — *Medieval Europe from 395 to 1270.* (Transl. Mary Sloan With Notes & Revision By George Burton Adams.)
New York: Henry Holt, 1902.

Berti, Roberto. — *Storia dei; Goti.* Venezia: Edizioni Helvetia. 1982.

Bosco, Giovanni. — *A Compendium of Italian History from the Fall of the Roman Empire.* (Transl. – 'and completed to the present time by J.D. Morell). London: Longman, Green & Co., 1881.

Bouchier, E.S. — *Spain under the Roman Empire.* Oxford: B.H. Blackwell, 1914.

Bradley, Henry. — *The Story of the Goths. From the Earliest Times to the End Of The Gothic Dominion in Spain.* London. New York, 1888.

Brownings, Robert. — *Justinian and Theodora.* London: Weidenfeld & Nicolson, 1971, Thames & Hudson, rev. ed. 1987.

Burnell, F.S. — *Rome.* London: Edward Arnold & Co., 1930.

Bury, J.B. — *A History of the Later Roman Empire. From Arcadius to Irene (395 A.D. to 800 A.D.)* Vols.I & II. London. New York: Macmillan, 1889.

Bury, J.B. — *History of the Later Roman Empire. From the Death of Theodosius I to the Death of Justinian (A.D. 395 to A.D. 565)* Vol.II. London: Macmillan, 1923 and Paper, New York: Dover Publications, 1958.

Bury, J.B. — *The Invasion of Europe by the Barbarians.* London: Macmillan, 1928. New York: Russell & Russell, 1963.

Byron, Robert. — *The Byzantine Achievement.* An Historical Perspective A.D. 330–1453. London & New York: Routledge & Kegan Paul, 1929. Reprinted 1987.

Planned by J.B. Bury, Edited by H.M. Gwatkin, J.P. Whitney. — *The Cambridge Medieval History*, Vol.I. The Christian Roman Empire and the Foundation of the Teutonic Kingdoms. Cambridge: Cambridge Univ. Press, 1911.
Volume II. The Rise of the Saracens and the Foundation of the Western Empire. Cambridge: Cambridge Univ. Press, 1913.

Canton, Norman F. — *Medieval History. The Life and Death of a Civilization.* London: Collier-Macmillan, 1963.

Collison-Morley, Lacy. *Naples Through the Centuries.* London: Methuen, 1925

Cotterill, H.B. *Medieval Italy. During a Thousand Years* (305–1313). London. New York, 1915.

Crawford, Francis Marion. *Ave Roma Immortalis. Studies from the Chronicles of Rome.* New Edition, Revised. London. New York: Macmillan, 1906.

Crawford, F.M. *The Rulers of the South.* Sicily, Calabria, Malta. Vol.II. London. New York: Macmillian, 1900.

Cuddon, J.A. *The Owl's Watchsong*, London: Barrie & Rockliff, 1960.

Davis, H.W.C. *Medieval Europe* (Home University Library). Second Edition. London: Oxford Univ. Press, 1960.

Davis, R.H.C. *A History of Medieval Europe from Constantine to Saint Louis.* London: Longmans Green, 1957. Revised Edition, 1970. Paperback – 1972–81.

Deanesly, Margaret. *A History of Early Medieval Europe from 476 To 911.* (Methuen's History of Medieval and Modern Europe Vol.I) London: Methuen, 1956. Second Edition. New York: Barnes and Noble, 1960. Reprinted, and as a paperback, 1969.

de Morgan, Jacques. *The History of the Armenian People from the Remotest Times to the Present Day.* (Transl. Ernest F. Barry.) Boston, Mass: Hairenik Press, 1918.

Dereksen, David. *The Crescent and the Cross. The Fall of Byzantium: May 1453.* New York, 1964.

Der Nersessian, Sirarpie. *Armenia and the Byzantine Empire. A Brief Study of Armenian Art And Civilization.* Cambridge, Mass: Harvard Univ. Press, 1947.

Der Nersessian, S. *The Armenians.* London: Thames and Hudson, 1969. (Ancient Peoples and Places, Vol.68).

Descola, Jean. *A History of Spain.* (Transl by Elain P Halperin.) New York: Alfred A. Knopf, 1963.

Diehl, Charles. *Byzantine Empresses.* (Chap.I–VII – Byzantine Portraits) (Transl. Harold Bell & Theresa de Kerpely). New York: A.A. Knopf, 1963. London: Elek Books, 1964.

Diehl, C. *Byzantine Portraits.* (Transl. H. Bell.) New York: Knopf, 1927.

Diehl, C. *Byzantium: Greatness and Decline.* (Transl. Naomi Walford). New Brunswick, N.J.: Rutgers Univ. Press, 1957.

Diehl, Charles. *History of the Byzantine Empire* (Transl. George B. Ives.) New York: G.E. Stechert & Co., 1945.

Downey, Glanville. *Constantinople in the Age Of Justinian.* Norman, Okla: Univ. of Oklahoma Press, 1960.

Duckett, Eleanor Shipley. *The Gateway to the Middle Ages.* New York: Macmillan, 1938.

Duruy, Victor. *The History of the Middle Ages.* (Transl. from 12th Edition by E.H. & M.D. Whitney. With Notes & Revisions by George Burton Adams.) New York.: Henry Holt, 1891.

Dvornik, F. *Les Slaves.* Byzance et Rome au IXe Siècle. Paris, 1926.

Eckstein-Diener. *Emperors, Angels & Eunuchs. The thousand years of the Byzantine Empire.* London: Chatto & Windus, 1938.

(Transl. Eden & Cedar Paul.) *Imperial Byzantium* (Byzanz, von Kaisern, Engeln und Eunuchen). Boston, Mass.: Little Brown, 1938.

Finley, George. *A History of Greece from its Conquest by the Romans to the Present Time.* B.C. 146 to A.D. 1864. Vol.I. Greece Under the Romans. B.C. 146–A.D.716. Oxford: Clarendon Press, 1877.

Finley, G. *History of the Byzantine Empire.* (Everyman's Library). London: J.M. Dent & Sons, 1935.

Fisher, H.A.L. *A History of Europe. From The Earliest Times to 1713.* London: Eyre & Spottiswood, Reprinted 1957.

Fletcher, C.R.L. *The Making of Western Europe. Being an Attempt to Trace the Fortunes of the Children of the Roman Empire. Vol.I. The Dark Ages 300–1000 A.D.* London: John Murray, 1912.

Foord, Edward A. *The Byzantine Empire. The Rearguard Of European Civilization.* London, 1911.

Forbes, Nevill. (et.al.) *The Balkans. A History of Bulgaria. Serbia. Greece. Rumania. Turkey.* Oxford: Clarendon Press, 1915.

Fraser, Mrs Hugh. *More Italian Yesterdays.* London: Hutchinson, 1915.

Funck-Brentano, Fr. *The National History of France.* (Transl. E.F. Buckley.) Vol.I. The Earliest Times. London: Wm. Heinemann, 1927.

Gibbon, Edward. *The History of the Decline and Fall of the Roman Empire* (first published in six volumes, 1775–88). Chapters XL, XLI, XLII, XLIII, XLV and XLVII cited.

Gifford, Augusta Hale. *New Italy. Her People and Their Story.* Boston, Mass. 1900.

Grant, Michael. *The Roman Forum.* London: Weidenfeld & Nicholson, 1970.

Gregorovius, Ferdinand. *History of the City of Rome in the Middle Ages*. (In 8 volumes – 1859–72). Vol.I (A.D.400–568). (Transl. from the 4th German Edition by Mrs Gustavus H. Hamilton) London 1900.

Guerdan, Rene. *Byzantium. Its Triumphs and Tragedy*. (Transl. D.L.B. Hartley) London 1956. New York. 1957.

Guggenberger A. (S.J.) *A General History of the Christian Era*. Vol.I. The Papacy and the Empire. St. Louis, Missouri. 1900.

Hare, Augustus J.C. *Cities of Northern and Central Italy*. Vol.II. New York. 1876.

Haussig, H.W. *A History of Byzantine Civilisation* (transl. by J.M. Hussey.) London: Thames & Hudson, 1971. (Kulturgeschicte von Byzanz. Stuttgart 1966).

Hazlitt, William Carew. *The Venetian Republic. Its Rise, its Growth, and its Fall 421–1797*. Vol.I. 421–1422. London. 1900.

Hearsey, John E.N. *City of Constantinople 324–1453*. London: John Murray, 1963.

Hodgkin, Thomas. *Italy and her Invaders*. Second Edition, Vol.IV & V. London, Oxford. 1896–1916.

Holmes, W.G. *The Age of Justinian and Theodora*. 2 Vol. 1905–7.

Hutton, Edward, *The Cities of Lombardy*. London, 1912.

Hutton, Edward. *The Cities of Romagne and the Marches*. London, 1913.

Hutton, Edward. *Naples and Southern Italy*. London, 1915.

Hutton, Edward. *Ravenna*. A Study. London, 1913.

Jones, A.H.M. *The Decline of the Ancient World*, London: Longman's 1966.

Jones, A.H.M. *The Later Roman Empire 284–602. A Social Economic and Administrative Survey*. 3 Vols. Oxford: Basil Blackwell, 1964.

Katz, Solomon. *The Decline of Rome and the Rise of Mediaeval Europe*, Ithaca, New York: Cornell Univ. Press 1963. (1955).

Kurkjian, Vahan M. *A History of Armenia*. New York: Armenian General Benevolent Union, 1958.

Lang, David Marshall. *Armenia Cradle of Civilization*. London: George Allen & Unwin. 1970. Revised 1980

Lessner, Erwin (and Ann M Lingg Lessner). *The Danube*. Garden City, N.Y: Doubleday, 1961.

Liddell, (John) Robert. *Byzantium and Istanbul*. London: Jonathan Cape, 1956.

Linsay, Jack. *Byzantium into Europe*. London, 1952.

Loewenstein, Prince Hubertus Zu. *The Germans in History*. Morningside Heights, N.Y: Columbia Univ. Press, 1945.

Ludwig, Emil. *The Mediterranean. Saga of a Sea.* New York: McGraw-Hill, 1942. London: Hamish Hamilton, 1943.

McCabe, Joseph. *The Empresses of Constantinople.* London: Methuen, 1913.

Marlowe, John. *The Golden Age of Alexandria. From its Foundation by Alexander the Great in 331 to its capture by the Arabs in 642 AD.* London: Victor Gollancz, 1971.

Mayne, Ethel Colburn. *The Romance of Monaco and its Rulers.* London, 1910.

Michelet, M. *History of France.* Vol. I (Transl G.H.Smith.) New York, Philadelphia 1847.

Morris, Jan. *A Venetian Bestiary.* London: Thames & Hudson, 1982.

Moss, H.St.L.B. *The Birth of the Middle Ages 395–814.* London: Oxford Univ. Press, 1957 (1935).

Norwich, John Julius. *Venice. The Greatness and the Fall.* London: Allen Lane 1981.

Norwich, J.J. *Venice. the Rise to Empire.* London: Allen Lane Penguin Books Ltd, 1977.

Okey, Thomas. *Venice and its Story*, London: J.M. Dent, 1903.

Oman, C.W.C. *The Byzantine Empire.* London & New York, 1892.

Oman, C.W.C. *The Dark Ages 476–918.* London 1949 (1901).

Ostrogorsky, George. *History of the Byzantine State* (Transl. from the German by Joan Hussey.) Oxford: Basil Blackwell. First English Edition 1956, Second Edition 1968. First Paperback Edition 1980.

Painter, Sidney. *A History of the Middle Ages 284–1500.* New York: Knopf, 1953. (Re-issued London, Macmillan, 1964.)

Parker, H.M.D. *A History of the Roman World from A.D.138 to 337* (Rev. by B.H. Warmington.) Vol.II. New York: Macmillan, 1958 (Vol. 7 Methuen's History of the Greek & Roman World. London, 1958.)

Pirenne, Henri. *A History of Europe. From the Invasions to the XVI Century.* (Transl Bernard Miall.) London: G. Allen & Unwin, 1967 (1939). New York: University Books, 1956.

Pirenne, Henri. *Mohammed and Charlemagne.* (Transl. B. Miall.) London: George Allen & Unwin, 1958.

Rackus, Alexander M. *Guthones (the Goths) Kinsmen of the Lithuanian People.* Chicago, 1929.

Randers–Pehrson, Justine Davis. *Barbarians and Romans: The Birth Stuggle of Europe AD 400–700.* London, Croom Helm, 1983.

Ross, Janet and Erichsen, Nelly. *The Story of Lucca*. London: J.M. Dent, 1912.

Runciman, Steven. *Byzantine Civilisation*. London: Edward Arnold, 1933. (7th Impression 1975.)

Salvatorelli, Luigi. *A Concise History of Italy. From Prehistoric Times to our Own Day*. (Transl. Bernard Miall.) New York: Oxford Univ. Press, 1940.

Schevill, Ferdinand. *History of Florence, from the Founding of the City through the Renaissance*. New York: Frederick Unger 1961 (1936).

Schreiber, Hermann. *I Goti. Garzanti 1981*. (Auf den Spuren der Gote.) Munchen: Paul List Verlag KG, 1977.

Sedwick, Henry Dwight. *A Short History of Italy*. (476–1900) Cambridge, Mass: The Riverside Press, 1905.

Sheppard, John G. *The Fall of Rome and the Rise of the New Nationalities*. London, New York: Routledge, Warne & Routledge, 1861.

Showerman, Grant. *Eternal Rome. The City and its People from the Earliest Timers to the Present Day*. New Haven: Yale Univ. Press London. Humphrey Milford. Oxford Univ. Press, 1925.

Showerman, G. *Rome and the Romans*. A Survey and Interpretation. New York: Macmillan, 1931.

De Sismondi, J.C.L. (Simonde) *History of the Fall of the Roman Empire Comprising a View of the Invasion and Settlement of the Barbarians*. Philadelphia, 1835.

(Simonde) *The French under the Merovingians*. (Transl. William Bellingham). London 1850.

Slesser, Sir Henry. *The Middle Ages in the West. A Study of European Unity*. London: Hutchinson, 1951.

Soisson, Pierre and Janine. *Byzantium*. (Transl. by David Macrae.) Geneve: Minerva, S.A., 1977.

Souttar, Robinson. *A Short History of Mediaeval Peoples from the dawn of the Christian era to the fall of Constantinople*. London: Hodder & Stoughton, 1907.

Spalding, William. *Italy and the Italian Islands from The Earliest Ages to the Present Time*. Vol.II. Second Edition. Edinburgh. London. 1841.

Stark, Freya. *Rome on the Euphrates: the story of a frontier*. London: John Murray, 1966.

Stein, Ernest. *Histoire du Bas-Empire*. Tome Second. De le disparition de l'Empire d'Occident à la mort de Justinien (476–565) Paris, Bruxelles, Amsterdam 1949.

Stephen, William. *Armenia. A Historical Sketch*, London 1896.

Stephenson, Carl. *Medieval History, Europe from the Second to the Sixteenth Century*. Rev. Edition. New York, London 1943. Third Edition New York: Harper, 1951. 4th Edition New York: Harper & Row, 1965.

Talbot Rice, Tamara. *Everyday Life in Byzantium*. London: B.T. Batsford. New York: G.P. Putnam's Sons, 1967. Dorset Press 1987.

Thayer, William Roscoe. *A Short History of Venice*. London. New York: Macmillan, 1905.

Thorndike, Lynn. *The History of Medieval Europe*. Third Edition. Cambridge Mass: The Riverside Press, 1956.

Todd, Malcolm. *Everyday Life of the Barbarians Goths, Franks and Vandals*. London: B.T. Batsford. New York: G.P. Putnam's Sons. 1972.

Todd, Malcolm. *The Northern Barbarians 100 B.C.–A.D. 300*. London: Hutchinson Univ. Library, 1975. Second Edition, Oxford: Basil Blackwell, 1987.

Trevelyan, Janet Penrose. *A Short History of the Italian People from the Barbarian Invasions to the Present Day*. Revised Edition, New York: Pitman, 1956.

Ure, Percy Neville. *Justinian and his Age*. Penguin Books, 1951. Westport, Conn: Greenwood Press 1980

Vasiliev, A.A. *History of the Byzantine Empire 324–1453*. Second English Edition. Madison, Wisc: The Univ. of Wisconsin Press, 1952. First Edition in two volumes, (1928).

Vernadsky, George. *Ancient Russia*. New Haven, Conn: Yale Univ. Press, 1959.

Villari, Pasquale. *The Barbarian Invasions of Italy*. (Transl. Linda Villari.) Vol.II. London 1902.

von Kalckreuth, Dunbar. *Three Thousand Years of Rome*. (Drei Tausend Jahre Rom.) (Transl. Caroline Fredrick.) New York: London, A.A. Knopf, 1930.

Vryonis, Speros. *Byzantium and Europe*. London & New York. Thames & Hudson, 1967.

Wallace-Hadrill, J.M. *The Barbarian West 400–1000* (Hutchinson's University Library). London, 1952. Oxford: Basil Blackwell, 1985.

Wickham, Chris. *Early Medieval Italy*. Central Power and Local Society 400–1000. London & Basingstoke: Macmillan Press, 1981.

Wiel, Alethea. *Venice*.London. New York, 1894.

Young, G.F. Brigadier-General. *East and West Through Fifteen Centuries. Being A General History from B.C. 44 to A.D. 1453*. Vol.II. London: Longmans Green, 1916.

MILITARY

Denison, George T. (Colonel) — *A History of Cavalry. From the Earliest Times with Lessons for the Future.* Second Edition. London: Macmillan, 1913.

Dupuy, Colonel Trevor N. — *The Evolution of Weapons and Warfare.* London – New York, Sydney: Jane's, 1982.

Fuller, J.F.C. Major General. — *A Military History of the Western World.* Vol.I. From the earliest times to the Battle of Lepanto. New York: Funk & Wagnalls, 1954.

Jones, Archer. — *The Art of War in the Western World.* London, Harrop, 1988. Univ. of Illinois Press, 1987

Liddell Hart, B.H. — *Strategy.* New York: Frederick A Praeger, 1957.

Liddell Hart, B.H. — *The Strategy of Indirect Approach.* (enlarged from the Decisive Wars of History, 1929.) London. Faber & Faber 1941. (Revised 1954.)

Lloyd, E.M. — *A Review of the History Of Infantry.* London. New York, Bombay & Calcutta: Longmans Green, 1908.

Montross, Lynn. — *War Through the Ages.* Rev. & Enlarged Edition. New York & London, 1946.

Oman, C.W.C. — *A History of the Art of War. The Middle Ages from the Fourth to the Fourteenth Century.* London: Methuen, 1898. (New York, 1898.)

Oman, C.W.C. — *The Art of War in the Middle Ages. A.D. 378–1515.* (Revised & Edited by John H Beeler.) Revised Edition, Ithaca, New York: Cornell Univ. Press, 1953.

Pratt, Fletcher. — *The Battles That Changed History.* Garden City, New York. Hanover House 1956.

Rodgers, William Ledyard. — *Naval Warfare Under Oars 4th to 16th Centuries.* Annapolis, Maryland: United States Naval Institute, 1939.

SPECIAL STUDIES/SUBJECTS

Bury, J.B. — *The Imperial Administrative System in the Ninth Century* (Published for the British Academy By Henry Frowde). Oxford University Press, 1911.

The Cambridge Economic History. — Vol.I. *The Agrarian Life of the Middle Ages.* (Edited by Chapham & Power.) Cambridge, 1944.

Chamberlain, Russell. — *LOOT! The Heritage of Plunder* London, 1983.

Clinton, Henry Fynes. *An Epitome of the Civil and Literary Chronology of Rome and Constantinople from the Death of Augustus to the Death of Heraclius.* (Edited by C.J. Fynes Clinton.) Oxford: Oxford Univ. Press, 1853.

Clinton, H.F. *Fasti Romani.* The Civil and Literary Chronology of Rome and Constantinople from the Death of Augustus to the Death of Justin II. Vol.I Tables. Oxford: Oxford Univ. Press. 1845.

Dunlap, James E. *The Office of the Grand Chamberlain in the Later Roman And Byzantine Empires.* (Part II of Two Studies In Later Roman And Byzantine Administration.) Arthur E.R. Boak & Dunlap. London, New York: Macmillan, 1924.

Gregorovius, Ferdinand. *The Tombs of the Popes.* Landmarks in Papal History. Transl R.W. Seton-Watson.) Westminster, 1903.

Haggard, Howard W. *The Doctor in History.* New Haven: Yale Univ. Press, 1934. (London, Humphrey Milford. Oxford Univ. Press.)

Hook, Sidney. *The Hero in History.* A study in limitation and possibility. New York: John Day, 1943. London: Secker & Warburg, 1945, (re-issue Boston: Beacon Press, 1959).

Lewis, Archibald R. *Naval Power and Trade in the Mediterranean. A.D.500–1100.* Princeton, N.J.: Princeton Univ. Press, 1951.

Lewis, A.R. *The Northern Seas. Shipping and Commerce in Northern Europe A.D. 300–1000.* Princeton, N.J.: Princeton Univ. Press, 1958.

Machivelli, Niccolo. *The Florentine History* with an Introduction by Henry Cust. Long Acre: David Nutt, 1905.

Machivelli, N. *The History of Florence from the Earliest Times to the Death of Lorenzo the Magnificent.* (Charles W Colby). Revised edition. Colonial Press, 1901.

Machivelli Nicholas, *The Works* of. Vol.I. (Transl. Ellis Faraeworth.) The Second Edition. London. 1775.

Muralt, Eduard von de. *Essai de Chronographie Byzantine, de 395 à 1057.* St. Petersbourg, 1855.

Oppenheimer, Francis. *Frankish Themes and Problems.* London: Faber & Faber, 1952.

Payne, Robert. *The Roman Triumph.* London, New York: Toronto: Abelard-Schuman. 1962

Pounds, Norman J.G. *An Historical Geography of Europe 450 BC–AD 1330*, Cambridge, 1973.

Smalley, Beryl. *Historians in the Middle Ages.* London, 1974.

Taylor, Henry Osborn. *The Medieval Mind.* A History of the Development of Thought and Emotion in the Middle Ages. Vol.I. Fourth Edition. Cambridge, Mass: Harvard Univ. Press, 1949.

Thompson, James Westfall. *Economic And Social History of the Middle Ages (300–1300).* (Century Historical Series). New York, London, 1928.

Treue, Wilhem. *Art Plunder. The fate of works of art in war and unrest.* (Kunstraub, 1957). New York: John Day, 1961.

Wallace-Hadrill, J.M. *The Long-Haired Kings, and Other Studies in Frankish History.* London: Methuen. 1962.

Wright, F.A. *A History of Later Greek Literature. From the Death of Alexander in 323 B.C. to the Death of Justinian in 565 A.D.* London: George Routledge, 1932.

Ziegler, Philip *The Black Death.* London 1969.

Index